THE ANGELICA
TOUCH

L. J. Sedgwick

First Edition | 2018

Janey Mac Books

Cover Design by Aoife Henkes
Formatting by Polgarus Studio

Print Version
ISBN-13: 978-0995702721
ISBN-10: 0995702721

Published by Janey Mac Books 2018

For Libby

Chapter 1

My name is Angelica Moone. I'm neither a vampire with gold eyes (and the need to drain cute boy-bands of blood) nor a werewolf. You could say my father was a whale but even that's pushing it a bit. I live with my mum, Molly, in The Drisogue Arms Hotel. It sits on a rugged peninsula elbowing into the Atlantic on the most westerly coast of Donegal.

This is the most westerly part of the west of Ireland and pretty far west, Europe-wise; making for a lot of thunder, hail and storms. We found an empty coffin once and a beach full of mannequin arms, all left handed. I'm sure drugs have washed up too and maybe a body or two, but nobody will admit it to me.

Apparently, I'm "*too young*".

Pointless to say I'm fourteen. People who say I'm too young smile when I do, as if my response proves to them that they are completely right.

But then they don't know me.

It's not their fault. I've been way ahead of them since the day I was born.

Being small and a little bit on the blue-to-purple range, I was swaddled tightly before I was handed to Mum. The paediatrician, with a mouthful of teeth that resembled a tiger, told her how much work I'd given him and that she must call me Michaela, after him. He was grumpy since he always gave up smoking and toffee in August.

As she unwrapped the blue blanket, beams of light flooded the room. Blinded, the doctor reeled away like a fish fighting a hook. Mum didn't notice. She was busy smiling at me and I was enjoying being born at last.

My mother didn't call me Michaela.

She was afraid if she called me Michaela I'd grow teeth like his and never write poetry.

No, she and Dad named me Angelica because of the beautiful downy wings with which I was born. Afraid they would make it difficult for me to wear nice clothes as I grew up, Mum folded them away and laid me down to sleep.

With my wings tucked away and my rays exhausted for the day, my angelic powers flowed into one hot little fist. It latched onto the thumb of the first midwife to lean down over my cot.

"What a tight grip, sweetheart," she said.

I held on so fast that she called for assistance. The doctor came running, wearing sun glasses because he didn't trust me and hadn't realised I was an angel. As his fingers unwrapped my hand from the midwife's thumb, they banged heads, met each other's eyes and fell in love.

Mum said she returned from the loo and they were kissing over my cot.

Me?

I was fast asleep. Thumb released. Job done.

My wings, not being used, fell away within days. All that's left are pronounced shoulder blades I could squish bison with, if there were any bison in Donegal.

Or I was into squishing, which I'm not.

Generally.

~~~

My father, Jeremy, was a film director. Mum said he was six feet four in his handmade Italian leather boots with tapered toes. (The boots had tapered toes, not my dad.) Anyway, his moustache tickled Mum's neck when they danced. She says this was nice; I'm not so sure. She was doing street theatre in Dublin during summer holidays from Uni. He said he would make her immortal.

They danced all through the pregnancy. "It was like dancing inside a moonbeam," she said. "My feet didn't touch the ground." I did not inherit my dad's talent for dancing. It's not that I have two left feet; only that my right foot thinks that it is his sole job/ duty/ goal in life to trip up my left. (Yeah, it's odd but my feet definitely feel male. Maybe because I can't trust them to get me into school in the morning without providing some sort of embarrassing *double flip, tip and bump* manoeuvre.)

Neither did I get his height, his film star looks or his charm.

Mostly all I share with Dad, genetic-wise, is his red hair. Unfortunately, it's not the sort of red that makes Hollywood directors go, "Wow!" It's the sort that causes people to tumble over laughing and it's ALWAYS tangled. Even brushed, my hair is snarly and it never, ever, stays up in a scrunchie.

This is a real disadvantage when you live in the windy West of Ireland.

Dad was filming something Very Big Out On The North Sea when I was born. He postponed the shoot for 24 hours to fly in and see me being born. When he returned to the set, he was shooting this scene from a boat in the water, a scene in which the heroine galloped along a coral beach pursued by scores of hunters.

It was okay; once she hit water, she'd turn back into a mermaid. Only Dad never filmed that bit because the tail of a whale whipped him into the foamy water. Before you could say, '*Action!*' or '*Cut!*' he had been swallowed whole.

Apparently, the water burped.

That's how they knew there was no point looking for him.

Mum cried for two days. Then she stopped and said that wasn't what Dad would have wanted. Not that he'd have wanted to be swallowed by a whale either but at least it was fast. And besides, she had me.

I hope his tapered boots gave the whale severe indigestion.

Her dreams of being a movie star scuppered by several hundredweight of blubber, Mum became a chambermaid with a baby on her back while she completed her degree in hotel management by night class.

Unaware of her tragedy, I and my gift blossomed.

Forget rays of light or banging heads, according to Mum she had only to leave me in the room with two mismatched individuals and love would erupt between them. In our first hotel, the concierge ran away with the maitre d' of the restaurant, after minding me for less than an hour while Mum changed the bridal suite.

Over lunch in the staff room at our next hotel, I notched up love between two waitresses, between the bar manager and gangly man from the bakery but it was only when the head chef ran off with owner's daughter on our third day that Mum was '*let go*'.

Again.

Everywhere I went, hearts beat faster, eyes dilated and hands shook. Mum didn't see it as a gift, which is fair enough since she was the one blamed for staff being distracted/ burning food / tripping over invisible gnomes and skipping away into sunsets.

We left a lot of jobs.

By the time I was seven, the rumour had spread throughout Dublin and county that staff trouble followed Molly Moone. The only place that would employ her as an assistant manageress was a backstreet hotel in which no questions were ever asked and everyone was too miserable to think about love.

Mum declared that it was time for the Moones to move out of the city.

We combed the papers and the websites; Mum put her name down with several agencies but, in the end, it was a simple ad in a newspaper. I'd have missed it too, if it hadn't been for the picture of a whale in the corner.

Mum was on the phone when I tugged her arm. Her coffee had gone cold, with this oily surface of dead cream.

"Mum, look!"

IMAGINATIVE AND ENTHUSIASTIC MANAGER WANTED.

REMOTE IRISH HOTEL. GEMINI'S ONLY.

Chapter 2

When you turn in from the road, you don't see the Drisogue Arms. Not at first. It's seated in a dip at the end of this curved driveway so mostly all you see is this giant oak tree, complete with loveseat. As you get closer, the painted gables of the hotel peep out either side. As if it's hiding.

When we arrived seven years ago, it was January 2003 and the sky was full of winter sun. We squeezed out of the banger we called William, having sat on and within all our worldly goods for nearly six hours. I don't remember much except this feeling of excitement, running from my toes to the tip of my head. As if I was a puppy facing the muddiest puddle; a puppy who KNOWS there is an enormous lamb shank underneath all the mud. Why? Because the Victorian romp of a hotel in front of us, with its pink and purple gables, was my dream home.

A fair-haired man with a very soft voice appeared out of nowhere and led us around the side, into a ballroom and up a wide staircase to a suite of rooms furnished like the Titanic. Then he vanished.

"Was he a ghost?"

"No," said Mum. "Ghosts don't usually smell of garlic."

"Unless he was a French ghost, marooned after his boat crashed into the cliff?"

"Shhh."

My fingers wanted to touch everything. I know now that the brocade and velvet drapes are full of moth holes and frayed, but it still felt magical. The walls were covered with old photographs but the one on the cupboard, of a couple standing so close they could be Siamese twins, drew me in for ages. This was Teddy, I learnt later; arm in arm with the person we were waiting for, Genevieve O'Malley, the owner of the Drisogue Arms.

Mum was fidgeting as if something small and many-legged had tiptoed up her sleeve and was making a nest. I put it down to her always being nervous at interviews but she told me years later that she had no plan B if she didn't get this job.

Everything we owned was in William or on his roof.

An elderly woman joined us, taking Mum's hand firmly in her own. "Molly," she said, as if Mum was a long lost friend. They stood like that for an age; she had a round open face and hair this side of marshmallow. "And you," she said, turning to me – which made sense because there was nobody else in the room, "must be Angelica".

"Is this your hotel?"

"It is. Do you like it?"

I nodded again. Because I did. Some whirling wind had caught me up and tipped me home, even if my shoes were purple docs, not sparkly red kitten heels and I hadn't tapped them together three times.

Mum still hadn't said a word so I spoke for her because there was NO way we were leaving this hotel. "Mum does too."

She directed us to this alcove with a bay window facing the Atlantic Ocean.

I can remember kneeling up on the scratchy sofa, to look out. The back and forth of introductions and Mum doing her spiel about her work ethic n stuff bored me to tears. I'd heard it too many times.

I was watching the surface of the water. It seemed so vast. "They like the warm water of the Gulf Stream," said our host, as if she knew I was looking for whales. Then, not a mile out to sea, as if he'd been waiting for her word, a whale leapt out of the water, spraying a spume ten feet high. "Mum."

Mum was holding a bag that seemed to have been woven from the Bayeux tapestry.

"Shake," said our host, "then tip the contents onto the table." Curious, I watched as the table filled with flattened milk bottle tops, a cork, twigs with desiccated berries and leaves, semi-precious stones and pebbles. After staring at the littered table for the longest moment, our host looked up at Mum. "It's very remote."

I turned back to the ocean.

"And we are very self-sufficient," said Mum.

"You've seen my credentials. You know I'm qualified. What I really want now is a home, Ms O'Malley. Somewhere I can work and look after my daughter, knowing she'll be safe. We're tired of the city and people who don't care where they stay so long as it's convenient and cheap."

When I'd almost given up, the whale leapt again. Then he flicked his tail back up and splashed it down once, twice, THREE times!

"Let me make the Drisogue Arms into the most special destination in the world."

"Exactly," said the old lady, "what the reading said. I hope you stay a very long time." She held out a hand. "My name is Genevieve Agatha O'Malley, but you may call me Guppy."

"Molly," says Mum and they shook on it.

I looked at the spread on the table then. Guppy was right.

It was a picture of Mum and me and the sea.

~ ~ ~

Chris, the man in overalls, had brought most of our gear to the apartment above the lobby before we found our way there. As if he knew we'd be staying. Mum's costumes were laid out on the sofa, like precious, velvety corpses; the crate we'd tied to William's roof had fallen apart when he'd tried to lift it off.

While he fetched the last bags up, Mum walked around, looking at everything. I chose the bedroom facing the sea and rummaged for treasure in all the drawers and cupboards. (One ten pence piece, an embroidered hankie and a birthday card, unused; I've done better.)

On his return, he introduced himself. "Maintenance man, janitor, general odd jobber, roof repairer, carpenter, plumber and front-of-house man, occasional chef, waiter, barman and singer of exotic love songs but only with a few glasses of local moonshine. Oh and I make a wicked Black Russian."

Mum said and I remember because it was as stiff and wooden as she gets, "Pleased to meet you". But it had been a long day.

He turned to me. "Fancy a look at your new home?"

"Mum?"I knew better than to push. Forcing Mum to agree to something never worked.

Chris gets it right though: "Might give you a chance to get organised?"

"Okay," she says finally and I am off the hook for all the cleaning that has to happen before Mum'll let us unpack, let alone sleep here. As we go out, she thanks him and warns me not to be "too long".

I don't know why. I'll never be *too long*. I'll always be short. I think this is why she likes me having long hair.

~~~

We fly around the hotel. He shows me hidden doors and secret passageways, a staircase through the hotel, down through the cliff to the beach, built so that Victorian ladies could get into the sea without being seen in their swimwear. Then down to raid the giant dessert fridge in the kitchen where he helps me to the largest slice of Banoffi Pie and decorates it with cream and marshmallows and chocolate chips.

Then he fishes out a little marble whale from his pocket that he'd carved. "A welcome gift."

It was only later, giving Mum a big sleepy hug as she tucked me, that I told her about the whale I saw during her interview. "Maybe it was the same one," I said. "Maybe it was Dad's whale?"

"Angelica—"

"I'm sure there were two, so at least he isn't lonely."

I had it all planned out. I was going to dream of swimming with whales and discovering sunken cities at the bottom of the ocean, stairways hidden behind walls leading to a secret treasure horde hidden by Granuaile, our pirate queen. Or dropping really hairy spiders down the shirt collars of all the hotel managers and guests who had ever been mean to Mum.

As she tiptoed out, I remembered the most important thing of all. The reason why the whale was in Drisogue.

"Chris says spirits always follow the people they love."

8

Chapter 3

Once a month, Mum and I shut ourselves away in our apartment. We eat pizza, toast marshmallows and pretend the Drisogue Arms is the most prestigious hotel in the whole universe. That any day now, Brad Pitt will book it for a hideaway and yes, I know that he's too old for me but he's her dream date and he became mine by default after we watched Meet Joe Black a gazillion times.

We often watch one of his classics, Mr & Mrs Smith, Legends of the Fall or the Ocean's trilogy. Since Mum hates sad endings, we've only watched Thelma & Louise five times but she makes an exception for Casablanca. This is her absolute favourite film; she used to watch with her dad, so we sometimes watch this instead of a Brad classic.

Other nights we make hot chocolate from real lumps of chocolate, dress up in costumes from her street theatre days and she tells me stories about what I was like when I was little or about life before me.

Tonight, it's New Year's Eve, the cusp of 2010. The hotel is so packed – we have two guests – that Mum and I are having the evening to ourselves and she has finally agreed to straighten my hair. Properly.

It's funny how you can be right next to something nearly happening, after which nothing will EVER be the same and yet have no idea. You would think there'd be a tingling down your neck or a warning bell in your head but there isn't.

I mean, right now, I'm wearing her Granuaile dress, the costume she was wearing when she met Dad. The last thought in my head is anything ever being different than the way it is. The dress is velvet; red and purple and green and gold. If it's less sumptuous than I thought it was when I was little, with a few unusual stains, it is still magical to wear. The weight of it makes me stand straight.

I feel tall and swirly.

Chris is managing everything downstairs. He designed special New York's Eve cocktails for the occasion and has sold exactly two.

To our two guests.

Guppy gave him several attics to make into a studio and he's still 'freeing' whales out of lumps of rock he finds on the beach. That's where he'd prefer to be tonight but Mum called dibs. When we came here, I thought he was this big friendly BFG but it was only the overalls. He's younger than Mum, she says.

When we came upstairs tonight, there was a storm brewing. The wind was rattling the arms of the oak tree; the loveseat tapping a rhythm on its trunk. But up here, right now, we can hear nothing except the soundtrack of Casablanca. Our own personal Brad Pitt, a plastic figurine that jiggles to noise and is only wearing a guitar, wiggles madly beside the CD player.

While I'm picturing my hair full of little Brad Pitts stomping on the tangles until they behave, Mum's in full swing nostalgia mode and it's the *me-being-named* story again.

"'Mais bien sur,' he said. 'I've never seen a more angelic baby!'"

"When did Dad turn French, Mum?"

"Didn't I mention that?"

"No, no. Dad was English and you said that he said—"

"'We must name her for an Angel of the Air!' Are we sure he's not French?"

"He's not. Wasn't."

"Pity. Always liked red-haired Frenchmen."

"No."

She grins and the hair straightening stops for a beat. "Are you sure?"

"You didn't." She does this to wind me up. Every time. "Tell it properly."

"He said, 'Why don't we name her Angelica?'"

"No. Dad thought I *was* an angel. You came up with the name."

"Why darling, you're absolutely right! He said, '*My daughter has wings on her back and feathers in her hair!*'" She turns me around to the mirror. My hair is liquid fire, running past my waist. In this dress, with this hair, I could make waves turn back and transform themselves into concert tickets.

Brad jiggles wildly. "He's excited about me turning into a siren," I say.

Mum says she has first dibs, being nearer his age but I'm growing up fast and by the time we meet, who knows? She's gazing into the mirror, past me, beyond me.

"You okay?"

She pulls back into herself then and smiles at me. "Just squashing cobwebs."

Before I can push her further – and I'm not sure I want to, Brad takes a tumble. He's very thoughtful that way. Mind you, he could have been trying to leap into my arms. (Well it can't be my bodice; there's hardly anything there. Sob.)

It's only when I stoop to pick him up that I notice lights outside. Mum snatches him from me as I pull back the curtains and look outside.

"Mum?"

She's dancing around the room, trying to make me laugh. "Don't you like my dancing?"

"I think there's a whale on the lawn."

Chapter 4

We race outside and there, framed against the moonlight, is an immense and majestic blue whale, lying on its side. For a moment I think it's the one I saw when I was seven but that's a bit scary. Especially if the whale I saw had actually been the whale that ate my dad and his bones were maybe inside still.

But I'm fourteen now, not seven. Whales don't leap up over cliffs onto peninsulas, even in tropical storms. Besides, a real whale wouldn't have a logo printed on its underbelly that says Paradoxical Films and neither would a helicopter be landing nearby.

But still! A whale has fallen out of the sky onto our lawn!

It's the best New Year's Eve surprise EVER!

The whole town is spilling up the hill to view the wonder. The only person untouched by this odd sort of miracle is Guppy. Arms folded, she faces off the man-in-charge from Paradoxical Films like a prize boxer; a man with the worst hairdo imaginable. It keeps fetching across his face and he has to flick it aside.

"One night. Two at the most."

He wants to stow the whale. It's built to go in the water for days on end but now needs to go undercover because it's damaged and could get water-damaged. Ironic.

"Tell you what, we'll put you down for a credit on the film. How about that? We'll take pictures you can use for publicity. Hotel Shelters Fallen Whale."

"It's not a real whale," she says. "And a credit doesn't pay bills. If it were a real whale, of course I wouldn't charge you a penny but fake whales cost €5,000 a night bed & breakfast."

"You have GOT to be kidding!"

"That's the cost of renting the ballroom."

I don't think it has ever been rented. Unless you kept the lights really dim, you'd see the plaster peeling with the damp underneath.

"Oh, right," he says. "So, how many fake whales have you had staying over lately? Or how many Balls?"

Guppy doesn't bother answering so they stand there in silence. Only the storm is really whipping up now and the whale needs to go undercover.

"Okay, Grandma—"

"Oh my!" Guppy winks at me. "I think it just went up to ten."

"You win. We'll sort something out tomorrow. For now, can we just get her inside?"

"If you think I was born yesterday then you haven't looked at my wrinkles. Molly!"

Mum's with Kitty whose daughter, Grace, is my best friend but I can't see Grace anywhere. Kitty runs The Pirate Queen pub in Drisogue. She's a single mum too but not so you'd know it and she NEVER misses out on an opportunity to talk to strangers.

"Molly, is it ten grand for the whole ballroom or twelve?"

"Oh we'll settle for two, since it our first whale this year," says Mum. "On condition you paint the ballroom afterwards."

The man, Marcus, agrees and hands are shaken all round. His hair is all puffy and long, but whatever the cut is, it should be placed on a Register of Banned Hairstyles. He doesn't let Kitty's fingers go for ages even though she has nothing to do with this deal. She has power over men and it's not only that she's blonde.

Grace says it's a genetic thing.

It just hasn't *exactly* revealed itself in her yet.

Guppy coughs loudly. Marcus lets go and runs his fingers through his hair. There's a lot of it; they get stuck half way down the back and it's not quite the suave gesture he meant it to be. Then he slopes off, hair swinging in the wind, to supervise the removal of the ballroom doors so the whale can fit through.

I stay with the whale. See, while I should hate whales because of Dad, I've always been drawn to them. Some dweebs from First Year are stuffing grass into a crack on the whale's stomach. "Look! Pubic hair."

I'm about to say something like, "*Grow up!*" which would NOT be worth the slagging that would follow or "*Leave him alone!*" when a voice echoes from the whale: "Don't do that" and freaks the boys out.

I have a peep around the back. It's Dylan, one of the new vicar's sons, speaking into the blowhole.

"Or I will eat you!"

He grins at me. It's a nice grin. Sort of the nicest grin I've seen on a boy in Drisogue. His dad only came here about six months ago but we don't go to church of any sort so I've only seen him in school and not up close. His jacket has a whale wrapped around the shoulders.

Pretty cool. For a boy.

"Angelica!"

Mum. She's looking around for me but I'm with Dylan behind the whale and I don't want to leave. Course I blush. Not because of Dylan. Because of Mum. That's when the whale starts talking to me. This is something that happens when I'm uncomfortable or things aren't turning out the way they should. I don't know why. Sometimes I have entire conversations with inanimate objects and animals who shouldn't be able to talk.

Mostly there's a REALLY good reason they shouldn't talk.

Pigeons, for example, they use really foul language.

"She's lonely, your mum. Look at how her shoulders droop, surrounded by couples holding hands; arms around waists; kisses on lips." So says the whale; a whale made from polystyrene and plywood. "Lonely and alone."

I answer anyway. "No, she's not. She's perfectly happy."

"Sorry?" says Dylan. I forgot he was there."Were you talking to me?"

"No. Sorry."

"It's okay."

In case I missed his meaning, the whale tosses in a dose of sarcasm. "Yeah, she's brimming with happiness."

I stay mute. Okay, so the last thing I wanted to do was get roped into helping out in the bar or making beds when there's bound to be some of the film crew staying. Right now, it doesn't feel like the worst option but the whale is on a roll. (Not literally. Literally he is lying on a broken fin and has a belly full of grass.)

"This is your seventh New Year's Eve in Drisogue. How often has your mum had company in all that time, other than you? Once. And he made her feel like shit. Or was that you?"

"He was a sleazebag."

"Who was?" It's Dylan, not the whale. Their voices are entirely different. Dylan's is smooth like butter and the whale sounds like an old man. A grumpy old man.

"Sorry. I was thinking aloud."

Besides, the whale has it wrong. Mum's gorgeous and funny and see, she's chatting away now to Marcus. This proves that if she really was lonely, she'd find someone easy.

"Hey Mouse, how about a picture of you with the whale?" says Chris, appearing out of nowhere, reading ten and twenty into the two and two that is me standing behind a whale with a boy. In the background, Mum points Kitty out to Marcus and he shifts like a rabbit in a landslide, leaving her totally alone on the crowded lawn.

"It's as if you dressed for the part!"

Damn. I forgot about the dress. I must look like a complete saddo. The sort of lonely teenager who still dresses up at Halloween, even though she hasn't been invited to a party.

"Chris, I can't. Mum's looking for me."

"One photo."

"I have to go," says Dylan disappearing into the crowd. "Nice whale-talking with you."

"Okay, one pic," I say, because it's not Chris's fault tonight's going belly up. Then I fetch Guppy to pose for him and Mum before the sky starts cackling. As the storm rolls in, everyone hares into the hotel, laughing.

The whale – I've named him Albert on account of his deep and grumpy voice, is carried indoors. A shaft of lightning hits the oak tree and splits the loveseat in half as we watch from the hotel lobby.

Can't be a good omen.

"Oh, fireworks!" says Guppy. "How lovely."

I'm glad they got Albert inside.

Kitty emerges from the bar with a phone stuck to her ear and mouths something to me about Mum looking for help before moving out of earshot. I still hear, "Well hello Big Bad Boy. What naughty things have you been doing?" before Grace thumps my upper arm by way of saying hello.

She's my best friend but she thumps like a pro and has a way of appearing without making a sound that's borderline creepy. After I've showered, I rope her into helping me make up some beds. It's the price of being my friend.

"I lifted one of Mum's work phones. Thought we could phone her clients back, like tomorrow?"

Grace's mum, Kitty does sex lines to make ends meet. These are immoral, says Mum, but I've heard them giggling about it when they think I'm asleep. I'm a single child and a daughter at that; it's my duty to pick up knowledge from whatever source I can.

"Come on, Licky, it'll be fun!"

Licky is her current nickname for me. Ange-lica, get it? I can't say it's my most impressive nickname but it beats *Anjj* and *Jelly* which were last year's efforts.

Doesn't take long to decide.

Not as if I have a whole lot else planned for New Year's Day.

"Ok."

ON FRECKLES

I have many freckles. If all my freckles held hands, I would look like a brown walrus without the tusks. If I had tusks, maybe I wouldn't have freckles.

In the summer, my freckles explode and multiply; for winter they stuff themselves back into their little skin suitcases and hide. Except they always leave a few behind and so every year, I have more. Even if I avoid the sun.

The purpose of freckles? None. They may be cute if you have four or five on your cheeks but not when it becomes difficult to see a space without a freckle. Grace says they're maybe Morse Code for an alien life form or the marks of a defunct and leftover plague.

Nice.

There is absolutely nothing but tat on TV.

First choice: *Famous Collectors* – the man has thirty-thousand banana-themed hats. Second: Plankton and their purpose. Third: The history of the New Testament. Fourth: Twelve singing dancing Wonder Kids in curls trying to win parts in a musical that only the insane with no taste whatsoever would actually want to go and see.

Then rom-coms, lots of rom-coms: *Pretty Woman, When Harry Met Sally, The Perfect Man.* Grace refuses to watch anything that isn't borderline horror.

The reception is abysmal anyway because of the weather and us being perched on the edge of the wild Atlantic Ocean.

We finally stumble upon a whale documentary. The presenter has a voice that could put ogres to sleep and make them dream they were slugs. "Whales are entirely sociable animals," he drones. "It is rare to see a whale alone, as if there is a shame attached to it." We turn the sound off and take turns to provide our own voiceover while bingeing on snacks.

"What is it with you and whales?" says Grace, when she's had enough and stomps off to bed down in our spare room. She says I talk in my sleep and that she's afraid I'll start singing whale songs at her or leap straight into a whale mating ritual, whatever that is, with her as the victim. My hair's still wet and I'm not tired, so I make hot chocolate and watch the whales.

Unfortunately, soon as I have convinced myself that I am in the water with the whales, voices filter through from the corridor.

Of course I peek out.

The hotel is full of film people tonight and a few locals who can't drive home because of Chris's cocktails. Who knows what I might hear?

At the end of our corridor, a door opens from our private quarters onto the first floor proper. Marcus props it open while Kitty tries to persuade Mum to join them. "Have a few drinks. Let your hair down. Have some fun. You have to have had some *once*!"

"It's been a long day and I'm tired. Besides, I don't want Angelica finding a stranger in my bed," says Mum who is weary of the joke that I am the only proof that she was once fun-loving.

Marcus winds his arms around Kitty's waist and tries to pull her away. He's made of patience. "So use another room," says Kitty. "It's your hotel! I'll do you a deal. If you don't like his friend, you can have Marcus." Marcus groans, which doesn't exactly bode well for the exchange. "Can't do fairer than that!"

"You do what you like. I've given you keys and Grace is staying with us." Mum walks away from them towards our apartment.

I close the door sharpish as Kitty calls after her.

"Angelica's fourteen, Molly! One day, she's going to leave home and what'll you have then?"

Chapter 5

The hotel is full for hours the next day. Breakfasts overflow into the bar and the film guys hang around making phone calls. The weather, unusually mild considering the number of branches that have come down on top of our newly serrated loveseat, is due to turn nasty again. They want to move the whale a.s.a.p., hangovers or no.

Everyone seems sloppy and sort of loose-limbed. There are three new leaks in the kitchen but nowhere near the electrics, which is good. Chris is fixing them now. It's as if the whole hotel drank a little too much last night and hasn't recovered yet.

I get roped in to help with the breakfasts since our chef, Eve zoomed off into the sunset last month with Sprite, the waiter we'd had for years. They sent a nice letter from somewhere sunny apologising, but we still haven't found a chef to replace her and Mum blames me.

(All I did was mention to Sprite that Eve was avoiding eye contact not because she was disappointed with his work but because she fancied him, like head over heels and belly- up-in-trifle fancied.) She should be glad I saved her two wages since the hotel has not been busy since, at least not until last night. Besides Chris is an excellent chef anyway.

The minute it quietens, I make my favourite breakfast: porridge with lumps of cooking chocolate melting in its heart, topped with cornflakes and cream mixed with milk. It's the best way to mark the start of the new year. I lift some veggie brekkie leftovers for Grace and head upstairs so we can picnic in private.

I told her about Marcus and she elected to stay upstairs until certain he'd gone. She didn't fancy seeing Marcus and her mum together. So when I come out of the dining room to see them snorkling the faces off each other in the lobby, it feels wrong.

"I wouldn't do that there." I point at the mistletoe over Kitty's head. "Seriously. That's been there for years."

Kitty smiles as if she thinks I'm jealous which is yuck and spurs me on.

"See the black bits? That's like a black mushroom mould, the sort bog bodies get between their toes. And behind their eyes. And – not sure if I should tell you this or if it's really inappropriate but kissing him under mistletoe like that?" I'm heading for the stairs, making it seem really casual, the sort of fact everyone knows, "You've probably made him infertile" as Mum comes out of the dining room

"You shouldn't even know words like that!" says Mum to my retreating back, but that's plain daft.

"I'm fourteen, Mum. Not twelve," I say as I disappear.

When you're an only child – and especially the daughter of a single Mum, you have no big sister to tell you anything. You don't get to see your parents argue and make up or talk about things they shouldn't. Besides, I read a lot. All the *'wrong'* books but by the time Mum notices or someone notices for her, it's too late.

What can I say except, "I've read far worse Mum". Which is when she sort of shrugs and gives up trying to inflict moral guidance on my reading material.

As for the mistletoe, teenagers can have fun too. Despite the bad press. And the spots. And the mood swings. And the nothing-fits-me-anymore. And the whole miserable shoulder droop life-is-boring routine. Though mine don't droop very well.

It's not a big thing, but it means I've learnt to have fun with words instead.

ON MULLETS

Marcus has a mullet. I know this because I asked Mum if
Marcus' hair had caught some strange styling disease and

she told me. Apparently, the mullet is a hairstyle from the 80s that has no reason to exist.

Think *'baby but very hairy mammoth'* landing on the head from a great height and you're close.

If I cut my hair short it would form itself into a mullet because it would be confused and lack the weight to keep it flat. Ish.

A mullet is also a smelly fish.

While Grace showers, I watch Albert being lifted onto a trailer pulled by a truck. His tail is festooned with a luminous pink scarf because it's sticking off the end. Story is that the crew needed to get their boss, Marcus, a present for his 40th. So when the whale was finally built, someone got the bright idea – *'bright'* as in *'dim'* – that they'd treat Marcus to a helicopter ride and dangle the whale along, thus saving on transportation costs.

The idea was that they'd lower Albert down before they undid the straps inside the helicopter. I'm guessing some of them weren't so securely tied. Chris wants us to buy Albert back when the film's finished and keep him out front as a tourist attraction. We could even put a door in his side and pipe whale sounds in; do a whole Jonah in the Belly of the Whale Experience at Easter and Christmas.

Maybe turn the whale into a unit for honeymooners with imagination.

He also wants to rename the bar after Albert, since we sold more drink, food and accommodation last night than in the whole three winter months.

Kitty kisses Marcus goodbye *again*, down beside the whale. I only realise Mum's behind me when she speaks.

"She's doing that deliberately."

"She doesn't even know you're here, Mum."

"Course she does. I'm sorry, love, you shouldn't have to see this."

There she goes, doing the moral protection thing again. You have to admire her for trying. And it is pretty gross. Forget 'kissing'; this is oral dissection; Kitty is sucking out all his internal organs and enjoying the wolf whistles of the film crew too much.

"I wonder what Grace would think of having Marcus for a dad?"

This is me trying to lighten the mood.

"I'd think yuck." Grace shields her eyes; right enough, in daylight, my hair is unnaturally bright. "My mum has rotten taste and did you SEE his hair? Besides, I already have one." Grace wants to be a unisex hairdresser. Maybe it's a previous life thing. Or a way to meet cute men when they're feeling vulnerable? "Hi, Ms Moone!"

Mum squeezes her shoulder and relaxes. Grace is far better with Mum than I am. She knows what to say. Like now Mum feels sorry for Grace instead of angry at Kitty and she knows she was totally right to say no to random frolicking last night.

Right then, when nobody is looking but me, the whale flicks his tail, knocking Marcus and his mullet into the ornamental pond and winks at me. The pink scarf ends up tied in a big bow on top of Marcus's head, turning his mullet into a Glee-pony's tail.

Then I blink and the whale is in the truck heading down the driveway.

I'm certain Marcus is entirely dry – but it's a shame.

~~~

Before I can sneak out with Grace, Mum nabs me to turn over some of the rooms so she can make a start on the laundry. She wants the bulk of it done before she goes to join Kitty for their annual New Year's Day lunch.

Grace says she did enough chambermaiding last night so we agree to meet at the dolmen in an hour. It sits on a sort of rise, surrounded by a circle of stones, only one of which stands upright, facing the dolmen. This is the Stone Man. He faces the dolmen head on; legend has it that he is the ultimate lover, turned to stone from grief.

This is where we go to talk about stuff we don't want anyone to hear. There's something about the ancient history of the place that feels comforting. Nothing can be as bad as being cremated under a rock thousands of years ago.

Or turned to stone.

Grace is sat on one of the apartmentter stones. It's minus 1 degree and my toes think they're being eaten by an aggressive budgie even if I know it's only pins and needles.

"What's wrong with you?" Grace doesn't feel the cold. That's okay though, I feel enough cold for us both. "Here." She holds out her mum's business phone but I'm not sure I want to know what's on the other end.

"My fingers are too frozen to hold a phone."

"It's just stupid," she says. "Nothing bad or sick. Promise. It'll keep one of your ears warm?"

I take the phone and listen. On the other end a man is singing Goosie Goosie Gander. At least I presume it's a man.

"I told him to sing every nursery rhyme he knew in a high pitched voice." Grace looks at her watch. "20 minutes ago."

We get bored more quickly than he does.

At *Baa Baa Black Sheep*, Grace hangs up and stuffs it in her pocket. "New plan. Let's go flirt."

Chapter 6

According to Grace, the first of January is officially THE best day to meet The One With Whom You Will Spend The Rest Of Your Life. Blissfully. As in boxes of chocolates and bunches of flowers every day AND he or she not only listens to all your music but actually likes it!

She reckons it has something to do with everyone spending too much time around elderly rellies over Christmas and wanting to feel alive again. We already have plans to meet incredibly wealthy and handsome twins from somewhere else who arrive on a fancy yacht that gets scuppered on a sandbank off Drisogue Harbour.

Grace says we need all the practice we can get at flirting, for when this happens.

I should explain why we need these twins to come in from somewhere else. Drisogue is grey. It used to be a market town so the main street is wide enough for cows to poop around on. Now cars tend to stop right in the middle for no reason other than that they couldn't be bothered parking. It's fun when the tourists arrive. You know they're lost when they stop behind a parked car in the middle of the road waiting for some invisible set of lights to change.

But the recession has made everything greyer. Instead of birds chattering, you can hear the squeak of For Sale signs dangling off their hinges. But if you ignore that the town is run down, Drisogue is on this really beautiful peninsula with a sea full of whales and dolphins with its own little pier jutting into the Atlantic Ocean like a welcoming finger. And everyone looks out for you. Everyone knows you. Okay, that's probably the downside.

But nothing really bad ever happens here.

We're like a beach at low tide.

Six roads lead off the main street but at the centre, past St Brigid's Catholic Church and opposite the Church of Ireland, there's a small cobbled square. This is the east end of the town, lowest and most sheltered. Here stand the war memorials for 1914-18 and 1939-45.

A rival memorial for local heroes of Ireland's War of Independence stands in a small tub of a dinky little park at the far end of the town where the winds of all Ireland converge. This is where Guppy last met the love of her life, Teddy Bannagher, in 1964. He was an American soldier. They were going to make a life together in Canada, only he never came back.

Guppy talks about Teddy as if he's still alive but if you ask her specifics, she gets defensive and sad. Mum says Vietnam happened and he got called up. She reckons he must have died in the war.

~ ~ ~

Needless to say, all the teens without chores are on Main Street today, converged around the nearest thing to a *'happening'* to occur in Drisogue since Fr Patrick ran away to France with Alice B. (Not my fault. I never said a word to either of them.) The event worthy of such an audience is the screwing up of a neon sign over a shop painted in all the shades of the brightest sunset ever: *Sup & Surf.*

This is the brainchild of Simon Clancy, the vicar's tall other son and Dylan's brother. He's twenty-five. He worked two years in one of the big American companies doing software before chucking it all in to travel. Grace heard him tell Kitty he wanted his cafe to have the feel of an Indian souk melded with an Arabian tent.

It's a big ask for a shop that used to be a bakery.

I feel sorry for Dylan, stuck holding the ladder while everyone stands around commenting.

"Yeah, like anyone'd go to an internet cafe in Drisogue!" says a voice at the back louder than the rest. It's Theo, who avoids eye contact and always has. Let's just say, he and I have history. No, not that sort. More the, 'Let's forget I ever saw what I just saw you do' sort. As in, I'd have forgotten it long ago and gladly if Theo hadn't been so odd ever since.

Unlike Dylan, Simon loves the attention. "Yo, dude!" he shouts down in the worst fake John Wayne accent EVER. Donegal and American accents do NOT mix. "Like you might be so wrong."

What does that even mean?

Grace peels off to chat up Tariq and I pick up a flier for the cafe from the windowsill nearby. Tariq's nearly sixteen, moody and known mainly for his hair. Rumour has it that he went to a hairdresser in Dublin after a school trip to the National Museum. He pointed at a prehistoric gold torc in the brochure from the museum and said, "I want that".

It's gold and all, though you can see the roots coming through.

He's cool and knows it. She has NO chance! Her latest plan is to persuade him to let her do his hair when it's grown out a bit. When she styles it, he'll see her for the babe she is (isn't). It's like watching a piranha at play, pretending to be harmless.

"This cafe," says Simon, climbing down, "is going to be the coolest, most popular venue in the history of the West. In years to come, you will be saying to your children, I was there when Sup n Surf opened its doors for the first time. Besides, you're wrong. Every town needs a net cafe just as every dude needs a baby brother."

"Stop talking like a turtle," says Dylan.

Simon ruffles Dylan's hair. "Beats being one, Shellfish."

Dylan goes red. Prawn red. Now I get the nickname. I study the leaflet for the cafe before he turns and realises I've seen.

'WHY WAIT?'

it shouts.

'Sup barista coffee in a louche lounge while surfing the internet. Make things happen with a website targeted for your business! Trace your ancestors, lost friends or family in Sup n Surf.'

It's a very busy leaflet and he forgot to put an address or email address on it so it'll only work for locals.

"Don't have to show interest in loony brother's undertaking because you fancy Dylan." I don't get how Grace can creep up on me like that.

"I wasn't."

"What does louche mean anyway? Does that mean he'll serve pot?"

"Doubt it. His dad would be all over him."

"Wouldn't be so sure. He's only a recent vicar. Mum says Mrs D heard from Big Brenda that he was a fashion designer in New York before he found God. Maybe he's atoning for a life of debauchery?"

"It means relaxed, rakishly; like 18th-century-aristocrat-relaxed. How'd it go with Tariq?"

"Gone for a pee in the pub."

"Too Much Information." But I forget it all instantly – Dylan is coming over. I can tell she's impressed. My technique of studying Simon's leaflet, even if it wasn't a technique, has hit the target.

"Then again," she mutters, "if it works for you. Hey Tariq!" Grace shouts to Tariq as he leaves The Pirate Queen. "About those roots?"

Dylan runs his hands through his hair as if he's trying to wipe off his brother's paw print. "I've to work most nights in Compton's," he says. "But how about doing something Wednesday?" He grins and I'm lost. Compton's is the posh restaurant in town. Makes sense that the cutest boy would be a waiter there. Tourists will love him; when we get some.

"If you're free?"

This is when I'd expect swallows to break out into a chorus of Alleluia! and roses to sprout through the pavement. The miracle has happened. I, Angelica Moone, aged fourteen, have been asked out!

Instead, Mum storms out of Kitty's pub across the road, with Kitty in pursuit.

"Yeah, well maybe the point is that we're not just 'single mums'. In case you hadn't noticed, Prince Charming doesn't *do* Donegal."

"Yeah, well I haven't given up."

Kitty's voice is deadly calm. "Meaning?"

"Oh come on, Kitty, how many men this month! You're saying that makes you more of a woman than me? Jeez, Grace mustn't know who to expect at the kitchen table!"

"At least she knows her mum is alive!"

"If by *alive*, you mean desperate!"

"Can't all be frigid—"

Kitty stops short, realising she has an audience. THEY have an audience. An audience of mostly teenagers that may not be applauding but that is very, very interested. Except for me and Grace; we are officially most MORTIFIED, frozen to the spot and staring at our mums.

Ideally, right now, a couple of eagles would swoop down and carry us off to a mountain eyrie as takeaway for little birdlets of prey and we would not be stuck on the kerb staring at our mums.

Funny how life never delivers enormous birds of prey when you need them.

Kitty clears her throat and retreats inside, leaving Mum stranded.

Simon offers Mum one of his fliers. "You should come over when we're open. Might be an idea to update your hotel website." He's trying to save her, which is sweet. Grace follows her mum inside. "You'd have guests pouring in from all over the world."

"Maybe later in the year."

Dylan, I can't even look at. He'll probably never want to talk to me again. Mum's heading home when she spots me and stops. "Coming or not?"

Guess I'm going home, so.

She doesn't say a word all the way home. I try to talk about the new cafe and how cool it is that we got so much money for putting the whale up, not to mention that the hotel was full on New Year's Eve which has happened, like, never.

All she manages are occasional grunts.

So I suggest we do something tonight, since we were interrupted last night. "Just the two of us, providing another whale doesn't fall out of the sky?"

"I'd be happy to do so, if I had a chef since we have seven tables booked tonight."

"Sorry."

Which is how and why we end up in the kitchen, preparing the vegetables for tonight. I pity the carrots. Mum shouldn't really chop vegetables when she has murder in mind. I try to slip her some peppers. Normally she rips them apart but today they go under the knife too.

"Being single is not a crime, Angelica!"

"I know."

"I am perfectly happy and fulfilled with my life exactly as it is." Mum stops, suddenly. "I'm sorry. I shouldn't take it out on you. I just—" The last pepper shuffles backwards towards the fruit bowl. "Funny but I always assumed I'd meet someone before you even realised you didn't have a dad. Not that I'd any notion that some big white wedding, sipping champagne off the back of a geriatric whale, was what I needed to be fulfilled as a woman."

Geriatric whale? The word 'why' comes to mind but it doesn't seem the right time. "It could still happen."

She smiles in that annoying way mums smile at small children who have said something daft but that's sweet too and they don't want the children to feel bad. "Yeah," she says. "Now you sound like Kitty."

"Seriously."

"Course it could. It's okay Angel, I am perfectly happy as I am, okay?"

"No, Mum, honest. You're gorgeous. You're beautiful. You don't have facial hair." Mum grimaces at my attempt at humour. "Sprite probably would have run away with you if you hadn't scared him so much. I mean, if you hadn't had a hotel to run." That gets a grunt. She's warming up. "And when you're not stressed…" I sneak a sideways look, "you're really fun to be with."

She puts the knife down and hugs me. "If I'd had to choose," she says, finally, "I'd have chosen my beautiful daughter over any man."

"Even Dad?"

"Even him. Now, let's get these veggies done."

"What it's like? I mean, how did you know Dad was the one?"

"You just do."

"But how?"

She gazes out the window at the oak tree. We'll have to replace the loveseat, says Chris. I suggested we could turn the old one into a feature in the bar. Seems a shame to lose all the history that was carved into it by lovers for decades. "Well, I guess, suddenly there's this person and he or she is all you can think of. Everything seems wonderful when they're around. Is this about some boy?"

"No."

"You're not being pressurised into doing something?"

"No, look, yuck, I just wanted—"

"You would tell me?"

"I said there's no one."

"I know you're all maturing faster than we did but it is still important, Angelica, to wait for the right person—"

"I said no. And I wouldn't. Oh what's the point, you never listen anyway!" And I am out of there.

It was her stupid fault for hiring a chef and waiter who were obviously going to fall in love. Not mine.

Chapter 7

When I call down next day, Grace is washing the windows of the pub and well grumpy. The minute she sees me, she dumps the rag into the bucket and peels off her industrial strength rubber gloves – it's important to have fantastic nails if you want to be a hairdresser, apparently.

"I go in, willing to completely forgive Mum for embarrassing me and comfort her if she needs it. I'll even tell her she's right and I'm glad she's alive. Anyway, just as I close the door, completely forgetting it's even on me, her phone rings – in my pocket! And there's Mum, all creeped up behind me, like some sort of praying mantis. It's not as if we really used it or anything."

"Praying mantis?"

"Y'know, the bird of prey that swoops down to snatch unsuspecting victims?"

"Vulture?"

"Whatever."

"Praying mantes are insects."

"Same difference."

"Who eat their lovers. Bite off their heads without even saying thanks."

"But they still get mates?"

I nod. Not sure '*mate*' is the best term, given the circumstances. "Now THAT is serious allure," says Grace, whistling. "Wonder if you could bottle it? Y'know, patent it as the Ultimate Spray-on Pheromone?"

"Could result in a serious shortage of dads." We exchange a look.

"Sure, there's that already," says Grace. "When you think of it, your mum was a sort of praying mantis. I mean, soon as she gets pregnant with you, your dad gets eaten by a shark."

"Not funny." One of Simon's fliers is on the pavement and I pick it up. Damp. "She was nowhere near him when he died. Besides, it was a whale. Whole lot bigger."

"Fair dues! But you have to admit it's a lot less messy than her biting his head off. Easier to explain to the Gardaí."

"I'm not sure you'd stay to talk to the cops if you'd done that. What did your mum say about the phone?"

"Oh she was furious and horrified and went into this big drive about how I have to turn out better than all the other kids because she's a single parent and she's stunned I could do this and did I answer it?"

She takes a deep breath and sits down on the windowsill though it's probably wet.

"So I said, because I was pissed off with her sneaking up on me and all that stuff with your mum and Marcus and because it was a waste of time stealing it anyway, 'Yeah, course I did'. So now I'm grounded till we go back to school. Plus I have to wash all the windows this morning and the floors this afternoon and she's inside thinking of a pile of other stuff to make me do."

We ponder the unfairness of life until Grace adds, "Least you had a good result".

"What?"

"Dylan. He asked you out, didn't he?" I nod. She punches the air. "I knew it! It was the way he walked over towards you, all seeming confident when he wasn't at all. So when are you meeting up? Just going to shift him or actually go on a proper date and talk and stuff?"

I shrug, reluctant to answer. It's just enough time for her to pounce.

"You said NO? You did!"

I shrug again; shrugs are the international language for avoiding speech and eye contact. Mine are not the biggest but I make sure they count.

"Oh I can't believe you Angelica Moone. You are such a waste of space.

He's cute. He's ADORABLY cute and he's into you. REALLY into you. He asks you out and you – YOU – say no!! The cutest – and newest boy in town is eating out of your hands, you're not even grounded and you're in a glump!"

I'd do a third shrug but she'd probably thump me. I'm not in the mood for being thumped.

"Well? Go on? Why'd you refuse? Must have had a super good reason?"

Instead, I talk about Mum. "You should have seen her when she and Dad met. There are these photos, taken for his next film, the one about Granuaile. She was going to maybe go to Hollywood and buy a big mansion and have a cocktail bar in her rooftop garden with an infinity pool. Instead, Mum has me, he dies and she spends seven years slaving in grotty hotels. Then seven more in a half-dead town on the edge of nowhere with no decent men for miles."

Grace pouts. "It's not that dead." I don't answer. "If we could get Theo to move out, it'd be fine."

There's slime building up on the top of the water in the bucket. The rag crawls up the side of the bucket, looks at me balefully and escapes over the edge.

"I don't see why that stops you seeing Dylan. Not as if your mum'd fancy him. Oh no – your mum doesn't fancy Dylan?"

"Yuck."

"Phew."

"Don't you get it?"

"Nope."

"How can I go out with Dylan when it's my fault Mum's single and alone? It'd be like rubbing her nose in it."

"She doesn't seem lonely."

"Yeah, well."

"Licky, nobody asked her to get pregnant. I mean, you weren't exactly expressing an opinion at the time."

We say nothing for a while. Across the road, Simon wires up the neon sign over the cafe.

"At least your mum sees men," I say. On the ground, her rag gives a groan and crawls towards the gutter to die.

"And sees them and sees them and sees them… And oops, was that a new one? Oh yeah, Mulletty Marcus."

Simon turns on his sign. "Tell me what it looks like from there!"

"Bright," I say, but a fuse blows and it dies. I look at the leaflet I picked up. The graphics are pretty tame; the words are cluttered. It's brave though. Has to be the first new shop to open here in two years. A pigeon sitting on the phone line above us craps directly on to it, which is a bit judgemental. The bird poo – and yes, I know it's only wee but it looks like poo – covers everything except the picture of a monitor.

I look up. The bird winks but I think she's eyeing the rag.

The internet? Is that the solution?

Grace interrupts but I'm already hatching a cunning plan, a super cunning plan. Well, okay, a minorly cunning plan that really isn't that cunning at all and I have no idea if it will work but still, it's something.

I have no idea what Grace is talking about but she has been talking all the time. "So, if you tell my mum we have to work on a project together?"

"What?"

"Then I wouldn't have to do the floors after this."

"Yeah," I say; my mind on other things. "Don't work too hard."

Instead of replying, she scoops the rag back into the bucket and stomps indoors.

Did I say something wrong?

Chapter 8

It's the perfect solution. All I need to do is find a website full of wonderful and thoughtful men. I'll persuade Mum to join up. As a dare. A bet. '*Something to do on a quiet night.*' No pressure and absolutely no judgement.

Gazillions of men will ask her out, but she'll be picky, cos she deserves the best and will find the one that makes her feel like a billion Euros. Job done and I can say '*yes*' to Dylan.

The tricky bit, see, about fixing Mum up is that Drisogue's a town run by women. Mrs D in Dolan's. Kitty in her pub, Mrs G in Gaffney's. Mum and Guppy in the hotel. Big Brenda (who's six foot three) in Hedges Hardware – grudgingly; her husband developed a fear of customers not long after they married. Now he writes love songs about mermaids and sheep.

He's even written one about a sheepy-mermaid but Mum says it's not for my ears, which would make you wonder.

Cathie's mum, who is as small as a pocket wristwatch on double time and never has the same hairdo twice, runs the estate agency/ legal firm/ takeaway/ laundrette and fish shop, while Denise's mum is our School Principal. As for the hotel, we only get couples. That's how we pitch it: the romantic getaway, far from it all.

But other people find love. Mrs D in Dolan's was windsurfing out of Galway when a rogue wind carried her all the way up the coast to Drisogue. Okay, it wasn't maybe Galway or even Sligo but she definitely blew in from somewhere and she fell in love with Damascus Dolan who talks in rhyming couplets.

Unless he has been to the dentist – Mamie Mac – which is lots.

Perils of growing up above your parents' sweet shop.

She hasn't windsurfed since. Not even when Mum heard her story and tried to coax her back out onto the waves for company. "It wouldn't be fair on Damascus," she said. As if she might be blown into another harbour and end up leaving him for another sweet shop owner.

The odds of that happening, even once, means it has to be possible for Mum to find love too. Even for a little time, so she knows it's possible. Thinking of the web as a giant wave washing men into Drisogue for her, I search 'romance', 'matchmaking' and 'dating sites'.

Up pops a dodgy mail-order-bride service, a company that organises weddings for cats and dogs – their exclusive package includes bow ties, top hats and honeymoon suite – and another site that suggests that the only 'tip top' way to find love is through nude table tennis.

Okay, I exaggerate. Halfway normal matchmaking sites pop up too but they're dull and their questions are lousy. Religion, qualifications, ambition, weight, height, income, profession and hat size.

I'm on page ten of 45 'links', beginning to think this is a bad idea – doomed, even, when there's a quiet knock at the door. Rather than engage in another pointless discussion about why I'm still on the computer at midnight, I turn off the monitor and dive fully dressed under my duvet.

It's a Monsters Inc duvet. I really must upgrade.

The bed's still bouncing when Mum comes in. There's a spring in the mattress that is out to get me and has already inflicted five scratches on my right thigh. I zone out, pretending, even to myself, that I'm deeply asleep, dreaming of dolphins.

Mum sits on the bed anyway. Does she not know that sitting on the bed when someone is asleep is likely to wake them up completely? Is this deliberate? Do they learn it at Mum School? I can feel her looking at me so I do my best to look angelic. It's too late to 'wake up' now.

"I never meant for you not to have a dad," she says, ever so quietly and kisses me on the head. Then she turns off my bedside lamp and leaves.

I wasn't thinking about dads. I was thinking about dolphins. Now she has me thinking about dads. Grrr.

~ ~ ~

"Guppy, if you knew what you wanted but not where it was or how to find it, what would you do?"

"I'd ask you. Now focus. What do you see?"

Guppy has been teaching me how to read her carpet bag of tricks for two years now. 12 is the magical age, apparently, to start. We had a ceremony with herbal tea and homemade brownies. Sometimes I think I almost have it, then I don't and never as clearly as I did on the day we arrived.

"You never know," she says, "when a twig or a stone will help you make the right decision."

I see my mother with a boyfriend. I see me with Dylan. I even, at a push, at a very long push made of being nice and knowing what my best friend wishes for, see Tariq with Grace on the broken loveseat. It's hard to clear your mind sufficiently to be able to accurately interpret a table-load of twigs, nuts and sea-curved scraps of glass when your entire future is at stake.

"Well?" says Guppy, all concerned when I don't respond except to sweep the spread back into the bag. "What did you see?"

"Grace coming up the driveway?"

She grunts something about ingratitude but I kiss her anyway. Then she has to hug me and we're good all over again.

By the time I get back to the lobby, Mum has cornered Grace. We only have four whole, glorious days of Christmas holidays left yet, somehow, she persuades us to take down all the Christmas decorations for her.

"It's too soon."

"You say that every year and every year, I end up taking them down after you've gone back to school."

~ ~ ~

Grace isn't impressed. "Can't believe I escaped Mum to end up doing this."

"Yeah. Sorry about that. How did you get off being grounded?"

"Said we had a project. If you can't be bothered helping me lie, at least you can cover for me."

"Sorry. I had something I needed to do last night."

"You rushed off before I could tell you," she says.

"Tell me what?"

"Tariq. Why do you think I was in such a good mood that I was going to forgive Mum for embarrassing us in front of everyone? He only said that I can maybe do his roots and if that works out, I can maybe cut his hair!" All glowering done – Grace never holds a grudge, or a grump; it's one of the most amazing things about her – but I note the double 'maybe'.

It's very hard to say no to Grace when she corners you.

Harder to make her hear you say 'no'.

Essentially, she'll hover till she gets you to agree.

We finish packing up the decorations. It's kind of satisfying. I shove the old mistletoe into the grate in the lounge.

"Isn't it bad luck to burn mistletoe?"

"Your mum and Marcus heavily smooched underneath it. It's contaminated mistletoe."

"Yeah," she says. "Bad mistletoe! It should burn."

Finally, Mum shoves us outside for some fresh air. Ironic, really, when she was the one keeping us inside all morning.

"What's your dad like, as a dad? I mean, I've seen him but…"

"Is this because of what your mum said?"

"Sort of," I lie.

"A sloth," says Grace, finally.

"As in furry and sleeps in trees?"

"As in makes promises he can't be bothered to keep." We're heading into town feeling completely Christmassed out. "Mum's as bad. Swears she's finished with him and then they meet up and poof! It makes for awkward breakfasts." She kicks a pebble that ricochets off the hotel sign.

"Thing is, half the time he thinks he's in with a chance again and sometimes she does too. Then they start argufying about something stupid and it seems as if I'm the only one who knows that they can't be bothered to fight about the serious stuff anymore or why it all went wrong. Y'know, they don't even look happy together in their wedding photo."

She kicks a second pebble out the gate.

"She put him off coming this week because Marcus said he wants to take her out and she doesn't want Dad to know, which is ridiculous. Like she still wants Dad, only then, when he's actually around, she doesn't. They're like a really crummy fairytale, the sort that got chucked out at the very beginning because it didn't work."

Grace kicks a third and final pebble with great force.

Only it's not a pebble, it's the nub of a massive stone and she stubs her toe badly. Quick as a flea, I suggest hospital, since everyone knows Tariq is doing work experience for Transition Year in A&E when he isn't helping Chris with odd jobs up at the hotel.

She growls at me and hops over to lean against the wall and massage her injured toe back into shape.

"You're better off without a dad. Unless you can find one that isn't defective. Why all the questions?"

"Do you think men aren't meant to be dads?"

She doesn't answer. Lots of our friends have dads who are at every school play and exhibition and boasting about them in the pub at night. "Your dad died. I'm sure he'd still be around if he hadn't," she says at last, which is hugely generous.

We walk – well, she hobbles – in silence for a while. "I used to think I was adopted," she says as we cusp town. I wasn't expecting this.

"Why?"

"Because I don't look like Mum."

It's true.

"And Dad, well I didn't want to look like Dad because he kept making her cry and I thought, if I'm adopted, that means she chose me and that Dad did too, even if he didn't realise it, so I was really loved. Despite what it felt like when Dad was around."

"That's pretty deep."

"Yeah. I was a cool child."

Simon is nowhere to be seen, so we peer through the windows. The inside walls are a shade midway between maroon and embarrassment. "How come you never told me?"

"It was sort of a secret, I guess."

The top rim of the walls are covered with swirly patterns that I think are Arabic script and the effect is pretty amazing. Grace says it looks messy. "Bet he got the paint as part of a job lot from Big Brenda's. A batch someone ordered for a nursing home but decided it was too cheerful. Or psychosis-inducing. Mum says she has a whole basement of paint nobody wants because she mixed it wrong."

I'm guessing Grace's salon will be white and black; no unnecessary ornamentation anywhere. That's when it comes to me in a whirl of genius and 'why didn't I think of that before?'-ness. Forget all the dating sites that already exist, why don't I start my own? Use it to find men she'd like and target Mum.

In a good way. Not like sniper fire. People get hurt by snipers.

As we cross over to The Pirate Queen, Simon pulls up to unload computers into the cafe.

A creative genius needs talented minions – and furry white cats, but Mum's allergic. I focus on the unfinished cafe. I need someone who can create a website for me, for example. Someone like Simon Clancy, entrepreneur and computer guru.

"When d'you think he'll open?"

"Who cares?"

"Just. Curious?" She can't know what I'm up to so I put on some lip balm, calmness personified.

"I can guarantee he'll be in there at eight tomorrow morning though. Hammering and drilling and blaring music across the street straight into my bedroom. Where I'm meant to be having a LIE IN!" she shouts across the road.

Simon turns around. "Talking to me?"

"No," says I. "She was just being grumpy." Thump. She thumps me a lot, does Grace, but mostly I deserve it.

"Thump me again and I WILL go over there and tell him you fancy him. Big time. As in lying on your bed, pining for the moment his music starts. As for the drilling—"

WHAT DADS ARE USEFUL FOR WHEN YOU DON'T HAVE ONE

Age 6 months – 3 years: Riding up on their shoulders; being taller than everyone and having a bird's-eye view of bald patches.

Age 3-12: Presents. Thinking you're a princess regardless. Treats.

Age 13+: Big fleeces to borrow. For complaining to when you fall out with your mum. Take you to boyband concerts at which your mum wouldn't be seen dead.

Age 16+: Lifts. Teaching you to drive. Reminding boyfriends to give you presents and treat you like a princess. Maybe.

Chris is in the lobby when I get back, mounting an extra large photo of me with the whale. When he steps back to see if it's straight, I snatch it off the wall.

"Hey! It's a beautiful picture! Captures your theatrical side."

"Use one of Mum." I nip in to answer the phone in the office.

He follows me in. "Mouse, come on! Give it back." I hand him the empty frame. Bad enough everyone thinks I'm weird without advertising it.

By the time I come out, he's losing the battle with Mum to hang the photo of her with the whale. "Use the one you took of Guppy. It's her hotel, after all."

They're sort of wrestling over it but Mum's winning because Chris is a softie.

He might as well give up. If he got it mounted, she'd only take it down when his back was turned. "What is it with you Moones! Anyone would think you were twelve foot ogres. With bad breath," he adds for good measure.

"Mum. The film guy called," I say, before a brawl develops. "Monkey something."

"Marcus? You know his name is Marcus." Mum hands the empty frame back to Chris, who grunts.

"Yeah. Him. He's sending painters along next week. Says you will have to put them up if we want the job done quickly."

"How many?"

"I dunno."

"And for how long?"

"Till it's done?"

"Chris," says Mum, "Never have a teenage daughter. They are only useful when you need help on the computer." She turns to me with her 'patient face'. "Did he leave a number?"

Chapter 9

Eight in the morning and I am down town before Mum even knows I'm awake. She poked her head in around seven to ask if I wanted to help with breakfasts but I faked some heavy snoring – think volcano with food poisoning and you're close. It's for her own good, even if she doesn't know it. Since we're back in school on Monday, all minnows and sharks, I know she's not pushed to make me do too many chores.

Unless I actually give her a reason to put me to work; as in I 'get found doing nothing'.

My task: to convince Simon that setting up a matchmaking site is the best thing since, well, since opening your own internet cafe. The more I thought about it overnight, the more perfect my idea was. I hadn't thought how odd it would look to him, to find me hovering like a dunebug outside his cafe at 7.55 am.

Being me, I put him at his ease immediately. "Don't worry, I don't fancy you. You're old."

"Good to know," he says.

"But I need to ask you a favour."

"I'm not doing your homework for you."

This is not going exactly as I'd planned.

"Anyway, I sucked at homework. You'd be better off asking Dylan. You're not the girl he fancies?"

"I dunno."

"He's the sweetest little bug of a brother, so if you want me to put in a good word or find out what his interests are—"

"Enough already. I'm not here for homework or to talk about Dylan and my guess is he's into whales."

"Correct. So why are you here—?"

"Angelica."

"Ah, the hotel lady's daughter. "

"In Computers, Dylan said you could design rockets for NASA with your eyes closed."

"Dylan tends to exaggerate."

"Course he does. You're his big brother." This disarms him a bit. "Can we go inside?" Grace's gossip antennae, even when she's in a deep sleep, will drag her over to the window to see us talking any minute now. Then she'll want to know why I'm talking to Simon and I'm not ready for that yet. "Please?"

He agrees reluctantly but leaves the door ajar in case he needs to flee. With no time to waste, I show him my research notes and my mission statement. See, I *was* listening in Business Studies, Ms Barrow. (We call her The Broomhandle on account of she's stick thin with a sort of sideways Mohican of hair.)

I'm stood there grinning, thinking he can't possibly turn me down.

But he does.

All I get for explaining my humungously clever plan is, "Sorry, not my scene".

"Doesn't have to be! And how do you know if you don't try?"

"Too many of them already."

"Not in the west. Not in Drisogue." I show him the rest of my plans and sketches of the various pages I've already thought up. "This is a great idea! We focus on people who want to live in the West. Also, you might not know this but Guppy – she's the lady who owns the hotel, she says Drisogue's matchmaker, Hughie MacHughie or something equally quaint, used to have his stall right outside this building. Which makes it fate, sort of."

"I know you're 14." I'm losing him again. "That makes it illegal." He is sooo IRRITATING!

"Here's the deal. You do the software, register the site. I'll do the matching. You've probably heard the rumours. I'm disgustingly good at it. That way it's legal and we both get to do what we're best at." He's wavering. "I'll do all the work, if you show me. It has to be safe and I have to control content."

I can see he's curious. Everyone knows there's money to be made in the love business. "We let people join for free but only for the first month or they won't value it."

"What about my time?"

"Once you've made back what it costs to design the site and all the bits that make it work, we split the profits 60:40. You can't lose."

"50:50"

"Okay." Silly boy; I was going to give him the 60. Sometimes I am way too old for my own good.

"Why?" he says, as if it just occurred to him to ask.

"To make money," says I, innocent as a smoothie. "What else?"

I don't like lying to him and I *will* tell him the truth but not yet, in case word gets out and tiptoes back to Mum all bright-eyed and bushy tailed.

So what he says next is absolutely okay with me.

"And Angelica, nobody knows, right? I mean you tell *nobody*."

"Cross my heart and hope to die. Or at least suffer mighty embarrassment which could be worse and longer-lasting, depending on who sees and what has actually happened and how quickly I realise what's happened and what the consequences are."

I have never been more serious about anything in my life. This way my future lies.

"By the way, if you put tables without computers in the window, you'll get the cafe trade too. You can't afford to alienate the computer illiterate yet."

Simon nods. I can tell he's impressed.

"Also, unless you make the counter top higher, everyone will bump their knees when they pull their chairs in. Then they won't be comfortable so they won't stay long. Besides, you might want colourful cushions on the seats for the harem look and then they won't be able to move the chairs in at all. Or you could lower the chairs, I guess."

I've always been good at this. A childhood spent bumping elbows and ankles into mis-designed hotel kitchens and dining rooms. "Now, if you mount the monitors on the walls, you'd have less glare and more space for coffee mugs. Why d'you have that shelf there?"

"Ornaments," he begins. "Books? Atmosphere?"

"Too low down. You really should have spoken to me before."

"Apparently."

"What coffee are you using?"

"Pure Arabica. Fairtrade."

"People don't like pure. They say they do but they don't. They want hint of chocolate, of mountain springs, Alaskan elk. Okay, I'm kidding about the last one. Besides, if the coffee's too strong, they'll only have one and you want them to have several. So you need to make really good coffee too. I can teach you if you like. Mum made me complete a barista course for her last summer but she says Kitty's a natural, so you have competition right there across the road."

We shake on it all. The website, my role as his new internal design consultant and his promise that I shall be the official taster of any new patisseries he's trying out for the cafe. Then, before he can change his mind on ANYTHING, I am out the door with a grin half the size of a house.

I forgot about Grace.

She's outside their pub, pretending to write up today's pub grub specials on their notice board. I KNEW she'd be watching! For all she says about lie-ins, she wakes with the crows. She just thinks it's cooler to lie in because it annoys her mother big time.

I head up the hill pretending to be so lost in thought that I haven't seen her. And I am, really. Thinking about how I'll find Mum the sort of men who will wine and dine and care for her.

As if she's a 1920s movie star and the only one to ever come to Donegal.

"He's not your type." She catches hold of my arm and her breath at the same time.

I smile and ask after her sore toe. It's good to cultivate a little mystery.

46

Chris told me that. Which may be why none of us know where Chris actually comes from, before he washed up in Drisogue. He says he'll tell me everything when I'm old enough, but that's probably him cultivating his 'air of mystery'.

"Oh please! You can't fancy him!"

"I dunno. He's 25. Single."

"You're 14," she says, weakly.

"Okay then."

"Okay what?"

"I won't fancy him." I walk off, leaving her seriously confused.

Life is good.

Chapter 10

Grace, knowing me better than I know myself, asks no questions but lures me back down after lunch with the promise of sharing in a ludicrously large bar of chocolate, which she then fails to produce. Instead, she launches into a discussion of mating experiments between different species of rat in the 70s.

"Only 50% of the offspring could learn to press the red and yellow button that would release food for them," she says. "The blue button played Tom Jones." I think she made that up. Her mum is a fan.

At least my mum's taste is Talking Heads and They Might Be Giants.

I let her think I've cracked.

Hey, I'm big enough to realise when I need to bring a graphic designer and co-creator into the process and Grace is the most amazing artist. She did me a stunner of Brad Pitt on the inside of my science book. I will never, EVER throw that book out.

The walls of her room are full of her drawings and the bar downstairs, though if you're not a celebrity, you're most likely Grace's victim. I'm always a little bit nervous when she draws me. Victims get lost somewhere between bubble-eyed lagoon lizards and the undead, with just enough reality to make you recognisable.

"You asked me what I was doing with Simon," says I, handing over my sketch pad.

She scans the page and leaps to the wrong conclusion. Granted, my sketch of the background to the home page is an enormous heart. I might have to lose it. "Oh my god! You're dating Simon," she blurts, then covers her mouth in case her mum might hear. As if she would. We heard her on the phone downstairs talking to Marcus; him of the flying whale and mullet.

"He's helping me set up a dating website." I turn the page. "See?"

RomanticHearts.com. ONLY TRUE ROMANTICS NEED APPLY.

"My idea, his computer whizzery. I thought you could do the graphics?"

"Pretty cheesy." Kitty wants Grace to go to art college, which is why she keeps framing Grace's drawings, but Grace still reckons her calling is hair.

"Look I'm not good at drawing like you, but this is the site logo. It's a cross between a heart, the male/ female symbols and chi – because you need good chi to make the energy work between people if it's to stand a chance; with seagulls to represent Drisogue. This section is for the new members' forum, like a chat room and they can join up here. There'll be a questionnaire but I haven't written it yet."

There could be lots of reasons Grace is looking at the pages I've drawn as if they were algebra and dog poo mixed in a big see-through bag with ketchup.

"I thought we could have ivy growing around the section for new members because it's evergreen. Maybe quotes from famous authors on the subject of love running on a loop across the bottom of the home page. In time, we can replace them with quotes from satisfied members."

"Why are you doing this?"

"To find Mum a man."

Grace frowns. "Her 'Perfect Man'?"

"Course not!" That would mean I was a romantic eejit and I can't have anyone thinking that.

"So you don't want your mum to meet her 'Mr Right'?"

"Nope. Just a man. Lots of men."

"You don't want *lots* of men."

"I KNOW." This is not going well. I thought she'd be excited. "All I meant is that I want Mum to start dating. That's all. Doesn't have to be True Love, whatever that is, but I don't want to be the reason she's alone anymore." Grace, being Grace, waits until I finish pacing and plonk down on her bed.

"You know you do that funny thing with your upper lip when you get angry."

"I wasn't angry."

She produces a large brick of mint crisp. At last. "You still did that thing, though." She splits the bar in half and we indulge. "Is this why you were asking about dads?"

"Not really. Maybe."

Grace flips a square into the air theatrically and catches it in her mouth. "This is NOT the way to go about getting a new dad! It's just wrong. Besides— Have you any idea the weirdos you meet on these things?"

Thanks Grace. Burst my bubble with a six-foot claw.

"Serial killers," she says. "Psychos." She's warming to the theme. "Morticians."

My protective balloon is not burst. It will not burst because there is nothing she can say. This is my best idea. "Which is why I need you to help me write the perfect questionnaire to weed them out."

"Oh no. Not me. I am NOT getting involved in another of your schemes! Like sleeping in a tent overnight to see if the Standing Man came alive during a full moon."

We fell asleep. It's still inconclusive.

"Or when you locked us into the ballroom overnight to photograph the ghosts."

"How was I to know the old camera needed film put into it? It seemed to work! Oh look, Grace, it HAS to be you! You're my best friend."

She smiles. I'm winning. (I usually do.)

"Besides—" Yup, here I go saying the wrong thing again: "Nobody knows as much about men as you– I mean, as your mother does; as you do because you've watched her making mistakes and stuff."

I needn't have worried. She stopped listening several seconds ago, when she spotted Tariq of the Torc Hairdo heading through town towards our hotel. Attention span of a newt sitting on a hive of ants, she grabs lippy, mascara, eyeliner, just a spot of white in the centre of her lower lip. She says it makes them look pouty.

In short, she transforms herself into a goddess – well, the sort of goddess who dreams of being a goddess.

"No way," she says, walking through a wave of perfume that settles after her like aerated ectoplasm. "I've got better things to do on the second last day of my holidays, even if you haven't."

And she's gone.

I sit back on her bed and put my feet up. Better to work on the content here where Mum can't walk in. Outside, Grace is flurrying like a snow cloud up Main Street to nip across the Far Field and *accidentally* bump into Tariq where the road curves up the hill to the Drisogue Arms.

Which raises the question, how far would you go, what would you do and who would you dump to chase after the man of your dreams?

Well, it's a question.

Chapter 11

"You've got your lunch?"

"Yes, Mum."

First day back at school. "Wrap that scarf around you properly. What's the point of wearing it like a necklace?" Mum has the Am-I-A-Good-Parent jitters. "And zip up your coat. No point catching a chill on your first day back."

And so, two weeks of holidays – during which I managed to forget almost everything I've ever learnt – end with Strangulation By School Scarf, courtesy of my over-zealous mother who fears colds more than she fears bankruptcy or ghosts.

I'm barely awake and Mum has deprived me of several precious minutes of dawdling. Instead of creeping down the driveway as if I hate going to school and it's a MAJOR punishment that should be reserved for really mean people who stamp on children's toes for fun, I'm forced to hare down the driveway and skid to a halt as the school bus pulls up.

Into a giant puddle.

So I get mud.

Lots of it. I land on the bus, shoes encased in liquid gunk, delicate splashes of thicker mud up my calf, over my knee and under my skirt. Yes. Under.

Not nice.

Jonas, the grumpy driver of our school bus manages a grunt that is several shades of porridge and milky tea. He's well named; the whale spat his namesake out, remember, so it's a fair guess that the biblical Jonas was probably smelly too. I am certain he aimed for that puddle. It was NOT a case of pulling in tightly so other traffic could pass. There is no other traffic at 8.30am. Since most kids in Drisogue need to take the school bus, all the 'grown ups' sleep on.

Well, okay, that's not exactly fair since most of our mums run businesses of some sort, but it's a Monday and it's cold and my bag feels like a ten ton Tessie with haemorrhoids.

So I'm not in the mood for fairness or logic.

Still, I give him my most winning smile. Everyone deserves to be loved; even if, like Jonas, they're so far past it as to hate adorable school kids like me.

Smile.

Grunt.

Swish and the doors close.

See, I like going back to school. But don't expect me to EVER admit this to any so-called adult (especially Mum) regardless of understanding eyes, compelling arguments or bribes. I miss my friends. I miss slagging off the teachers. I even miss the routine in a sort of way.

But I only like 'going back'. I don't actually like BEING there. 'Cept maybe Computers. Or History. As for homework, don't get me started. Well, okay. The rot began in Fourth Class, aged 10, when we were told to draw a map of Ireland with the rivers and coves and stuff.

"No pirates," said Ms Squidgy Fingers, "and definitely no whales."

I was drawing whales in every project; writing about them when I couldn't draw them. It's sort of my specialist subject and if a given topic is boring, as, let's face it, most school essay topics are, it's my way of making it interesting. You could say whales are my Personal Teaching Aid.

Only, I wasn't really paying attention and I missed a crucial element of the homework she gave out. Listening is HARD WORK. If we were meant to listen for nearly seven hours straight, we'd have ears the size of small aeroplanes with flaps and spinny bits so they could tune in to whatever a teacher was saying, regardless of whether she had a low voice or was standing at the back of the class trying to catch us doodling.

Or maybe ginormous cat ears, but without the fur and we wouldn't want to lick our bums clean or spit out fur balls; we'd just have the ears.

And I do doodle EXCESSIVELY well. Even Grace does not doodle as well as I. Mum has threatened to have my doodles entered in a national competition but we haven't found a doodle-friendly one yet. Maybe I should try street art. If I could do with a spray can what I can do with a pen, I'd be infamous.

"What if I need to doodle in order to hear what people are saying?" I said.

Mum chose that moment to stop listening herself and start making scones. See? If our mums can't manage to listen to us for five straight minutes, how do teachers expect us to listen to them for hours?

So anyway, I spent an entire weekend meticulously copying a detailed map of Ireland by hand from the geography book. And what were we meant to do?

Trace it.

Did I even get extra marks? A big, *'Well done. REMARKABLE achievement!'*

I got a 'C'.

Apparently I'd ended the River Shannon in Clare instead of Limerick and put Offaly in Westmeath. Which are both silly names anyway. I mean, there are heaps of counties *west* of Meath and why should one be named after innards?

Is it any wonder we HATE being asked, "Anything happen at school today?" or "How was your day?" by parents when we get home! We are tired!

Grace is three rows from the back, right-hand side. She sits somewhere else on the school bus every term. Last term, it was to get further from Jack, who was going through a niffy deodorant period. This time, it's probably to get a better view of Tariq diagonally across the aisle. Since he's TY and we're Second Year, it's her only chance to openly ogle.

"Guten Tag," she says.

Loudly.

Tariq does German. Grace doesn't but she wants him to know she's up to new experiences.

I scootch in beside her, forcing her into the corner so she has no choice but to listen to me. Without Grace's help, I'll end up creating some sort of monster website that gobbles up all my friends and spews them into a war zone without mascara because I'll get so obsessed I can't talk about anything else.

Or worse! A site that only attracts losers or gold diggers, who all make a beeline for Mum and she finds them utterly desirable. So I end up ditched at the side of a road while they explore the World's Greatest Five Star Hotels.

"We make the matches," I say, "so you don't have to."

Grace manages a shrug.

This is progress. I can take a shrug and build it into a 'count me in'. While I'm working on my next counter-attack, Jack lands on to the seat across from us and leans over. He has pressing issues of his own that are not all to do with acne or b.o. such as living in a haunted house on the edge of town with two mums. Overall, this makes him more interesting than the grunt of boys in our class, now the deodorant issue has been sorted out by Grimmx.

"Do you think I should ask Denise out?" he says.

Angelica, Fount of Wisdom in the Matchmaking Stakes, is right on it. "Nah," I reply, having waited a moment to give the topic requisite attention. "Try Cathie."

Jack nods and moves back to his seat. Grace waits, arms crossed. So I explain, "Cathie is more open to ideas of the supernatural. She has a vivid imagination. Denise is too pragmatic for Jack." I can tell she's is impressed, but she's not saying anything as I'm still blocking her view of Tariq, the man-boy wonder. "What is it between you and Denise anyway?"

Grace shrugs.

"It's not easy to meet someone. Jack's parents were introduced at Lisdoonvarna. What if one of them had changed their mind and not gone? Cathie's met through a mutual friend who'd slept with them both."

"How do you know?"

"Never mind. Theo's parents spewed on each other in the church when they were three."

She shrugs, mellowing a little.

"Look, my mum isn't an extrovert like yours. How is she meant to meet anyone in Drisogue?"

Nothing.

Not a shrug or a flinch or an eyebrow tilt.

"It was hard enough for her to meet my dad and that was when she was living in Dublin without a child!"

"How did they meet again?"

"Street protest. He was trying to cut across this scuffle between the pro-choice and pro-life protestors. She was doing street theatre only nobody was listening, so she rescued him from being trampled by some enthusiastic buggies instead."

Time to use my master card. Not the money kind. That would be too impressive and I'd have to have one first. "Brad Pitt was on a site." Granted, it was an agency site for actors, but she's not likely to look for specifics and let's face it, he might have been on a dating site too.

"Course, nobody picked him. Your mum and mine, now they'd be hot properties." I let Brad's name sink in and weave its magic. It's something we will ALWAYS have in common. "Hell, might settle your mum down too."

She looks wistful. Dylan pops his head over the seat behind us. Is there a sign hanging over our seat that says, *Stick your Head Into Our Private Conversation Today?*

"Dad paid €500 last year to a dating agency. Had to stop saying he was a vicar. He was attracting the wrong sort of woman. I could talk to him for you?"

"No!" we both say at once.

Must remember to check who is sitting where before I open my mouth. Fortunately, the bus pulls up at school. Everyone spills out with a combination of grunts and groans, "Don't poke me's" and "Ow, you stepped on my foot!"

Dylan makes it inside the gate before he is mobbed. His jacket with the whale is less neat but more noticeable in daylight. The whale curls around its entire width but in the full force of a January sun, it looks as if his waist is being hugged by a hot water bottle cover. Of course I don't say anything and I elbow Grace to stop her saying it either. She's very good at picking up what I don't want to say and saying it for me.

"Nice jacket," she says instead.

"Very coolious," says I.

"I call it the Albert." He hands me this squeezy thing with a tube that disappears into the lining of his jacket under the whale's tail. "Squeeze it."

So I do. A solar powered jet of water squirts out of the whale's blowhole, catching Grace in the eye. I can't help laughing.

"Super coolious."

Grace is not amused. Her mascara is RUINED.

ON MASCARA

Most likely, though no historian has admitted it, mascara dates back to Stone Age men applying mud to their eyelashes to prevent them cracking with frostbite. Maybe the first ever fake eyelashes were stolen from cows, who do have luscious lashes.

According to Grace, mascara makes your eyes big, your face beautiful and everything about you irresistible. Except that Tariq is resisting very well and I haven't noticed any other mini-men in Drisogue collapsing in a heap. Still, it is an art form and she's an artist who wants to work with hair. It's a start.

Mascara has never liked me. I generally manage to rub my eyes before I get on the school bus. By the time I get to school, I look like a panda and have to remove it with soap and lots of loo paper.

Or I reapply and do the same on the bus home so that Chris assumes I've fallen out with Grace or with some speckly boy and tries to give me worldly wisdom about not being in a rush.

"They'll appreciate you more if you make them wait. Cultivate an air of mystery. Don't let them see you cry."

Grrrr.

Double Science and what are we doing first this term? Reproduction. Brilliant subject for a mixed class. They really should have thought this out first. It takes ages for Ms Brennan-as-in-bread to stop everyone teasing and messing and generally finding inventive ways to wind each other up under the pretext of science.

But she does and we do it. Nobody actually looks left or right at anyone until it's over because it's EMBARRASSING. Finally satisfied that we've had our introduction, she asks for questions. Theo's first up with his big gammy hand.

"No, Theo," says Ms Brennan. "Celibacy does not cause cancer."

I caught Theo weeing behind a hedge near the hotel years ago and he hasn't forgiven me yet. I told Mum. She said since I hated him so much, I'd most likely marry him.

"Isn't it a fact that if your mum's single, chances are you'll never form a proper relationship?"

Grace sticks her tongue out at him. It's a long tongue. She can touch her nose. Ms Brennan doesn't even understand the dig and initiates this class discussion about relationships and what we would all look for in a so-called *proper* relationship. She talks about relationships with a sort of wonder, which tells me she hasn't had one yet. I wish I didn't notice these things.

"I heard," says I, when my turn comes, "that having yuppie parents is likely to turn you into a dork." I don't even bother looking at Theo because everyone knows who I mean. I catch Grace's eye and she grins.

"'*Dork*' being?" says Ms Brennan.

I leave this catch to my best friend in the world.

"Like Theo, Miss."

Chapter 12

Worst thing about going back to school this term is trying to avoid being alone with Dylan, despite wanting to be alone with him more than any other wish on my wishes list. If he asks me out again, it will jinx everything. Since I won't be able to explain why I'm saying no, he'll think I actually don't want to go out with him and my life will be ruined.

Stompingly, depressingly, mulletly ruined.

However, if I can avoid him asking me out until Mum's met Mr Perfect, then I can say, '*Yes, absolutely, anytime you want!*'

And yes, I lied to Grace. Of course I want Mum to meet Mr Right. If she has to meet someone and I'm adult enough to know it's only fair, then I want him to be the right one.

But it was only a little lie.

I tell Grace and Cathie to stay close; that we have to have lunch together under the weeping willow. Somehow, in the time it takes me to excavate my lunch from the too-small locker, they vanish. I eat my lunch behind the tree and then go scouring for them, walking straight into The Boy Himself.

He is even more adorable now that the jacket is in the locker. Funny how school uniforms can look dorky on most of us but okay on others. (NOT me.) As for how I look, based on the heat of my skin at this moment, I'd say I'm a carnival of pink and puce from my neck to my nose.

"Hey," he says. "Talked to any whales lately?"

"What?" Oh. Okay. Talk, Angelica. Talk normally. "Nope. All out of whales." I'm stood there clutching my sandwich box as if it were a life-raft. Say something. "Yeah. Whales. Hard conversationalists."

He laughs. I made him laugh!

"Dad said it's going to rain."

"Oh."

"He's really into the weather. Always bringing in the washing seconds before it rains. Mum used to say Dad must have been an albatross in a previous life. Maybe you'll get lucky and it'll rain whales again."

I try to laugh but it comes out more 'strangled rat'.

"Tomorrow is definitely going to be fine." He grins. I dunno what's so funny about the weather. "I mean, if you thought it was going to rain today, which it might. Sky looks pretty mean. No sign of mammals yet. Or fish of any kind." We gaze out the window at grumpy sky. "So if you wanted to go for a walk tomorrow or something, it should be okay? I'm still free Wednesday."

No no no NO! He is NOT meant to ask me out yet! This is so wrong.

"Mum's really strict about school nights. I'm really sorry. Oh there's Grace and she looks really upset. I better go see if she's okay. But definitely, some time, love to, yeah?" I grab her arm. "Look upset!" and spin her 180 degrees and down the corridor.

"I AM upset! You turned him down *again*."

If Grace was into wagging fingers, she would be wagging a whole handful at me now but we're late for Computers and I need to learn all I can about designing websites.

If The Broomhandle gets suspicious, I'm going to say Mum wants to set up a site for the hotel and I want to surprise her.

~~~

I hop off the bus in town with Grace and half the class. Usually, we hover around hers for a bit, then she and I walk halfway to the hotel before we split. Unless it's raining and I get off at the hotel.

"Let me get this right? You've decided you can't see Dylan till–. Hey, it rhymes! See *Dyl till*." 'Unimpressed' is written across my face so she assumes a more serious expression of concern. "Till your mum is dating someone, right?"

"Yeah."

"So set her up with someone yourself? Do your *stuff?*"

"I can't. She's my mum." I kick a beer cap on the pavement. It flies up the exhaust pipe of the school bus. That can't be good. "Especially since she made me swear on Dad's whale that I would never EVER, not even if she were the last woman on earth and had to be paired with a man or get eaten alive by aliens, ever try to matchmake her. Besides," I say, drawing her across to the other side of the road. "Have you noticed, Drisogue isn't exactly TEEMING with attractive men under the age of 60?"

She shrugs, point made.

"This has to come from outside. She HAS to think it's all her own idea."

~~~

When I've the worst of my homework done, I head over to Guppy's apartment to say sorry for running off the other day. I save Maths for later because it's my favourite subject, though you won't find me admitting it to anyone. Thing is, when it's right, it's right. If homework generally serves no purpose other than the chew up our minds and make us feel inadequate, at least Maths makes sense.

By way of testing exactly how apologetic I am, she suggests I try another reading. "And concentrate this time?"

So I do.

It's pretty impressive, if you don't question the fact that you're trying to read the future with bottle caps and bits of twig. "A shipwreck?"

"Which means?"

"Deep water. Hidden depths. Dramatic change."

"Good girl."

It could mean my web plans are totally misjudged and that I should stop now before I run aground on a reef and suck cobwebs from the sea floor with dead pirates.

"Guppy, what's love like? I mean, in your day, how did people meet and fall in love?"

"Oh," she says. "Goodness! What a question. When I was your age, I was far more interested in escape. Independence. I'd have fallen for anyone offering that."

I'm confused. "Didn't you love Teddy?"

She smiles as if I'm four years-old and teething. Funny, she and Mum have the same look when they do this. "My parents must have paired up half of the county at their dances. Every first Friday people came. On horseback some of them. I remember thinking, *When I'm old enough, I'll go to the Ball and meet the man of my dreams. Then we'll travel the world.*" She gazes across the lawn, past the oak. "They were a good couple, my parents. Respected each other. But I knew, deep down, that I wanted a more exciting life. I wanted to be unique."

"So why didn't you leave?"

"Oh by the time I grew up, I'd fallen in love with the hotel."

"You'd have left it for Teddy."

She nods and shoves the thought aside.

"One time, during the dance, there was so much rain that every guest had to stay overnight."

Mum and Guppy are really good at this. Chris not so much; he can only focus on one thing at a time. Instead of changing the subject like Mum and Guppy, he closes down, which is really frustrating.

"The Roman Catholic graveyard in Drisogue was flooded and coffins floated across the road into the Protestant cemetery. The most magnificent rainbow appeared when the men went down to try and tidy things up the next day."

"I could try and find out what happened to Teddy for you?"

"No, love."

"We're looking at websites in Computers, learning how to find stuff. There are missing person sites. Or I could google his name and see what came up?"

She stops me with one raised hand and a slow smile. "Shall we try another spread or do you have homework to finish?"

"Maths."

"Best go then before your mother comes looking."

By the time I slide into bed, I have convinced myself that the shipwreck is an entirely excellent omen. Here, on the Donegal coastline, historically, shipwrecks have meant treasure washed ashore, Spanish sailors to adopt for dads and heroic rescues. (I won't think of the 'wrecking' part.)

I go to sleep thinking of how much I wanted to say to Dylan, "Yes, please!"

~ ~ ~

Grace plumps down in the seat beside me on the bus next morning. "Okay."

"Okay what?"

"Okay I'll do your stupid site."

I don't REALLY know why she's changed her mind but it doesn't matter. Maybe the shipwreck I saw was the film set with the whale, Albert; which foretold of Marcus coming to town. Which, in turn, means Grace has decided she needs to settle her mum down quickly with someone (anyone) else.

I can't help hugging her!

"Get off! Seriously, OFF! You stink of garlic."

"Left over pizza for breakfast. What's not to like?"

"That. Weirdo."

"We tell no one, mind. I don't want people thinking I'm a sad loser."

"People like Tariq." Thump. "You mean you're not a sad loser?" Thump.

I love having a best friend. When you have a best friend you can insult them enormously and slag them but they take no offence. Even if they do, you laugh about it afterwards. The first thing Grace did to me when we met was trip me up so my face landed in her birthday cake. We've been friends for life ever since.

We were eight and it was a really nice birthday cake.

I think I got the best bit.

Chapter 13

"So where do we start?"

"We pick a template, decide on all the different sections we need; graphics only come then but I think they're almost the most important part. Least till we design the questionnaire."

"But how do we get people to find the site and log on?" says Grace.

Way ahead of her there. "You do really hot graphics and Simon makes them whizz around."

Grace interrupts before I can tell her about my latest idea for flying cherubs and roses literally growing up the side of the home page. "Won't be enough. You have to think global. What do people really want to see?" She's lost me and she knows it. "Most popular things on the internet?"

"Cute cats. Singing dogs. Laughing babies."

"So we make a trailer full of ninja babies, dogs dancing with ducks and cats reading Shakespeare! Everyone looks at the trailer, clicks on the link and they end up on our site—"

"Because they think we're a dodgy puppy farm martial arts adoption agency."

"You have no imagination."

"I imagined a website."

We mope into Irish but then we frequently mope into Irish. It's the sort of class you have to mope into.

Bouncing into Irish feels wrong.

~ ~ ~

"We need to make sure that we weed out people who would define 'romantic' as paring toenails into a turf fire. Ask the wrong questions and we might as well sell your body to science now."

"Why mine?"

She shrugs. "Your nose is crooked. You have that winged shoulder thing. There's bound to be something interesting about your insides too."

Before I can decide to be insulted, we're neck deep in double Science. Reproduction continues its merry incursion into our psyches. Wonder if someday we'll find our future partners by DNA? Swapping globules of spit in Petri dishes with wannabe mates, to test for compatability.

I have my answer for her on the corridor before English: "We ask questions no other website would think of."

"Such as?"

Okay, so I hadn't got much beyond, '*Are you romantic and will you be nice to my mum?*' and only in my head. "I dunno. We do some research. Ask people we know what they'd want to ask?"

"Great idea!" Grace sweeps her eyes to the sky and nearly crashes into Ms Willow, who scowls. I don't think she actually likes kids. "I am NOT asking my mum what she wants in a man! Whatever we might learn, it could not be good for me to know!"

"I didn't mean our mums. I meant friends. And we don't have to tell them why." We pull out To Kill a Mocking Bird, a novel of which we are already sincerely bored. This is a shame because I loved it the first time we read it. Mr Quinn is still rummaging around in his desk as if he's looking for a small rodent that has been at his notes.

Then it comes to me – first brainwave of the day! (I'd usually expect at least one; something to do with being fourteen and female.) "We use Brad Pitt and Angelina Jolie for role models and come up with questions we would like to hear them answer?"

After English we get a ten-minute break before PE with The Rabbit, who hates me. He is teaching us – okay, TRYING to teach us basketball, teamwork and sporting spirit. Apparently the school used to have a great reputation for athletics. Something to do with pulling barrow-loads of seaweed off the beach to feed the fields in force nine gales.

Oh and potatoes.

Last time he told me to get more involved, a basketball hit me on my left ear. I heard bells for a week. Sport is not for all. It ought not to be pushed down the throats and up the noses of teens.

In the changing room, Grace grabs space on the bench beside me. "It has to be foolproof."

"Foolproof as in it filters out the fools?"

"As in only intelligent, kind, genuinely romantic men – and women – get through." We shove out into the hall for the latest dose of sport-related torture. "I mean, we need women to lure the men onto the site that you want your mum to nibble, right?"

"Ugh."

"I meant figuratively," says Grace.

"OOOh posh words." Theo pushes past. "Probably means you're a lesbian." He has a thing about lesbians. Grace says it's only because he really, REALLY wants to be one.

"Hope so," she says.

I pull her aside. "I don't want Mum to nibble. I want her to date. That's all. She's choosy and particular."

"Like my mum isn't?" says Grace.

"I didn't mean that!" She just DOESN'T get it. "Nibbling is what happens to a fishing line. You have no idea what is nibbling but you land it anyway and hope it's not a crab or an old boot." I know this because Chris dragged me fishing three times when I was ten. I didn't see the 'why'; he always threw the fish back when we caught one.

"So you want her to hook a proper fish, with all his own fins, flippers and fantasy pecs?"

"Sorta."

~ ~ ~

66

"Isms," she says as we change after PE. "If we actively filter people or turn them away because we don't like the answers they give, we could be charged with ageism or sexism or a whole pile of other isms."

"Isms are not good," says Cathie as the lunch bell goes. She still uses long words and has the most amazing dreams that she says are like an alternative reality she can actually navigate.

Grace nods wisely and waits for Cathie to leave. "If word spread that we were elitist, the site would get blacklisted! Nobody likes being rejected."

"So how do we attract the right people?"

"You're the one with the gift. How do you know when two people fit together?"

That's a good one. I chew my fingernails while Grace checks her mascara for the umpteenth time today in the bathroom mirror. It's a rare moment of calm: I only chew the second last finger nail of each hand. They're the most invisible of nails. I'm very disciplined this way.

"It's something they have; some energy or way of connecting."

"Can you write a questionnaire to find that out?"

I think back to Eve and Sprite, our former chef and waiter. All they needed was to be told what they already knew deep down, that the other person felt the same way. "Dunno. Usually I need to see them together. It's something in the air between them and I just know."

"So, let me get this straight?" says Grace as we leave the changing room. "You're planning to flash into cyber space and sniff every person on the site like a rabid dog so you can match them?"

"What a great idea!" Thump.

I might start wearing upper arm shields under my school jumper. Either that or I need to stop saying things that make Grace retaliate with a thump.

"You know your thumps are getting weaker," I say, diving into the canteen and the safety of the horde. Funny, everyone smells of b.o. today and at least three people on my table are eating egg sandwiches.

Egg sandwiches should be banned from schools.

ON EGG SANDWICHES

Eggs are supposedly good for us – protein and stuff – but think of the moral implications of eating dead – okay, not-quite-fertilised-but-could-have-been-baby – chicks. I mean, they haven't even had a chance to be born before they are boiled, mashed up, mixed with onion and mayo and squished between bread. Is this why a hen lays an egg?

This can NOT be the reason hens lay eggs.

More importantly, not only do egg sandwiches smell like sick but they are innately eco-unfriendly by flooding the environment with putrid air which is probably really bad for the ozone layer. What's left of it.

That they taste nice and are vaguely healthy are not good enough reasons to allow them in any enclosed space containing teenagers.

Chapter 14

Brainwave Number 2 hits in Religion I pass a note across to Grace: We use BP!!!"

Grace gives me a look that says, *What ARE you on about now?* but a bit too graphically because Ms Willow is on to us.

"Something interesting, Grace?"

"No, Miss."

"Oh I'm sure it is. Why not share Angelica's note with the class?" This is revenge for Grace doing an essay on atheism when the assignment was to discuss a recognised world religion. And for looking universally bored the length of every religion class.

"Sorry Miss." Grace is a good friend but she's never going to get away with this. Everyone swivels to watch Ms Willow. "It's not worth reading. Really," she says, scrunching it up.

"Angelica's a lesbian, Miss," says Theo. "It's probably a love note."

Sniggers. Nice.

"If you were a typical example of mankind, Theo Maguire, I'd very happily become a lesbian," says Grace. That stops him. Stops Ms Willow too who grabs the note. This can't end well.

"We use BP?" she reads, to me. "Are you planning a career in oil? To fill your mother's car up and flee into the wilderness?"

Like Thelma and Louise. It's tempting.

Grace, Theo and I get detention. Fortunately, Theo has a 'get out of jail free' card that he cashes in. I'm not sure the three of us in a room alone would be a good idea right now.

~~~

"This had better be worth it," says Grace.

Our task: to scribble a page of deep thoughts about adding spirituality to our daily lives. We rattle through it and then Grace turns on me. "BP ?"

"Brad Pitt. We connect the site to him and it will attract the sort of women who will appeal to the sort of men we want on the site."

"He'd sue for defamation."

Grace's dad is a solicitor for some big law firm in Dublin that nobody can really afford. She says they give out handmade chocolates to visitors with their coffee, rather than biscuits.

"Way past you. We dedicate RomanticHearts.com to him. You do a portrait for the home page, we tag and tweet it everywhere. That way we get hits from everyone who types in his name. All we have to do then is make them believe this is the site on which they will meet the man or woman of their dreams."

"I'm not sure."

"Think of it as the first public platform for your work, sort of a first exhibition. You couldn't exactly put your name up on it just yet, but still?"

The rest of detention flies past as we construct a list of the information we need to make our site so fantastic that even Brad would join without thinking more than twice. Chris comes to collect us so neither of us has to explain to our mums why we got detention, which is just as well, though it means I owe him big time. Work has started on the ballroom so Mum probably hasn't even noticed I'm late home.

Grace suggests we ask Chris what questions he'd ask but I tell her it'd get back to Mum.

~~~

Grace and I invite a few trusted friends for a Very Important Discussion. It will be held behind the shed Wednesday lunchtime, barring hailstones, rogue tornados and prowling teachers. Cathie arrives last, which makes Jack sit up straight but she's more interested in Dylan's jacket. Grace invited him to join us. I try to keep focused.

Everyone's buzzing. There's a rumour that I'm organising gigs in the ballroom or a walk out from Religion and it takes ages to stop them all talking long enough to explain.

"We need a list of what you would want to know or need to ask if you were looking for the perfect boyfriend or girlfriend." There follows three whole minutes of absolute silence.

"Who cares?" says Denise. "Boys are stupid."

"Thanks." This from Dylan.

"Well they are. They're smelly and loud and make fart jokes constantly." Jack gives his armpits a quick sniff. "I don't."

"Neither do I." Dylan tugs his jacket around him.

"Squirt me again, Dylan Clancy and you are dead." Grace moves over beside Jack, who now looks scared.

This is going nowhere.

"Guys! It's a project, okay. For CPSE. Right, Grace?" Grace is shaking her head; everyone does CPSE so they'd know. "Sorry, History; it's for a project about the changing needs of Irish society."

Cathie starts the ball rolling. "What are their hopes, wishes and dreams? Psychos say candlelit dinners, cannibals sushi."

"What do normal people say?" says Grace and Dylan leaps in.

"Make the world a whale sanctuary."

"Find true love," says Jack, surprisingly. Denise catches his eye and he blushes. Sweet. "Or to meet a real alien." This completely spoils the effect. "Y'know the ones with the green eyes and their innards all on the outside full of purple slime you can eat."

"Jack!" we squeal.

"What?"

Cathie looks sort of impressed and gives him a goofy grin. Grace misses it completely, which is just as well. She'd only tease them later. And for days.

"You said hopes and dreams!"

"For your ideal *date*." says Grace. "Not about you!"

"Howabout kids; do they like kids?" says Dylan. It's the first sensible and usable thing anyone has said. So he's deep and thoughtful as well as divine.

"Especially teenagers," says Grace. He is such a good influence on her when he's not squirting water in her eye.

"Can't ask that. They'd be afraid to answer. Nobody admits to liking teens. Even teens. We are the best of humans but not everyone can see it."

"Like adults are so balanced and rational."

"Or nice!"

"We should start a campaign to reinstate teens as future world leaders."

"Awesome inventors," says Denise, smiling at Dylan.

"Wicked litigators."

"Returning to the questions?" says I.

"Turned out feet." Denise says this as if it's obvious why, but we all sit there, waiting for her to explain. "You don't know?" We shake our heads in unison. "Dad says it's a sign of a split personality. Like cabbage ears."

Jack pulls his woolly hat down over his ears – not cabbage ears but not the neatest either – and makes himself look small.

"Or a wet nose," adds Grace. There is NO END to the knowledge my best friend has! It's a worry.

"We're not talking about dogs."

"I know, '*Is he or she a good listener?*'" says Denise. "Mum says that's the one thing she'd change about Dad."

While this goes down, Dylan lets Cathie press the squirty thing. She's been hinting for days. And guess what, the water squirts Grace in the eye again despite her being as far from him as is possible in a small space.

"Ah, really?" She storms off inside. Cathie moves over beside Jack as if she needed to stretch her legs but then neither of them can look at each other. It's just as well the bell goes.

Best thing to happen in school today: Art. Last class. We unveil the still life we had to do over the holidays to the unflinching eye of The Growler. All goes well. A little grunt, a minor growl here and there. Until she gets to Grace.

"Inappropriate."

"But Miss!"

"Grace Cluskey, I asked you for a still life."

"He's very still, Miss."

It's a naked man. Actually, it's the statue of Christ in Rio but with Tariq's hair, a green and gold bandana and a pint of Guinness in each hand.

Chapter 15

**GENERAL ADVICE for use of
ROMANTICHEARTS.COM**

Do not use your real name. Neither should you call yourself the Devil – Brad was the BEST, Duckling or Mr Big.

Meet in public. Coffee is better than dinner.

Dylan clued us in on this, based on his dad's experience. Coffee doesn't cost much and no need for babysitters, so it doesn't matter who pays and you aren't stuck together for hours if it turns out that you don't have lots to talk about.

Correspond only through the site at first.

Be honest about everything but do not give out your personal contact details immediately.

There is someone out there waiting for each and every one of us. If you get together with another member of RomanticHearts.com, please let us know.

It will give hope to everyone else and keep the karma flying.

"D'you think they'll do that?" says Grace. "I mean, it would be great and all, but I can't imagine my mum telling the world she'd met someone on a dating site."

"That's sooo 20th century prejudice," says I.

"What dating sites did they have in the 20th century?"

"I dunno. Look, by the time people have experienced RomanticHearts.com, it will be the trendiest, easiest, most fascinating way to meet someone special."

"You mean by the time your mum meets someone?"

"Oh she'll say they met in a cafe. Which is technically true, since the website started in a cafe."

"You said nobody else would know," says Simon, coming up all sneaky behind us. Must be the tai chi he does. Or the bare feet. Did I mention he doesn't wear shoes indoors? Which is kind of strange since it's January in the west of Ireland and not exactly balmy. He says he doesn't mind honest dirt, but sometimes it isn't.

Sometimes it's dog poo or petrol gunge. Now he can see exactly how dirty the floor gets. It's like some sort of wildlife special on the sole of each foot, so he might be in shoes yet.

Would it be weird if I got him slippers?

"Grace isn't anyone. She's my best friend and she's more streetwise than me, so I need her help."

"Have you told anyone else?" He looks severe, the sort of severe you see on a Santa when someone's little darling wees on his lap ten minutes into his shift.

"Course not," we say in unison. I cross my fingers and toes to ward off evil, which gives me a sort of wobbly hobble as he steers us into the back room. I mean, none of our friends KNEW what they were lab rats for.

"Something wrong with your feet?" says Simon. "You're walking weird."

Full moon tonight.

Must remember to howl.

"Promise you won't tell anyone else and I'll set up a computer in here for you to work on."

"I promise and so does Grace. Don't you?"

Grace nods. The back room is perfect. This way nobody can spot me or ask Mum why I'm on a computer in Simon's cafe when I have a perfectly good one at home. I persuade him – it's not hard – to make us a couple of fancy flat whites. Turns out he's utterly addicted to the barista process and a complete natural. I've heard him talk to the coffee machine in very soft tones and I think he calls it Mike.

We set to work.

"Dreams," he says, when he sees what we're working on. "You need to ask them what they last dreamt about. Dreams are very indicative of deep-rooted issues. I can't believe I'm doing this," he says, for the twentieth time this week.

Even though even Grace has twigged that he can't stop now.

Which is good for us.

He insists on decaf, regardless of protests. This is probably good and a sign of maturity on his side. As he puts it, Grace and I are sufficiently wired by nature without adding anything extra.

'*What was your most recent dream?*' I type.

"What if their dreams are full of gory stuff?" says Grace. So we add a clarification.

'*What was your most recent dream? (No naked, gory or offensive stuff.)*'

"What about subsections?" says Grace. "Y'know, food, childhood, ideals?"

"Maybe. Can we do them tomorrow. Need to help Mum in the kitchen tonight."

"Still no chef?"

"We interviewed." Which reminds me: "Simon, we're getting a new chef. You have to come up and meet him."

"I wouldn't bother," says Grace. "He won't last long. All their chefs run away with waiters. It's a health hazard of working in the same place as Angelica."

Thanks Grace. Best bud in the world and most irritating. "That has only happened three times and the first chef we had ran away with a guest anyway." I turn to Simon. "He's Finnish. Name's Onni. Starts next week. Probably has a moustache. Sounded like he had a moustache."

"How can you tell?" This from Grace, the future hair dresser who should surely know such things.

"It was the way he was speaking, like there was something muffling his upper lip or making it too heavy to move. He was the only applicant we all liked, so Mum hired him over the phone."

"Oh."

Back to Simon. I owe him and it's clear he's romantic at heart because this site has become more than a favour he's doing me or a money-making scheme. "I can bring him down to meet you, once he's settled in?"

"Why?"

"Just because."

"Okay."

Grace walks out with me as Marcus pulls up outside their pub opposite. "Guess you're playing happy families too," says I.

She sneaks a thump in as she heads across, scowl in place.

~ ~ ~

"Maybe you should rethink this mating-your-mum business," Grace mutters next day when she lands into school; Marcus having given her a lift.

Seems he whisked Grace and Kitty off to Sligo for a meal. She was not impressed. It was a fry-your-own-cow restaurant and Grace is strictly vegetarian, except sometimes at Christmas. Then there was the polite conversation and seeing her mum laugh at all his lousy jokes.

Now she's going to get into trouble for only having her homework half done and yawning in Religion.

Though she often yawns in Religion.

I reckon she's allergic.

~ ~ ~

Turns out Simon is on 45 chat rooms. This should make spreading the word easier. I tell him this as if it's a good thing.

"No way."

"Why not?"

"Privacy. Ethics. Legality. Not wanting anyone to know I'm involved."

"Oh, that."

~~~

Grace thinks the site should look like a glossy woman's mag because her mum loves them. Simon and I veto this with scarce a breath between us. For a start, Mum hates women's mags and she's the priority here, even if Simon doesn't know. "Besides, we want all sorts of cool men as well as women," says I.

My heart motif has been replaced. First by seagulls. Simon ruled them out as we live near the sea and this might be "too much of a clue" to the geographic location of the site. Then by swifts. "Nah. They move too fast," says Grace. "We want men who will stick."

We've settled on swans since they mate for life. Their long necks ALMOST form a heart if they're facing each other. Which they will, on our site.

"Isn't it too cheesy?"

"Completely."

"Might put men off," says I.

"What sort of men?"

"Men like Marcus."

"Yeah," says Grace immediately. "I like it. It's a FANTASTIC logo. We should have a dozen swans and make them pink and put them on a millpond."

"Not enough space." Simon frowns. He's not used to Grace's humour yet. I suspect he thinks she fancies him because she keeps going on about his hair and wanting to, 'do something' with it.

Chapter 16

I wake up in the middle of the night plagued with doubts like some old-fashioned hermit sitting in the desert on a lump of poo. These doubts sit on my shoulders or bounce on my chest and generally transform things I was sure about into things unreal and savage.

What if I'm wrong?

What if using technology to alter Mum's fate leads to something disastrous and dark like a homunculus crawling out of the ether and swallowing her up?

Yeah, sometimes I can be a bit medieval but this is Mum's life and therefore mine. If I bring the wrong man into her life, who suffers? Me! In the middle of the night, these possible men are not just wrong, they have horns and tails and beat up children for fun.

When I finally sleep, I dream about having the stepdad from hell who packs me off to boarding school on the Hebrides where I meet the sons and daughters of English lords and become a complete snob.

~ ~ ~

Just to put my mind at rest, I drop into Guppy with a cup of tea before I leave for school. She has moved in with us until they've finished painting the ballroom. The fumes were filling her apartment above, making her have the most amazing dreams.

Dreams about Teddy.

"Isn't that good?" I asked her, when we were moving her things in.

"Oh no, love," she says, with this heaviness in her limbs. "Because then I wake up every morning being alone and old again."

She spills the contents across the table. "You want a reading to tell you, '*Am I doing the right thing?*'"

I nod.

A sprig of lavender lands on top of a lump of sea-weathered quartz but everything else is cluttered. Even I can see it's inconclusive. Are all the bits paired off? I decide they are, mostly and that this is a good sign.

"Maybe you need to make your question clearer? Is this about a boy?"

Why does everything have to be about a boy? I'm fourteen. Not thirty-five!

"Oops. School bus!" I tear out.

Conversation postponed.

Indefinitely.

~~~

Marcus drops in to 'supervise' the painting but we all know his visit is an excuse to call into Kitty. I heard Mum ask him about the film shoot. They're waiting for the lead actor to commit.

Which seeMrs Daft as stuffing mushrooms to me.

Surely the cast should have been tied down before they built and transported a forty foot whale? Chris agrees, but he doesn't say this to Marcus because he's still hoping to 're-home' Albert here when the film is over.

Kitty says the whale-flying was a publicity stunt to bring in more investment as well as a birthday treat. It was dark by the time they set off, hence the dodgy strap-tying. Albert decapitated at least three trees before the strap that wasn't secure completely snapped. They got publicity, just not the sort they'd planned.

Chris's latest plan is to turn the whale into a honeymoon chalet. "For honeymoon couples who happen to be whale spotters?" says Mum. I think it's a cool idea and I can tell, for all her sarcastic tone of voice and frown, that Mum does too.

See? Underneath that hard shell of self-sufficiency, a romantic heart burns.

It just needs a bit of encouragement, oxygen and lots of flowers. Unfortunately, when Chris finally asks, Marcus informs him, in a really snooty way that I don't much like, that the whale is not for sale.

"Oh we weren't going to pay," says Chris. "We were going to rescue it."

I cheer, but quietly in my head.

The publicity around Albert's visit has temporarily put us on the map and the hotel is doing a bit better than expected for this time of year. Chris now wants Mum to throw a Valentines' Ball to launch the newly painted ballroom when work's finished on it.

She keeps fobbing him off. Too expensive, too difficult to organise, not enough time.

He's taken her lack of decision as a bone fide 'YES' in capital letters, fluorescent lights and dancing the Merengue.

I'm not sure I want to be in the room when she breaks it to him that it's not going to happen.

~ ~ ~

The questionnaire is nearly done and Simon says we need to have a list of 'possible sources of publicity'. Fortuitously, we have a free computer class, thanks to The Broomhandle having a tummy ache and get to download emails and links to newspaper and magazine websites and blogs.

"She's probably pregnant," says Cathie. Cathie thinks everyone who has a tummy ache is probably pregnant. Grace says this is because her mum always is, but then she has a dozen businesses to pass on and it might as well be family.

Dylan dropped into the cafe after school, ostensibly to help Simon. I ducked into the backroom and Simon sent him home saying their Dad had rung wondering where he was.

"He thinks you're avoiding him," says Grace. She wears her disapproval like a halo of small storm clouds. I know she won't understand but I try to explain.

"Chris says it's important not to be too eager or you can scare away the very person you're mad into."

"Oh right. So Chris, who hasn't had a girlfriend in forever, has scared everyone away?"

"Maybe."

"If they scare that easily, I'm not interested."

While I hide in the back room, I tell myself that it's only a matter of time before cool romantic people everywhere will be signing up to our website and inviting Mum out. Then I won't have to avoid being alone with Dylan.

Even if he's going to ask me out.

~~~

Saturday night. Youth club. Parish hall. Dylan's dad, the Reverend Clancy and Father Lefarge run it. I think it's more so that parents can have a few hours off from us Teen Adorables than to keep us entertained because all we do is play board games, eat crisps and play table tennis.

Grace and I slip out and over to Simon's and finish the questionnaire. By the time we split up at 10pm, it is truly a work of genius, guaranteed to attract men and women with imagination, courage and good taste.

> What is your favourite flavour of crisp? Which do you prefer, Tayto or King?
>
> Do you or have you ever bitten your nails?
>
> What is the most chivalrous/ romantic thing you have ever done?
>
> When was your first kiss/what is your first memory?
>
> What are your hopes, wishes and dreams?
>
> Who is your favourite person?
>
> What was your most recent dream (no naked, gory or offensive stuff)?
>
> Are birthdays important to you and do you like buying presents?

What's your favourite day of the year?

How would you define love, romance, spaghetti bolognaise?

How would you feel if you met the right person?

Do you have/ have you had pets? If so, what kind were they, what happened to them and how did you feel?

What is your favourite food and can you cook?

Mum catches me heading home, totally whacked from staring at words on a screen for two hours. "Where the hell were you? I went to meet you at the hall and nobody knew where you were!"

She NEVER does this. My brain, slow and sluggish, digs me out: "Grace broke up with her boyfriend. She was too upset to stay at the youth club so we sat in Simon's cafe. Then we went to hers for a while. Ask Kitty."

It's a risk, but chances are Kitty was busy with the bar and wouldn't have noticed if we were upstairs or not.

Note to self: remember to warn Grace.

"What boyfriend?"

"I can't say. She made me swear. But she's soooo upset. She didn't even reapply her mascara AND she forgot to brush her hair." (Act of genius. Grace is going to kill me.) "Can I get a new duvet? My toes are sticking out of the end." When you're on a roll, keep rolling.

"Sure."

~ ~ ~

Every step I make down the school bus Monday morning feels weighted. As if my feet are in lumps of concrete. I am SOOO dead. More dead than if I'd been drained by a really thirsty carnivorous ghoul who then sold me for gristle to a werewolf with exceptionally sharp teeth and a family of starving cubs.

But at least I'm getting a new duvet?

"You told your mum that I broke up with someone at the youth club?"

I nod.

"Dylan? Jack?"

"Eh, not exactly." (I am DEAD.)

Steely silence. "Who?"

"Theo."

"Oh thanks. Thanks a bunch. You are SUCH a good friend. Theo! Theo Maguire and she believed you?"

"Well I couldn't say Dylan and she knows Jack isn't allowed out after nine so…"

"You owe me, Angelica Moone."

Chapter 17

"So, we're ready to go. For real?"

Simon nods. We're sharing the same grin. All the glitches have been road tested and removed. He is finally happy that nothing on the site could get us reported, that it is the best matchmaking site there is and completely untraceable to us or even to Drisogue.

Grace is talking to me again but only because her mum has been very sweet and is actually treating her like a grown-up. Of course this also means Mum can't keep a secret, but at least she'll blab about going on the site when she does join up and I'll be able to steer her in the right direction.

If I tell anyone else that she went out with Theo, Grace says she will dump me in it over this site. I make us three flat whites with big romantic hearts in the crema and bring them to the computer in the back room of the cafe.

"I can't believe we're doing this," says Grace. "It has to be illegal. We're fourteen."

"We're helping people, not breaking the law. There's a difference."

"Yeah, of five to fifteen years."

"Really?" says Simon.

I'm impressed. Grace has managed, at the very last minute, to put the scares up the person we need most on this project. "No. She's joking. You're joking, right Grace?" She nods. "It would only be illegal if we downloaded bad stuff. And technically, it's your site, not ours and you're way older than fourteen."

Then I activate the site before he changes his mind.

ALTERNATIVE ACRONYMS

LOL: Love Only Lollipops (especially toffee apple flavour)

FYI: Flick Your Index (i.e. index finger, like flicking an irritating bug off your desk)

ASAP: As Squishy As Poo

EG: Extra Gooey

DPY: Don't Pee Yet.

I.E.: If Ever.

"I have to get my hair cut," says Grace, by way of nothing in particular. "I need to show Tariq that I'm the girl for him."

"Bit drastic."

"You think?"

"What look are you going for? A matching torc or a dolmen?"

"That's an idea!"

"I was joking."

She's not even listening. I fear the worst.

~~~

Simon is a dark horse, despite his hair being various shades of orange and yellow at the moment. He has been bigging the site up in all his chat rooms. Under an alias, of course. Several. As if each had just discovered this amazing and magical new site and wanted to tell the world.

I think he's into this even more than we are now. Not that he'd admit it, him being a 'grown up' with a cafe to run and a vicar for a dad. I wonder how it is to have a vicar for a dad?

There are just so many things to learn when Dylan and I start going out. I daydream my way to bed, imagining the months to come.

~ ~ ~

Sunday rolls by. So people don't like to go on the internet on a Sunday. Day of rest. Old-fashioned but it could be true.

Monday. They're all too busy catching up with work. Everyone knows Mondays are frantic.

Tuesday. Seriously?

Wednesday morning and not one person has joined the site.

"Well," says Grace, "that was fun. What's your next big plan?"

"People are looking at it." Her tone of voice doesn't make me full of human kindness; of glumness, maybe, if I wasn't already full to the brim."We've had hundreds of hits."

"Oh wait, so it wasn't a mammoth waste of time? Doesn't matter that NOBODY has bothered to sign up. Maybe we can submit it as our computer project – that's overdue, by the way! Oh yeah, we can't because it's a dating site. Oops."

~ ~ ~

Brainwave Number Three *finally* lands in History. To prevent misunderstanding (and detention), I draw my best version of a little fluffy sheep and pass it to Grace. Course she doesn't get it and looks all befuddled but it's clear as day and I should have realised way back.

"What's this?"

"Sheep."

"I know they're sheep. Even you can draw sheep"

"Your mum's always saying people are like sheep, right?"

We're changing. PE definitely comes around too fast, but at least The Rabbit can't give homework.

"'Cept without the three stomachs and the ability to digest grass."

"That's cows. Sheep are the ones with the multicoloured bums."

"Oh. Right," she says. "Silly me. What have sheep got to do with the dating site?"

"Nobody wants to be the first. Would you join a dating site that hasn't any members? Once we have a few, the rest will follow. It's a mathematical equation."

"But if no one wants to join—?"

"We create some."

I'm a genius, so why does Grace's face wrinkle up all gargoyle? "That's wrong. It's like, entrapment. Honey-trapping.

"Not really. We'll delete them as soon as we have a critical mass."

"What are you two hatching?" Denise has the nose of a bloodhound sniffing a frankfurter in a mall.

"Licky thinks she's gifted."

"Oh," says Denise, losing interest. "D'you think Dylan fancies me?"

"No!" say Grace and I in unison.

"Absolutely not," says Grace, in case Denise missed the point. She swings me a warning look to make sure I understand the risk I'm taking playing it cool.

And I was wrong about PE. The Rabbit wants us to do ten stomach curls and ten press-ups every evening after school. He has entered us into some Teen Fitness reality show and if our school gets picked, he wants us to be ahead of the game.

~~~

Grace still isn't convinced when we spill off the bus. "Are you going to tell me how we do this?"

"Watch and learn."

Unfortunately Simon's not easy to convince.

"Come on, Simon. You have to! You have at least five different names in the games forums."

"He has?"

"Yeah."

"Wow!"

Simon does not know how to take Grace's admiration. He still thinks she fancies him or something. I need to remind him he's ancient; that it's only his hair she's after.

"Actually, I have seven. Plus a few that are dormant."

"See? You're the only one who can do this!" I sit him down on a high stool.

"Do you really want to see this site fail after all your hard work?" The idea appeals, if not the ethics. "You'd be helping to spread world peace and happiness."

He's still reluctant; his toes play with the bottom bar of the stool. Every nail is painted a different colour. It's probably so the dirt doesn't show, from being barefoot n all.

"It wouldn't take long anyway. You told me, they all have totally different personalities. I bet all of your avatars have been chatted up lots!"

He weakens enough to give a shy smile.

"Think of it as bringing your own avatars to life! Soon as we have, say, 40 members, we delete your avatar's profiles. Promise."

"Okay, but as soon as some members come in, we pull these off."

"Absolutely. Sure we wouldn't need them anymore."

"And nobody knows."

"Nobody."

Now we have him onside, we act fast. I run through our questionnaire, once for each of his avatars since he's adamant they all sound like different men. Grace pretends not to approve but she inputs all his answers and even adds stuff of her own so they sound more genuine.

To keep it fair, we make up several women – based on nobody we know. Within an hour we have give new, REAL members but the real Simon is looking stressed as a water buffalo in a vat of oil before he realises it's only a beauty treatment for rough skin.

"See how hot you are?" says I.

Chapter 18

The trickle becomes a steady stream. Grace and I keep out of his way so he won't ask us to pull the avatars yet – he could do it without asking anyway but I think he's seeing it like a game now because he doesn't pull them and by Thursday evening, we have two hundred and fifty genuine members! We are a skip and a lopsided jump away from having serious multitudes!

Even Simon seems surprised, in a sort of happy-delighted-moony way, that his alter egos proved to be such a pull.

"Must be Valentine's Day is coming up."

"Maybe."

Grace wants to put Kitty on the site, in disguise. "Just to see who would go for her."

Course I say no and she goes all huffy.

"Don't see what harm it would do. Not as if she'd ever know."

"I take it she doesn't like Marcus?" says Simon. He can be SO astute.

"I don't think he's her ideal father figure, no."

"He has a mullet," she says.

By Thursday night, the trickle is a steady stream.

It worked!

RomanticHearts.com is bright-eyed, bushy-tailed and absolutely live. Which may be why I keep thinking of it as a squirrel. Y'know, the cute bouncy sort that comes up really close but could also bite your hand and give you rabies?

Ignoring this feeling, I print out a few dozen profiles for Grace and me to match up during lunch next day. If we can get a few successful matches under the site's waist, those lucky few will soon recommend the site to friends.

~ ~ ~

Grace is not a natural. "No way! You can't match them!" She points to the two members I've pinned together. "She's into partying; he likes stamp collecting."

"Grace, Grace, look beyond superficial hobbies to their inner romantic. She likes fancy dress parties, he collects European stamps – therefore, they both like colour and adventure, both like the idea of escaping normality temporarily and superficially."

She picks up the next match I've made.

"He's into sci-fi and dressing up as an alien; she's into celebrities."

"Not celebrities, *stars*. So they both like space. They're made for each other!"

"Thought the site was meant to match people."

"No harm in a helping hand."

The Water Witch rounds the corner, eating the most enormous chocolate muffin. I imagine an army of chocolate-loving rodents following in her wake looking for crumbs. "Homework behind the shed or planning a revolution?" she says. And, "Would you prefer to do it in detention?"

The bell goes as we file past; eyes down like prisoners of war.

Back of the shed is out of bounds but nobody has ever enforced it before.

Out of the corner of my ever-watchful eye, I see The Growler bend down to pick up a flier that must have fallen from my pocket. I'm waiting to be called back and asked all sorts of awkward questions – but nothing happens.

Nothing at all.

So I sneak a look back and get this, she doesn't bin it. She doesn't tear it up and feed it to the shredder.

She tucks it into her pocket.

~ ~ ~

As the numbers flood in over the weekend, we allow Simon to remove his avatars in return for two caffeine-free double macchiatos with froth and chocolate flakes. Late Saturday, the site hits the three hundred members mark and crashes but Simon brings it back up in super quick time.

Simon makes us promise one thing then, his face as serious as a weather forecaster talking about an incoming monsoon. "No real person gets put on this site without their permission. A vague nod or an 'okay love' when your mothers are juggling a full set of wriggly puppies does NOT qualify as permission."

He's learning fast.

I like to think we're good for him.

~~~

Time for Phase Three: getting Mum to sign up.

For this to have a chance, it has to be something she becomes aware of without me telling her so I slip fliers into the Saturday newspapers sitting on the front desk before she has even started breakfast, so it looks like an insert delivered with the paper rather than by a spooky teenage daughter.

I can be sneaky when I need to be, but only in a good cause.

Dylan is DEFINITELY a good cause!

Before school on Monday, I drop fliers through various letterboxes in town before grabbing the school bus with Grace. This way, it'll look as if they came with the post. It's not that I want a whole pile of Drisoguens on the site, but word is king and they might all have cute cousins or single uncles they are dying to help find love.

Any day now, I think, as Jonas snarls at my sleepy face.

Any day now, I think as I flop down beside Grace and give her my beamiest beam.

Any day now, my mum will sign up, find a nice man and everything in my boyfriend-empty life will change.

Then I cross my fingers and toes.

~~~

"Might as well advertise my desperation on a bus shelter!"

Mum's waving one of our fliers at Kitty when I get home, as if she were trying to swat a fly. Kitty, it seems, has been trying to persuade Mum to join the site with her.

"Molly, trust me. I've seen plenty of these sites – for research, of course. This one seeMrs Different." Kitty calmly tries to talk Mum out of her ivory tower with its matching Laura Ashley blinds. "Something about the design of it and the questions. They're fun and wonderfully sweet. It's a site for romantics, not one-nighters."

This is where Mum says, 'Jeez Kitty, you are so completely right, I must join up immediately'. Only Kitty's not finished yet.

"If you got off your high horse you'd see it's perfect!"

I have a sneaky feeling this is NOT the way to convince Mum to join.

And I'm right.

Sometimes I hate being right.

"Course it is," says Mum. "If you're sad, sex mad or psychotic."

So, wisdom comes with age? They're like two kids pinching each other to get hold of the last Big Girl's Swing in the playground.

"Guess I'm all three so!" Kitty snatches her coat from a nearby chair. "Chill out, Moll, before it's too late."

"Does Marcus know he's another notch on the bedpost?"

Kitty leaves without answering. Mum dumps the flier in the bin. Dumps it so hard, it un-creases and bounces out again. (Good idea Grace – high grade paper, doesn't like being bullied into bins.) I need to fix things. Fast. I'm sick of them falling out over men or, more accurately, Mum's lack and Kitty's abundance.

"Mum—"

"Not now, love."

What are the chances? An elderly guest approaches Mum with another flier. "Is this a service offered by the hotel? I have no wife, you see. I did have one and she was very sweet, very tiny but then she died. At least, I think she died. I'm sure someone said she'd run away but I think she died. Maybe she ran away and then died," he concludes, chirpily.

Mum snatches the flier. "No, we don't." She steers him back into the lounge, shouting to Chris to bring him a complimentary cup of tea.

"And some nice biscuits," adds the man. Then this tiny woman joins him and takes his arm. "Ah there you are, love," he says.

I guess his loss-of-wife is an occasional and temporary thing.

Mum sweeps through the lounge and bar like an avenging angel, grabbing fliers wherever they've fallen out of papers. My fringe stands on end with the draught she's making but that's probably not worth mentioning.

"Angelica, did you have something to do with this?"

I force myself to laugh, casually. "Like I need a website, Mum!"

"So why has my hotel been targeted?"

"There was a couple in Room 5. Matching hats and gloves saying 'his' and 'hers'? Didn't they say something about helping others find the happiness they had found through some dating website?" Yup, I can improvise when faced by an avenging angel. It's a useful skill to have.

"I remember those," says Chris, changing the bar menu to the evening one. "Don't remember the website bit." Way ahead of him. I'm on the point of 'happening' to remember the name of the site they met on, doing an 'oh my!' and pointing at the flier – way to turn a negative situation into a promotional one – when Mum snaps.

"I want them found and dumped."

"I think they checked out yesterday," says Chris.

Ha ha.

Chapter 19

Two days later, Mum is still going on about the website. You'd think someone had decided to build a penthouse suite for Saddam Hussein and fifty wild orang-utans – in polka dot bikinis – on top of our hotel.

I keep my head down and TRY not to say anything. Chris is the same. Mum vetoed the Valentine's Ball this morning. Onni, our new chef, arrives this aft. Since I'm not meant to be home from school yet, Mum ropes me into tidying up the kitchen before he arrives.

I've never heard a walrus sigh. But if one were to sigh, I bet he would sound like Mum. I'm really trying hard not to react but she has sighs that sneak under your skin and turn you grumpy too.

"It's just a website. Why the fuss?"

This is hardly the most explosive thing I've ever said. From the way she turns and stares at me, you would think I'd asked her to build that penthouse suite or train the orang-utans to serve breakfast.

I pretend not to notice and keep busy chopping parsnips for lunchtime wedges as if all I have ever dreamt of doing for the past fourteen years is fragmenting parsnips.

Chris mutters something about doing an inventory of the stock room and gives my arm a squeeze in passing, which earns him a dirty look from Hers Truly.

She waits until he's left. "Have you been talking to Kitty?"

I shake my head. Well I haven't. She didn't ask if I'd eavesdropped. "She's

95

your friend, Mum. And—" Here's my big mistake: "At least she's trying."

Oops. Big heavy stomping 'OOPS'.

"What do you mean?"

"Who was Dad, Mum? What did he do that made you so scared of trying again?"

"You know who he was."

"I know some fairytale about my father saying I looked angelic because I had wings. Which is physically impossible; unless one of you was a swan. So it's not exactly a huge amount of useful genetic information. Especially since it's a fun way to explain why one of my shoulder blades sticks out and hurts sometimes.

"Oh wait, yes, there's more! He was English. He had red hair, was a mega dancer and totally impulsive and that ever since he died – fourteen years ago - you live like a hermit, dress like a nun and the most exciting 'outing' you've had in the last few months you spent straightening my hair!"

Whose mouth IS this? I never meant to say any of this. But now I'm worked up.

I wish I wasn't.

"Which I have decided to get cut, by the way!"

I haven't.

I like having long hair. Mostly.

It's as if a well of putrid water had fermented in the belly of my soul and now it's spewing out in one massive purge. "I dunno, maybe you made him up and that's why you can't fathom trying again. Nothing's going to come close to some fantasy you made up after a one-night stand?"

Oh, this is NOT going in the right direction.

"Maybe Gramma was right. You didn't know his name, so you made one up!" We haven't seen Gramma since she said that; it is SO not something I should ever say to Mum.

And guess what, she slaps me across the face.

She has never, EVER done anything like this before and I know she regrets it quicker than anything, but I can't stop now.

"Well," I shout, because I'm still as riled as her. It's not easy, in this condition, to stop yourself saying stuff you don't know you're going to say and that you will wish you could take back later. "That solves everything. REALLY answered my questions."

And I'm gone as fast as my little runners can take me.

"Angelica!"

There's a cry in her voice but I haven't heard it yet. I won't really hear it until I've calmed down. Don't even know why I'm so angry, except maybe it's all the hard work I did to get this website going. It was all for her, even if she doesn't know it, but of course she thinks it's rubbish.

So what does that make me?

Now she'll never meet anyone and I'll end up just like her, single and lonely and life passing by till I'm too old to care.

Probably won't even manage to have a child.

Not that I want one. I mean, I want to travel the world and meet all sorts of people and do any number of jobs and mad things but sometime, somewhere at the end, I'd like one.

Not that it matters now. Might as well sign on at the local nunnery. Some Enclosed Order based on a remote island where you have to lick the pigeon poo off rocks as a penance for being so stupid as trying to do something nice for someone.

As for Dylan, he'll have to become a monk because his heart is broken and both our lives will be ruined forever.

Way to go, Mum.

～～～

I sit on the dolmen, firing pebbles at the Standing Man. He was clearly as stubborn and unreasonable as Mum. They bounce off him with tiny thuds but it's less satisfying than I expected. See, I fancied swopping cards with Dylan on Valentine's Day.

With Chris's help, I was planning to carve him a rudimentary whale from driftwood that would remind us forever to that first fateful meeting behind Albert, the skydiving whale.

None of which can happen until Mum starts dating.

I climb down to restock my artillery.

There are many versions of the Stone Man story but essentially, in Jonas' version, when he starts telling stories for the tourists, it all starts with a young girl. Beautiful, of course; hair like the crest of a wave tipped by a sunset. The man seduces her, goes on his travels promising to return and she dies of a broken heart.

For a grumpy man and a grumpier bus driver, Jonas an excellent storyteller. Tourists love him. I heard him tell tourists that Granuaile was his ancestor once. They bought him drinks all night after that.

In his version of the Stone Man myth, the man was shipwrecked, stoned and sullied by Sirens but still fights his way home. Only she's dead. Drowned. In her own tears. Probably. He stands grieving by her dolmen night and day until his heart turns to stone and he becomes the Standing Man who guards her grave forevermore.

Alternatively, when he's a little further into his cups, he claims that the woman was a mermaid and her lover stood here to try and catch sight of her again so he could call her back to shore.

Only he stood too long and calcified.

Mermaids are mythical and myths are less scary than abandonment and death.

Bet the truth is that he left kids like me and Grace all along his travels. Maybe he was really Oisín and 300 years old when he bothered to return on his white stallion. Either way, I hope she had moved on and said to him, "Ah no, sure I only fancied you when I was young and foolish, but I'm fine now. I can manage on my own, but thank you for asking."

If he did get turned to stone, I bet the minute he felt his heart calcifying, he said, "This is foolish. She wouldn't want me to do this! I should go get myself a nice strong whiskey and a new wife."

"Careful," says Mum. "He might come to life with all that deep emoting."

How does she always know where to find me and what I'm thinking?

I shrug. A mighty un-peachy shrug. "Pretty stupid to turn to stone just because someone died."

"You shouldn't judge other people's behaviour before you've had the experience."

Yup. There it is. The old 'experience' card she uses when she's stuck for an answer.

"But I have to admit, I think you're right. Seems a pretty extreme reaction. But then grief is a strange creature."

I'm back up on the dolmen, apologising mentally for bringing our emotional garbage to this sacred spot.

"I was thinking of taking the board out. Surf looks high. You want to have a go?" she says.

I shake my head. Never in a million, gazillion years.

"I don't get it, Mum. You risk your life on a ridiculous piece of wood that's neither a boat nor a raft and you do this on the Atlantic Ocean, beside cliffs and whirlpools and huge whales. Yet you won't stick your nose out in case you actually meet someone you like! How can I ever hope to have a proper relationship when you're not even capable of trying?"

"Have you considered that I'm perfectly happy with my life as it is?"

A pigeon dive bombs a harvest mouse darting out from the hedgerow.

"Dad's dead, Mum. Let him go!"

Chapter 20

Grace has tortured her long hair into a series of small bumps around the crown of her head. It's a stone circle, apparently; to match Tariq's torc; in period if not in shape. Dylan notices as soon as we get off the bus. "Cool hairdo."

All she replies is, "No squirting".

Everyone stares at it when she passes, which she takes to be a compliment. Except Tariq.

He doesn't notice her at all.

Nobody realises it's meant to represent a monument except Mr Walsh in History, who takes one look and smiles. "How nice to see you participate in class at such a Neolithic level."

There's a problem with the toilets and they let us all off home, I'm barely in the lobby when Guppy beckons me into the lounge and extracts one of our fliers from an inside pocket. "Tell me how this works."

Her eyes have that away-with-the-fairies look Mum worries about. "It's a site that people who want to meet someone can log onto, anywhere in the world. They fill in a questionnaire and then they can choose to get in touch with each other or the site recommends dates."

"But you don't need an office or an address?"

"No. It's all over the internet."

"And this internet reaches hundreds of people?"

"More, if you're lucky." No, wait. Maybe? "Is this about finding Teddy?"

She shakes her head, taps her nose and tucks the flier away again.

Okay, that was strange. So now Guppy is finally over Teddy and wants to meet hundreds of men? She's seventy-three! Then I find myself grinning. Well, why shouldn't she? And wouldn't any of them be lucky to meet her?

Cool, but strange. I make a note to call into her later. It's quiet in the apartment now she's moved back to her own.

Mum's in the office. SHE'S looking at a flier too. I mean, eye contact, concentration, the lot. Not sure why this is happening but not wanting to break her mood, I step back out of sight, cross my fingers and toes and do my wobbly walk towards the stairs.

"Angelica?"

I slouch in, as if I'm still grouchy. Don't want to give too much away.

"Look, I hate fighting with you." I give my 'so-do-I' shrug. "You want to go out this week, catch a meal in town? Unless that's too dull for you?"

"Sure."

"Sure yes or sure okay?"

"Sure yes." I do a quick scan. The flier is NOT in the bin. If it isn't in the bin, it's in the drawer and if it's in the drawer, there IS hope! "I'd like that."

"I've been thinking about what you said. Not that everything you said was right and you really shouldn't talk to me like that." She holds up a hand to stop me interrupting and closes the door behind me. "Have you thought about what it would mean if I were to meet someone?"

"I guess. I mean, not really, but it happens, right, to other people and they survive."

"I'd have to make time for him too. There'd be less time for us to hang out. You might feel left out."

I nod and she's off, listing how things would change. To be honest, I hadn't thought beyond it meaning I can have some class of the best boyfriend in the world for myself, i.e. Dylan. I mean, it's not like I really want a dad. I hadn't really thought about someone moving in with us and Mum's pretty busy all the time anyway. This is only meant to be a start.

They don't have to be permanent partners just so long as they break up AFTER I've agreed to go out with Dylan. And it's not a break-up with serious tears and poor me but because she's bored and knows she can do better; that type of break up

Then I'd be fine.

I have a feeling this may be a flaw in my '*doing-this-to-make-Mum-happy*' argument.

~~~

"Are you sure she was actually looking at the flier?"

I nod. I've called into to Grace with my news. Such momentous tidings are not suitable for mere telephonic communication.

"She wasn't shredding it into hamster hay?"

"It went into her drawer." I grin broadly. That's when I spot Mum parking up outside the pub, lifting the most luscious Black Forest Gateau from the back seat.

"That looks hopeful," says Grace. Our mums fall out regularly, but generally not as spectacularly. This may explain why neither is as slim as they should be, despite all the running around and worrying that they do. We adjourn to the landing to listen in.

ON MAKING UP, WOMAN-STYLE

Women who fall out should always make up with long walks and/or cake. 'Making up' must always be face to face. Phone calls and texts do not hack it. The most permanent falling out happens by phone and text; often parcelled with not knowing whether the other person is joking or serious. Smiley emoticons don't help.

'Making up' mainly requires jumping off high horses, kissing the soil beneath the other woman's feet and swearing hormones were responsible. Or lack of cake. Then producing a cake and suggesting a walk.

"I'm sorry." Mum holds the cake out to Kitty. "I'm so used to doing everything for myself and Angelica. How do I let someone else in? Maybe I'm afraid of reminding myself of all I've missed. If it doesn't work out? What happens then?"

"Let's go to my office," says Kitty. "I fancy some big wriggly ears are twitching around the corner."

Soon as they actually close themselves into Kitty's bedroom, with the cake, Grace and I disappear across the road. Simon doesn't open the cafe on a Sunday but he told us he'd be going in today to keep an eye on our burgeoning site.

"How did she know we were listening?"

Grace shrugs. "Least they're talking again."

~ ~ ~

If he's surprised to see us, Simon doesn't say it. He's making us decaf lattes when Dylan bursts into the back room. "Why didn't you tell me! If you fancy my brother—"

"I don't!" I'm as shocked as Grace. "Honestly! Grace, stop looking."

"Me?" she says, but she turns back to the screen.

Difficult situations require brave responses. Dylan's staring at me, pink all over with the embarrassment he's trying to ignore. He's adorable. So I kiss him. I really do. A little one, nothing major, but still my first. I can't believe I just did this, but there's no time to wonder if it was the right thing to do because Dylan is grinning like a lemur.

Which is better than grinning like a leprechaun or a lemming.

"You kissed me!"

I did! He has a lovely smile. Nice teeth. Maybe I'll be a dentist. Mum has a brother in Australia who's a dentist but they haven't talked in years. I don't think there's any particular reason. I'd have heard if he'd murdered someone or tried to extract all her teeth in a fit of pique. Course I try to act nonchalant and mature, like a 1940s film heroine, but I can't stop smiling.

Even Grace is grinning. I can see it from the way she holds her shoulders.

"Thing is, I can't go out with you while Mum's single."

"Ok." You can see his brain ticking over, trying to make the connection. "That's different."

It's as if he has heard all the excuses – a dinosaur ate my mobile phone, my mum grounded me for eating green chillies and four cacti chased me home. I take him outside the cafe and explain; leaving out the row with Mum so I come off slightly better. Also, I don't mention that I got the idea of finding a website for Mum after a bird crapped on his brother's leaflet. Or that Grace had been grounded for borrowing her mum's sex phone and that she thought I fancied Simon too.

"What can I do to help?"

"Hey, lovebirds!" says Grace, somewhere in the background. Not sure where. At this moment, only Dylan and I exist in the whole wide world. "Cooing swans?"

We block her voice out. "Must be something," says Dylan, smiling mischievously.

"Yes." His eyes have flecks of green right at the centre, orbiting his pupils. As if there's a whole galaxy of stars inside each eye. "There must."

"Earth to Romeo and Juliet?"

"What do you think, are we Romeo and Juliet?" says I to Dylan, since we're in this 'moment'. It feels like a dramatic one with the sort of deep underlying music beat that could explode into cymbals any time now.

"I don't want to die," says Dylan.

"No death pacts so," says I.

"Nope."

"Ice-cream would be good, maybe."

"Chocolate chip fudge brownie."

Hmm. "That's an idea."

"Licky, you REALLY need to come in and see this."

"Double chocolate?"

"Absolutely!"

Dylan gets called inside by Simon who's had a call from their dad asking if his brother was down there skiving off when he'd most likely homework left to do. Soon as he's gone, Grace thumps my arm.

"What?

"Your mum."

I can feel goosebumps skiving up my arm as she drags me inside and points to an entry in the New Members box. "You might not have to wait that long."

There, in red and gold, is a new profile: single mother, hotel manager, blue eyes, brown hair, likes to windsurf. Nickname: Granuaile!

"She's on!"

Grace gives me a little hug.

My mother's on!

Chapter 21

Childhood secret: When I was ten I wanted to be an exotic dancer or a woman wrestler.

First kiss: My cousin Richard's bum. It was a dare. Don't worry. He was dressed. We were five.

"You shouldn't be reading this," says Grace.

I turn it off to focus on Dylan. He's at my elbow, grinning in a way that makes me melt somewhere between my stomach and my lungs.

"We need intelligent, interesting men." I hand him one of our fliers. "But not your dad; I don't want to be your sibling." To be fair, he barely reacts, but his grin gets broader.

"Dad's brother Colm works in The Advertiser," he says. "If there's space, he might put in a bit of copy. Dad says it's time he found someone else to nag anyway. I mean, for my uncle to nag other than Dad – tho' a woman wouldn't nag, that's not what I meant," he says quickly. "Only if he met someone, he'd have company so he'd be happier and wouldn't feel the need to nag Dad. Except maybe about him meeting a woman again. That could be bad."

"It's okay, Dylan," says Grace. "Stop digging before your neck gets really muddy."

"All I meant is that it looks good if the paper looks busy and everyone would see it, so you might get good people?" I'd hug him there and then only Grace is watching so I give him a thumbs-up instead and walk him to the door.

He takes a bunch of fliers, "To leave lying around the place—"

"When no-one's looking."

"Yeah." He looks pretty pleased with himself. "Knew you didn't fancy him. He's my brother after all. Doesn't even wear shoes. Much. And you have no idea how much he snores. Not that you'd want to know. I mean, I'm not saying you're that type of girl—"

"What type of girl is she?" shouts Grace.

I open the door before he can consider answering. "Bye, Dylan." I watch him walk off, like some lovelorn bride whose man is going off to war.

But there is work to be done and a mother to fix up.

"What I want: "Someone kind, thoughtful and fun."

Grace grunts disapproval and she's right so I turn off Mum's profile, virtuously. Once as she's gone to get 'celebratory chocolate', I concentrate on looking through the member profiles for men that the site could 'recommend' to Mum. The algorithm is fine for everyone else, but a little helping hand can't hurt.

And I'm taking out the question about first kisses when we do our next overhaul. I really, really didn't need to know that my genes were quite that mixed up.

"What are you doing?" Grace can move without disturbing dust.

"Nothing."

She clicks the return button and the screen lights up with men's profiles. Jack, John and Jeffrey the jazz guitarist. "That's not nothing." She turns off the monitor and swivels my chair round to face her. "Either the site recommends men to her or you let your mother choose her own."

"Oh I'm going to but—"

"No buts. You've got her this far, Licky. It's time to let the birdling fly."

"That's not a word."

"It works."

"It's really not even a real word."

"You got what I meant."

"You could have said baby bird and I'd have got the picture."

"You want chocolate?"

"Yeah."

"So walk with me out of this cafe and let's pretend we are normal, healthy fourteen-year old girls who do not run a dating website aimed at pairing our mums up with strange men."

For chocolate I will do many things. I will even stand in drizzling rain by the war memorials, trading snipes about school until my hair frizzes up like a wall of tangled thread.

"Nice men," I say. "Not strange. Nice."

~ ~ ~

Walking the long way home, I'm daydreaming about Dylan and me so I'm almost on top of Guppy before I see her. She's staking out a patch of grass in the Far Field. This is actually the fallow field nearest to the hotel but farthest from town, hence the name.

She smiles when I stop alongside but all she says, by way of explaining what she's up to is, "Oh, I was hoping to grow a spot of grass in the shape of a woman's body. It's harder than I thought it would be".

"Oh. Really?" What else is there to say? "Great, I guess, but why?"

"You're right."

"About what?"

"Far too showy and rather pushing the point. So long as the patch can clearly accommodate two bodies lying down. Tough they were smaller then and they would have moved about, most likely, so a body form isn't necessary. Maybe if I concentrate on a patch the size of a small bed. Do you think five foot by four would be enough?"

Because I'm puzzled and hoping she might tell me more, I help her stake out her plot. We spread fertiliser inside the string, while she natters on about Queen Maeve. "You do know that it is highly likely she had a base somewhere in Drisogue, possibly even under the bones of the Drisogue Arms Hotel?"

"Okay. That's cool. What's this for, Guppy?"

"When I was wee, guests were always reporting the ghost of a wild looking woman with red hair – not unlike yours, I imagine, which brings me to my next point," says Guppy. "What are you doing Saturday fortnight, about noon?"

~ ~ ~

Mum's making up the Honeymoon Suite when I get home, for Americans due over from Dublin. We think they're both men; it's hard to tell from the names. I catch the side of the under-sheet and tuck it in. My 'hospital corners' are wicked, but I still think elasticated sheets and duvets would be easier. (Mum says we have to turn a profit first. By profit she means money beyond that needed for roof repairs. Enough to refurbish the hotel so it will match the now gorgeous ballroom.)

Chris sticks his nose in to mention the Valentine's Day Ball again. "You said we needed a fundraiser, given the recession has eaten away more of our clientele than you expected."

Mum grunts something about the work involved and the necessary outlay. I'm not sure he understands or maybe he was born under a wishing star.

"I've ordered some decorations, just in case."

I wait until he's gone. "Mum, about Dad—"

"Jeremy was six foot three, three years younger than me. Very impulsive. Always deciding to do things on the spur of the moment. He was the one who introduced me to surfing. Rotten balance though, despite the dancing. Could be finicky. Had a wee scar the shape of a whale's tail on his inner left thigh—"

"I get it."

"Pâté made him sing like a fish, wine made him dance until he fell over and he had a spot just below his right ear that if you pressed—"

"Enough!"

She leaves me to finish the bed with a grin that tells me she knows full well that this is TOO much information. I can hear her attacking the bath with venom. She has always hated cleaning bathrooms, convinced spiders hide under the plug hole waiting to snap at her fingers. "Kitty says she saw you with some boy in the cafe?"

Here we go again.

"Why don't you invite him for tea?" she says. "I can scare him off."

Ha ha. So I call her bluff. "Can't meet mine till I meet yours! They could come for tea together."

Soon as I've said it, the carved bird on the bedpost swivels, Chucky-style. "Yeah," it says, in this heavy American accent, "as if that's ever going to happen."

Mum sticks her head around the bathroom door. "What was that, Mouse?"

"This pillow case, it's stained. I'd better get another."

"I joined that site," she says, as I leave, to no one in particular. She could be talking to one of the carved birds but, if so, the birds don't reply, so I have to.

"Cool," says I, as if I didn't know and don't mind.

Cool.

Chapter 22

"Well?"

"Four men have contacted her."

I cross my fingers behind my back. Grace thinks checking up on Mum's account would be wrong. So I haven't told her. Mainly because there's nothing to tell. Mum logs on, roots around a bit and logs off.

"Two are cute. Not that I'd know, of course." Grace squints at me, then at Tariq (who still hasn't noticed her new hairdo) and back to me.

"Has she contacted them back?"

"Nope."

Her new hairdo is painful to sleep in and may not last long. Perhaps that's why she chooses now to lecture me on Dylan. At least he's down the front of the bus, so he won't overhear; even if Denise is sat beside him.

"I don't get it. You have a chance to date the most divine salamander, my own Tariq excluded."

"He's not your Tariq."

"Irrelevant. He will be. You should be listening to soft music with Dylan or going for long slow walks in places where the oxygen is in short supply, because you two belong together; though he is," she adds in case my head gets too big, "way cooler than you. By his newness alone—"

"Thanks."

Thump. There's not much space so it's a feeble one.

"They're definitely getting weaker."

She ignores me. "He's hot; you're cool; okay, majorly cool sometimes and I might only be saying that because I'm your bestie, but while he's pining for you – it's okay, everyone knows; and NOBODY gets it, by the way – you have transformed him into some sort of tragic romantic hero and all the girls are starting to notice that he's hot."

"We're waiting. He understands."

She takes a deep breath and turns to face me, as if I were an infant in need of direction to the loo. "Denise has been trying to sit beside him for days and now she has. Fortunately for you, he hasn't even noticed, whereas if you were to ask him to dress like Lady Gaga and yodel Galway Girl backwards, he would."

"I don't want to peak too soon," I say quietly.

Four days and counting. That's all.

~~~

"Wait till you see this!" Simon is skittish with excitement. "Our first paying ad." Down the sidebar, flashing little red hearts, is an ad for *'The Pirate Queen Bar', Where Love Stories Begin!'*

Grace goes pale. "That's our pub!"

Simon grins. "Cool, isn't it."

"No. This is terrible. She must know we're involved!"

"Relax. It was all done through the site, legitimately paid for via PayPal."

"You sure she doesn't know?"

"'Blind Date weekends'," I read. "'You've tried online. You've tried your best friend's slightly odd array of cousins. Now try residential matchmaking in romantic Drisogue perched on the edge of the Atlantic Ocean'."

"Gross," says Grace.

"You teens have no sense of romance," says Simon.

"It's not that romantic," says Dylan, looking out at the rain. I give him a look to tell him I'm finding it hard too. For five days now, Mum has declined every 'match' the site has suggested.

"Seriously guys—" Guys? Guys! "This could be the start of something huge. Say these weekends of hers take off? We would have tourists choosing to come to Drisogue, which is good for the town, good for business. There might even be coffee aficionados willing to fall for yours truly."

He blushes and changes the subject back to the site. "It shows we are a viable site, worth putting ads on. Advertising revenue would allow us to cover our costs, even pay ourselves something down the line and it increases the number of hits we are likely to get."

Which wasn't exactly our goal, but Simon doesn't know that. Grace manages a nod, but Simon is not letting her away with that. "I think it's awesome that your mum is giving something back. Drisogue could do with some help."

"I guess," says Grace, mellowing or blown aside by Simon's enthusiasm.

I'm still trying to introduce him to Onni. I had it all figured out. I would invite him on a walking tour of the town, we we'd wind up in Simon's cafe for a coffee and I'd suddenly remember on urgent errand and disappear.

But it's impossible. Mum never leaves me alone with him. It's as if she's protecting him from me lest he fall in love with someone and run off. She doesn't understand. If Onni falls in love with Simon, he's more likely to stay cos Simon lives in Drisogue.

And I was right about the moustache. He's got the sort of moustache you see on photos of Victorian weightlifters.

"We should do one for the hotel too? I should drop your mum an email, say I've just come across this site—"

"You can't. She'd suspect something."

~ ~ ~

Chris has hidden the boxes of decorations upstairs with the Halloween and Christmas gear. He still thinks Mum will come round. It's a good time to borrow the power drill.

"You won't do anything silly with this?"

All I know is that it has to be the power drill because Guppy wants to drill in a place that doesn't have a socket nearby. She won't tell me any more than that. "Said I'd hang a few pictures for Guppy," I say, innocent as light.

"I can do that."

I cradle the drill. "It's important I learn to do these things for myself." Chris has said this to Mum about me learning to plaster or tile or unblock a sink, so he has to agree.

When I hand the drill to Guppy, I repeat Chris's warning and she reminds me to dig out Mum's Granuaile dress for the weekend after next. I'll be serving lunch in it, for some reason she won't disclose. Now she has me keeping secrets from everyone, even from myself since I don't know what I'm being roped into.

Maybe it's a new Association for Half-daft, Drill-wielding, Grass-growing Women of a Certain Age.

Which, I have to admit, would make an interesting alternative to watching Mum tiptoe around the site like a ghoul in wellies stomping on hope. I'm not worried. Mum's a grown-up and hates to lose; she'll see it through until she meets someone.

Hopefully soon.

My job on Saturday week is to "provide colour and sandwiches". What is it with adults in Drisogue?

All for the good of the hotel, she says.

Karma, thinks I.

And boy do I need karma.

~ ~ ~

"That patch of grass, the other day? What's it meant to be?"

Guppy grins and tries out the drill in the air. If you put her in khaki, you'd think she was a freedom fighter. "You know how Queen Maeve tested her soldiers in bed, to see if they were good enough for her army."

"Not really."

Guppy sighs. It utterly confuses her that our education system doesn't include such facts. "Well, if they didn't impress her, she reputedly had them killed. And now I've found the spot she used to test them in. Right here, in Drisogue. Isn't that remarkable?" she adds with a grin and a wink.

"I'm calling it the Leaba Dhrúis or Bed of Passion."

"Guppy, what are you up to?"

"Saving the hotel with myth and legend, love and lore. Your mother has done wonders, but now it's time to be more inventive. How long will this last if I charge it up overnight?"

~ ~ ~

"Maybe it's not for her."

Cross-legged opposite me at the end of her bed, Grace's hand is flying across the sketch pad far too fast for the result to be flattering. "Are you drawing me as a rabbit again?"

"Nope."

"We could put something up on the home page that says, 'Weirdos, psychos and morticians back off. Angelica's mum is not interested. Brad Pitt, sorry but you're wasting your time'."

I smile crookedly. "Sounds about right."

"Have you tried reverse psychology. Works with my mum."

"So you've told your mum you're really fond of Marcus and hope he becomes your new dad?"

"Last night, before I went to bed. When I came down for breakfast, she was cancelling dinner with him tonight."

The last few lines she drew looked like rabbit ears from here. Either that or she's drawing me as a water buffalo with pigtails.

"You could try with your mum. What type does she want anyway?"

"Hotel managers, surfers and romantic clowns who believe babies can be born with wings."

"Okay, so you go home tonight, repeat over and over how you hope she'll never go near any of them and bingo, she will. But skip the clowns. You do not want a clown in your life, BE-LIEVE me." Grace has a fantastic cache of stories about the men her mum has sort-of introduced her to over muesli and toast. "Put it this way, last time the clown stayed over, I went to school hungry."

Speaking of which: "Any chocolate?"

It's a safe question. Grace always has chocolate. It's one of the many things I love about her. She digs out an ENORMOUS bar. I'm guessing it's a gift from Marcus because the Christmas stash is long gone. Normally she's uber-protective of her giant bars, hoarding them for bait or reward.

"Go on."

"He turned my toast into a balloon, my milk into a cauldron of blood and my muesli into a rabbit – white, big ears, no watch – that bit my finger."

"Is that why you hate rabbits?"

"It's why I hate clowns."

She puts the charcoal down and turns the pad around. Okay, so I'm not a rabbit or a water buffalo. I'm a sabre-toothed Munchkin.

"We should have a sleepover."

"We should get this maths done. Have you ANY idea what loony O'Lunney wants?"

"Apart from being head-butted into a stagnant pond by a gazebo?"

"I think you mean gazelle."

"No I don't."

"The animal that looks like a deer and has four legs and horns, or a wooden structure in the garden for cocktail suppers?" Though I do like the idea of a gazebo charging across a lawn aiming for O'Lunney's broadside.

"Reverse psychology wouldn't work. Mum would only think I was validating an opinion she already has. She'd probably drop the site altogether. Come on, Maths!"

And that's us done till it's the witching hour. Kitty drops me home because it's all dark and stormy out.

Thinking I'm sad, Mum decides we should have one of our evenings and wrestles me from my room. "You spend too much time on that computer. You are still doing your stretches? It's not good for you, being scrunched over."

I have winged scapula, see. It's why I hate that photo of me with the whale. I look like a hunchback. "Yes and yes."

After toasting marshmallows and making smores, she gets all soppy over Dirty Dancing.

See? She's getting in the mood.

Any day now, she'll respond to someone.

~ ~ ~

I've been in Simon's for an hour when Dylan pulls a chair in next to mine. "How's it going?" He smells of seawater, which is kind of nice. I pull up Mum's statistics box for him to see: Number of dates: NONE; number of ongoing conversations: NONE.

"What if we focus on places where your mum's sort of man might hang?" He passes me a printout of blogs, chat rooms and forums for people who love windsurfing, body boarding and other water sports. "If we could get on these and casually talk about the site, who knows?"

"You are amazing."

He blushes, that lovely shellfish pink and goes all focused so I know he's embarrassed – but happy too because he's smiling. "What are her other interests?"

"Casablanca," I say. "She loves Casablanca and whales. And acting and music and marshmallows—"

"Brilliant." He grins. "There's bound to be forums for people who love old films and plays and marshmallows. I'm already on some of the ones for people who love whales, so that's easy."

I drift away, watching his lips move. There's this feeling in my stomach that's warm and fuzzy and totally overpowering.

"What about good food? Didn't she start the restaurant at the hotel?"

I nod. "And dancing. She loves dancing." My fella – okay, my someday-fella, is utterly wonderful.

Within days, numbers are rising. As for me, it's time to do what I do best.

Chapter 23

From what I've seen so far, once the site's algorithm has suggested a few matches (or I do), members dive in and manage themselves. We've nearly four hundred members now yet the site hasn't suggested anyone Mum is interested in. It has to be possible to find a handful of men she's at least curious enough about to contact.

The algorithm doesn't know Mum as well as I do.

And I only agreed with Grace that Mum should *choose* who she met.

Suggesting dates wasn't forbidden.

~~~

I'm still scanning male profiles at midnight when I hear Mum approaching. This is a really weird thing to be doing when you're fourteen. By the time she comes in, the monitor is off and I'm pretending very intensely to be asleep. She leans over to kiss me on the forehead, sighs and leaves. When I hear her bedroom door close, I return to my task.

At least she didn't say anything about dads this time.

It's a long night. I manage to find four okay men and drop them into her on-site in-tray – one surfer, one lover of black and white films, another dancer. When I sleep, I have inappropriate dreams about hairy mountains and giraffes.

Don't ask.

By the time my alarm goes for school, I'm just glad to be awake.

Fortunately, I don't actually have to speak to anyone when I get downstairs. Mum's in the kitchen talking Onni through our regular dishes while Chris takes delivery of a vanload of boxes. Still, I nearly miss the bus because Mum lands into the lobby and pulls s this grotesque red-haired gold cupid out of one of the boxes.

"What the hell is this?"

"Good luck cherubs." Chris catches my eye and winks. "For the Valentine's Ball? Our February fundraiser."

She doesn't say anything. Something else has caught her eye. Chris takes it from her quickly – must be bad – and stuffs it back in. "Okay, forget the Ball. How about this year, to start with, we organise a Valentine's evening? Soft music in the bar, some comic matchmaking, show Casablanca on a big screen?"

That bit got her – it's her favourite film of all time – until she unwinds a purple banner that reads: Hopping Vasectomy Day.

Which I imagine is the last activity you would want to do, after a vasectomy.

I have to sprint to the bus. Hardly able to breathe properly, I land beside Grace, blocking her view, again, of Tariq; I'm teaching her how to play hard to get and get a small thumb as repayment, but it's still worth it.

ON THE BENEFITS OF CHOCOLATE

Chocolate helps us love each other.

Chocolate, provided everyone is given the type of chocolate they like best, would prevent wars. If the conquistadors had found only chocolate in South America and gold didn't exist, the history of the world as we know it would have been a kinder one.

It helps mood swings, stomach pains, depression, moroseness; it soothes and comforts us. Oh and everyone should have a friend like Grace who has an endless supply.

I bounce home all hopeful. I've probably flipped over into the dark and merry side of over-tiredness but there is no way Mum can't have found someone interesting from the men I sent her last night. I've been thinking about it all day. All I'm doing is making it a little easier for her.

After all, that's my gift. I matchmake!

She's on the computer in the office. That's a good sign. "Any luck?"

"Unimaginative serial killers, bored psychos and mummy's boys."

There goes my bounce , slithering across the floor and through the vent. She sounds like Grace. Maybe I need to think of Grace when I'm matchmaking Mum? No, that'd be too weird; like putting mustard on a Caramac.

Might work, though best not to mention it to Grace. I don't mind being weird if I can get Mum dating but I'm not going to advertise it.

"Give it time, Mum. Rome wasn't built in a campervan." It's okay, I dunno what it means either but I'm too tired to be quoting clichés accurately.

~~~

The way I see it, the web is a giant arcade machine, only instead of guiding the claw down to catch a misshapen Pooh Bear, this particular game is full of possible dates. Dylan's plan yields an extra 80 within days. I pluck the most eligible ones up and slip them into Mum's inbox.

Trouble is, she fires them squealing back through the trapdoor to be gobbled up by someone else. My mother is a one-woman execution squad who seriously loves her job too much. It's like a blood sport.

~~~

We said we wouldn't try to work out whether locals were using the site, but it's hard not to notice when strangers are arriving in your town for dates with locals and confirmed bachelors start patting little babies on the head outside Dolan's. Simon says people are pairing up in the cafe and on the street, in the local restaurant and Kitty's bar. But that makes it harder. If it works for everyone else, it has to work for Mum.

Not that Simon's immune to love, being smitten with our Onni, though that has nothing to do with the site.

Yeah, I called Simon up to the hotel when Mum was at the wholesalers. "You need to come up here. To do with the site? Well, sort of. Look, it's serious."

When he arrived, I took him into the kitchen to get a coffee before we started. He saw Onni, Onni saw him.

I scarpered before Mum came home.

~ ~ ~

I will not lose heart. I am the master Love-Bringer of the Drisogue Arms. I only need one man Mum can't resist. That's all I need. Once she starts dating, she'll have fun and feel fantastic and it will all have been worthwhile.

Before I go to bed each night, having fired the latest batch across, I create a new password on my computer in case Mum decides to check up on the content I'm watching. Not surprisingly, most mornings I am as dopey as a boiled frog and less intelligent.

As for Mum, day after day, she clicks on the profiles in her inbox and deletes them, one by one.

Chapter 24

Grace carries her disapproval around like a dark black rain cloud full of sleet. "You're trying to fix her up, aren't you?"

I give her my most world-weary shrug as if I haven't noticed the rain cloud, but I'm sick of it. I can't answer anyway because the bus has stopped and we're all piling off into Drisogue's Main Street.

I'm sick of being judged. All I'm doing is trying to make Mum happy. Well, okay, trying to get me my perfect boyfriend who is, incidentally, very supportive.

"Anything that gets your mum a man is okay by me," he said.

Well, not exactly, he's more subtle than that. But I know he's waiting with bated breath. Which sounds kind of disgusting, really. And difficult. If you think of bait, as in for fishing, it must mean wormy breath but I don't think that's right. (Note to self: look up 'baited breath' when I get home.)

I only went fishing three times. Why am I remembering it now, with nostalgia, when I hated it at the time? Okay, I didn't hate it exactly, but if I liked it, that was only because it was Chris and me and no one else. He didn't mind me chattering about all sorts of new species of fish-snakes and boar-salmon and how I was going to travel the world on the back of a whale.

"You have to let her choose her own."

"Chose Dad, didn't she?"

We wait till everyone has dispersed and Jonas has gone into The Pirate Queen. "He didn't abandon you," she says. "He died."

"Which shows he was a dodgy genetic choice, right?"

"Means you're a dodgy genetic daughter."

"Unless I sort Mum out."

"Right. Your logic is insane and I think you're barking like a lunatic dog with rabies and twenty-five different types of mutant forbears, but that's the dodgy genes, right?" I nod. "Seriously, Licky, you have to stop doing this. What if she found out?"

I shrug. It's not as if I haven't thought of it.

"Unless I can get Mum to actually respond to someone, everything I did this is worthless. I'll never go out with Dylan or anyone else. I'm this close to giving up. You leaping on my back and pummelling me from a height with everything that's wrong about what I'm doing is not helping!"

ON THE CREATION OF MEN

1. According to Fr Lefarge, men were created by God. Since this is not true of dinosaurs, Dobermans or ducks, it proves categorically that man would never have evolved without divine intervention. Ergo, men are an inferior species.

2. Woman needed only one of man's ribs to evolve into an entirely new, far more evolved species with brains capable of doing fifteen things at once AND giving birth.

We are clearly the superior species.

3. Men are better at reading maps. This may be true, but women know how to ask directions and cause connections to happen.

4. Adult men are allowed to have hairy armpits, legs and faces to mark them out as the more primitive species. Chris is the exception. He carves whales, can make my mum laugh when she doesn't want to and knows how to fix a leaky pipe. If I could make him an honorary female, I would.

However, right now and despite all the obvious flaws of the male species as a whole, if I could get Mum to say yes to coffee with just one man on the website, I'd whoop like a kangaroo on an airborne trampoline.

Simon bursts out of the cafe and freezes. "Inside. Now!"

"Me too?" says Dylan.

Simon barely keeps a straight face long enough to say, "Sure!" to his baby brother; his CUTE baby brother. It's amazing they came from the same mum. But at least he's over the fact that Dylan knows about the site. Simon ushers us through the heaving cafe and out into the back lane.

"What have we done now?" says Grace.

As the door closes behind us, he whispers, "MSN. They're going to feature RomanticHearts.com site." He shows us an email on his phone, shaking his head as if he can't quite believe his luck. The bells around his neck jingle like reindeer. "As one of their 'Sites To Watch'!"

He takes a deep breath and looks down at his bare feet. No, not bare; he's wearing slipper socks. They look Scandinavian. A gift from Onni, perhaps?

"Great," says Dylan.

"Brilliant," says I. My voice sounds like an empty cup.

"No, no, bigger dudes! This is the Oscar nomination of the Internet, little-brother. Try saying something slightly more awesome than 'great'. I mean, brilliant's okay but WOW! would be better. Mega, fantastic, AMAZING! Any of those would do."

"Don't say 'dude'," says Dylan. "People don't say 'dude' anymore. Haven't for a gazillion years."

We're a bit deflated. No matter how great Simon's news, we know that if my mum won't date any living man outside of Brad Pitt, Dylan and I are officially doomed as a couple.

"Little brother, I have created one of the best – albeit necessarily anonymous websites in the known universe! I can say dude as often as I like!" He seems to have forgotten this site was my idea but right now, I couldn't care less.

Before we can say *boo*, he wafts back into the cafe, still riding his little silver cloud of happiness. I plonk myself down on the window sill. If I count to ten before I check Mum's stats again, I'll find she's agreed to meet someone. A really kind someone.

Simon pops his head in again. "Oh you can say 'dude' too, Angelica. It was your idea! And Dylan-dude, I need your help inside."

"Come on." Grace throws my coat into my arms. "We need to talk and I need to escape those maroon walls. Do not try to tell me again that the hieroglyphics he has on the walls are some ancient Indian rune to make us all happy and content.

"Because if that's what those runes are meant to do, they don't work!"

~ ~ ~

"Your mum's taking her time. That's all. Bet you, when you get home, she'll be waiting to tell you she's been in contact with, oh I dunno, a wee multitude of men and they all want to take her out for five star meals and buy you enormous boxes of chocolates to keep you sweet."

I know Grace is trying to cheer me up but it's impossible. From the stone circle, looking west, we can see Guppy drilling at a bit of rock beside a wee waterfall where an underground stream rushes forth. Well, it rushes when there's been rain; today, it sort of splutters.

Last week, Dylan spotted her drilling a hole in the west end of the estate wall.

"Should she be doing that?" says Grace.

"Probably not, but she's standing on a wooden chair so that's good." I climb onto a standing stone lying on its side and survey the world I will live in for the rest of my days.

"Maybe she's happy being single. If she isn't interested, there's nothing you can do."

Hardly worth saying really.

"Especially as you're not even meant to know she's on the site."

Yeah and I really needed to hear that, Grace, oh best friend in the known world. I really needed to.

"Come on. You've sent her all the best men you can find. Don't pretend it was only one or two, because I know you, Licky Moone. Hey! Licky Moon! That's not bad. Maybe we should form a band. The Licky Moons. We could, like, tattoo moons on our tongues."

"Yuck."

She shrugs. "How many have you sent her?"

"30 or so." We sit on my stone for a while to let this sink in, sink in ten feet below the ground and tickle the toes of a troll; a kindly troll who will alter history and make Mum happy.

"Maybe she's rusty," says Grace at last. "Which sounds weird. It's not like we can actually go rusty. If we did, sure all we'd need is some WD40 and problem solved. Are you even listening to me?"

Sometimes friends don't know when they're helping and when they're not, so Grace has no idea why I grab her in a bear-with-twelve-arms-from-a-mutant-chemical-explosion hug. "That's it!!" From grump with no hope to impulsive hugger. It's clear as beagle spit speeding towards you in a southerly wind – Mum's date-o-phobic! How did I not see this before? All she needs is practice. "You're a genius."

"What did I say?"

"Can't stop. Talk later!" I need to enlist the most efficient dater in the county in Mum's cause. It's probably better if Grace isn't there when I broach my new and deeply-meddling plan. "Thank you!"

I race off with a grin on my face that would put the Cheshire Cat into a home for depressed felines.

"Don't electrocute yourself, Guppy!" I shout as I fly past, but I think I'm too late. She has this wet look that doesn't look intentional while her hair's akin to an upside down Dumbledore.

Kind of suits her, though.

Chapter 25

Kitty's adding their daily specials to the table menus when I skid into The Pirate Queen and assume an expression of innocence as if I'd tumbled from a misdirected spaceship. I even make small talk.

"You didn't run here to talk about the weather."

"Mum needs to remember how to date."

"And you're telling me this because?"

"It's, well, I mean, you know how to handle men. Okay, that didn't sound right." I force myself to take a deep breath and try again. "You're good with them. I mean, dating doesn't freak you out or offend you or scare you or anything. You like it, even. Maybe? But Mum doesn't. Hasn't. Not for years and years. One first date and she'll be fine but right now, she hasn't the confidence to go on a date because she's REALLY rusty."

Kitty's looking at me as if I was speaking Sumerian.

"So it came to me, what if all she needs is a bit of practice?"

Slowly, Kitty nods. "Makes sense, but what can we do about it and why are you suddenly so concerned?"

"That's where you come in." I ignore the last bit she said. "If she thought I was behind it, she'd make soup of me. With broccoli." (I hate broccoli and so does Grace's Mum.)

She frowns. "Behind what, exactly?"

"When you fall off a horse, you get straight back on, right? Only Mum never had a chance because of me."

"You want me to take her horse-riding?"

"Yes. No. I want you to teach her how to date again. No, wait. Hear me out. It's not totally insane. What if we set up a pretend date and you coached her through it. With someone she knows and doesn't fancy, who knows what the score is because he doesn't fancy her either because maybe he's known her for years."

"A mock date?"

"Exactly.

"And where do you propose finding our disinterested guinea pig? I presume he has to be disinterested?"

I nod

And I was thinking Chris would be perfect."

"Oh I'm not sure."

"It's perfect. They're friends, right, so it's safe. I'll square it with him too but I know he'd want to help. It's in his nature. Mum can practice dating with him under your tuition and expert guidance." Okay, I might have overdone the apartmenttery; she's frowning again. "If she doesn't get over her fear of dating. Look, I know it's a bit weird but she'll never meet anyone on the site—"

Oops.

"How do you know she hasn't?" starts Kitty.

"Oh, you know." Think fast! "She'd have told me. She's not singing to herself in the shower or giving me happy hugs for no reason and she's not eating chocolate." When in doubt, deflect. I learnt this from Mum.

"Or borrowing my make-up, which, let's face it is much better than hers."

Her phone rings before she can push for more information. "Stay where you are. I have to get that."

"This Saturday," I say, backing away.

"The Blind Date Weekend? Yes, we still have a few places available." She covers the mouthpiece and mouths, "Too soon," as she pulls a red notebook from her pocket.

I grin. "All you have to do is persuade Mum to agree to it. I'll look after everything else."

I bump into Grace on the way out. "Thanks a mil. I traipsed all the way up to the hotel to find out you weren't there. What were you talking to my mum about?"

"If I told you, I'd have to kill you."

"Licky."

"I'll explain tomorrow." I hug her again and run off before she can throw in a thump. "When it's all sorted. Oh and did I mention you're a genius?"

"I don't get you, Licky Moone."

"Neither do I, mostly. Got to go."

~ ~ ~

Chris is replacing tiles on the roof of the ballroom when I screech to a halt full of plot and persuasion, but this can't wait. I scamper up the ladder behind him, hoping he won't get such a fright that we both fall off. The sky is blue as blue and there isn't a hint of rain, which is an excellent omen.

Especially here.

We get a lot of rain.

"Chris! Didn't you do acting?"

"What are you doing up here? Angelica, get down now."

"Not till you agree to something!"

Oh yes. Plot, persuasion and a ladder into the eaves. That night, for the first time in weeks, I sleep like a newborn lamb that doesn't know it's probably food.

And I don't dream.

AT ALL.

Chapter 26

It takes Kitty two days to convince Mum that a practice date is not the daftest idea since the last daft idea she shot down. Mainly because Kitty pitches it in such a way that she thinks it might be fun, because Kitty will be there the whole time and because Mum knows, maybe, deep down, that she has to do something.

I've sworn Chris to secrecy about my role in the whole affair.

Not because it could still go wrong but because my involvement would give her the best excuse to change her mind.

The non-romantic and entirely pragmatic training tryst will take place in The Old Barn at 11am on Saturday. By then breakfast is over and, at present, it doesn't look like we'll have any checkouts that day.

The Old Barn in the Far Field isn't as dodgy as it sounds. It is only ever used for hay so it doesn't smell bad or anything. Besides, Mum won't want anyone to know she's doing this and nobody has any reason to pass through the Far Field in February except sheep. Or maybe Guppy now and then, with her power drill and fertilizer.

On Friday, Chris drops a table and two chairs to the barn and the scene is set. Mum will be too busy now with everyday hotel stuff to change her mind. This is my last rational thought. We're in the apartment when we hear a bus pull up outside and exactly twenty-two excuses to cancel romance disgorge noisily onto our stoop in sturdy hiking boots.

It's as if they'd been sent by a malicious little elf who wants me to be single all my life.

"Am I hallucinating?" says Mum.

"Nope."

"It's definitely not another whale or Brad Pitt?"

"Nope."

Mum grabs her cardigan. "Maybe they're lost?"

I follow her downstairs and it seems they're in the right place. The Drisogue Arms. Mum takes a step back into the office on the pretext of checking the booking on the computer.

"How many rooMrs Do we have made up?"

"Maybe ten."

She returns to the front desk where the Leader of the Pack brandishes a 20% discount voucher and the printout of an itinerary entitled *Walking Tour of Drisogue's Myths and Magical Townlands*. "Group booking, Friday and Saturday night. Maybe I could speak to Genevieve O'Malley."

As if on cue, Guppy sweeps in the main door before Mum can respond. "Jacqueline Maguire! Well I never!"

Hugs and kisses transform the lobby into a seething mass of goodwill. Guppy is togged up like a 19th-century country lady. The look is scatty but intriguing. I suspect the velvet wraparound over-skirt is a tablecloth.

"You realise you're a week early!"

"Are we?" Jacqueline looks around at her colleagues. "Long time since I've been that early!"

"You were a week early for your wedding, dear," one of her companions explains, but Jacqueline is gesturing at Mum for Guppy's benefit.

"I thought your manager was a bit odd!" she says.

Before Mum can do a wobbly – and it IS there, forming in her mind, Guppy shoos her out from behind the desk. She fishes out a guest list and places it on the counter. Next, she produces a bundle of leaflets from her pocket that she hands to me to pass out.

"Hot off the press this very afternoon!"

Mum's too shocked to do much else except calculate in her head how many beds they will need and whether we have enough sausages and rashers for breakfast or will need to grab some downtown.

"Now, leave your bags over there, under the picture of myself with the last whale to stay in the hotel" There's an appreciative ripple of laughter that seems to set the mood as she ushers them into the bar. "Let's get you some nice hot ports in the lounge while we sort out the rooms."

Mum's reading one of Guppy's leaflets. *FOLLOW THE FOOTSTEPS OF IRELAND'S GREATEST LOVERS*, it screams in calligraphic swirls.

A walking tour of Drisogue – lust, love, myth and magic.

This is what she's been up to!

Leaba Dhrúis, where it all began, the Cúirt Field of Dreams, Lover's Stumble, the Sighing Wall, The Stone Man and his heart's desire.

Mum's wide awake now. And who does she attack?
Me.

"I suppose you knew about this?" She turns the leaflet over to look at the price list. Oh well. This makes her stop; who would have thought people would pay so much to go tramping around fields? "How many rooms will we need?" she says, when Guppy returns.

"Twenty-two," says Guppy. "For tonight. Maybe less after that, once Drisogue weaves its magic." The noise level in the bar goes up several notches. "It's a singles walking club." If this is flirting for the over fifty-fives, it's scary! "They might double up tomorrow."

"Angelica, second floor, rooms 12 to 20; not 21, it's too damp." There goes my Friday evening in a blur of sheets, pillow cases and towels. She holds open the restaurant door. "Guppy, can I have a word?"

It's never good when she says that. Never never NEVER. So it's in Guppy's interest, really, that I spot Guppy's shawl and follow them to give it back. She's seventy-three. Someone has to look after her.

"First," Mum is saying, "You should have told me. What if the hotel had been full?"

She should have closed the kitchen door if she didn't want me to listen.

"Oh, Chris and Angelica would have helped me. Most of the hotel has been empty all winter. Besides, they came a week early. I was waiting for the leaflets to arrive and they only got here this afternoon. The website is barely live. That lovely vicar's boy helped me out. Unless I got the date wrong."

Mum remains mute.

"See, they're my test group. I got in touch with Jacqueline is the daughter of an old friend. Runs these single meet-ups. The dating website gave me an idea. I pitched it to her and she leapt right in. We're not getting full price on the rooms but if the weekend comes up to scratch, they'll spread the word faster than a scoop of butter on a warm windowsill."

"That's not the point. Would you have told me before next week?"

"Of course I would."

Mum doesn't sound convinced. "So everyone knew except me?"

"Technically, Angelica and Chris didn't know. Simon only knew of necessity but I swore him to secrecy."

"What about Father Lefarge and the vicar and Big Brenda?"

"I never told Big Brenda."

Mum lets out a loud sigh. She has a range of sighs almost as extensive as I have shrugs.

"Well, I had to okay it with the religious," says Guppy in her own defence. "To make sure I didn't step on their toes when I claimed that St Mary in the Grotto was actually Brigid, the pagan priestess that the Church sucked up. Fr Lefarge said it was fine, so long as I did the same with something in the Church of Ireland grounds too. So I did."

Mum sits down, defeated. "This is a madhouse."

"It was a meant to be a nice surprise," says Guppy. "You've been telling me how worried you are about numbers since the recession hit. Well, that's my responsibility too. I've left you holding everything together and it's time to harness our horses."

"The minute they leave, you will walk me through the package before another lot arrives. I don't want to look like a complete fool again." Mum sticks on the kettle, a sign that the storm has run its course. "Is any of it real?"

"Oh it's all potentially real. Who's to say Maeve didn't test her men's virility in the Far Field, where the Leaba Dhrúis lies? Could have been how the town got its name and the men their reputation."

"If they expect clean sheets each night, we're scuppered." Mum pulls out a packet of chocolate biscuits from a filing cabinet drawer full of recipes and kitchen paperwork and gobbles three without pausing. So that's where the secret stash is. This is the point when I should produce Guppy's shawl.

"Did you love him?" says Guppy suddenly.

"What?"

"Angelica's dad. Did you love him?"

"That's none of your business."

"So you want to end up like me?" she says, so quiet I almost miss it.

"You're your own boss. You live in a beautiful place. Everyone loves you."

"Forty-six years of sleeping alone, waking alone, buried in my books. This hotel was all I had until you and Angelica came along. I know she's worried about you."

"You had Chris," says Mum.

"I did," she says and, "Just don't leave it too late," says Guppy.

I hardly dare breathe as Mum opens the door with me behind it and strides out. Guppy follows but before I move, she says: "Shouldn't you be making up beds?"

She closes the door, so I'm revealed. I hand her the scarf and take the back stairs up so I can arrive on the second floor before Mum.

Chapter 27

Breakfast is anything but quiet. Guppy's walkers have the appetites of scavenging bears fresh from hibernation. But they eat fast, which is good though I saw them sneak little jams into their rucksacks, no doubt for when they get hit by exhaustion half way across a boggy field.

By the time Guppy leads them off to see the sights, Mum is having cold feet. Kitty, primed by me that this would happen, refuses to take no for an answer. I slip away to the barn while Kitty calms her down.

Having laid the table with a lovely linen tablecloth, the nicest cutlery and wine glasses, I go out back and climb the rickety ladder up to the mezzanine generally used by courting couples in summer who want to watch the sun set over the peninsula. And, yes, I know I shouldn't listen in, but it's my duty to know if anything goes wrong. Then I can steer Mum around the broken pieces of glass.

I promise the ladder that I'll plant it someday and pretend it's a tree if it stays put.

Chris arrives first, with a bottle of plum-coloured cordial, as organised by Kitty. She wants them to go through the motions as if it were a real date. He peels off his overalls to reveal a fairly decent pair of trousers and a polo shirt. I don't like the polo shirt. He doesn't suit a polo shirt. Not unless he plans to jump up on a Connemara pony and hack the heads off dandelions with a hurley.

He checks his breath by breathing into the palm of his hand, which is kind of sweet. Grace lands in behind me in a heap.

"What are you doing here?"

"Making sure you don't do something stupid, like interfere," she says with a cheeky grin.

"At least you didn't have to get up at six to make breakfast for strangers first."

"AND I have some news. Big news. Two pieces.

"Shhh. Here they come."

Mum and Kitty linger right at the base of the ladder. Thirty seconds earlier and they'd have spotted Grace climbing up. Please don't move it. Please don't move it!

"You don't think he fancies me do you?"

Kitty steers Mum towards the entrance. "God, no!" Pepper the pill with kindness, why not!

"That's okay so."

"It isn't," whispers Grace. "You heard her voice. She's disappointed!"

"Don't be silly."

"First piece of news. Jonas has done something weird with the school bus." I'm not really listening. "He's filled it with flowers and pasted Star Trek posters inside over the windows."

"You were inside?"

She shrugs and snaps a bar of 86% dark chocolate. "Energy food. D'you think he's met someone on our site?"

Below us, Kitty ushers Mum inside and Chris stands up.

"I suppose it'd be unethical to try and find out, through the site?"

"Yes."

"Thought so." She sighs. I worry about Grace sometimes. "Pity. But wait till you see this!"

She's pulling a newspaper supplement from her coat pocket. It sounds noisy enough to give our location away to anyone within a five mile radius. "Shhh."

"But."

"Not now."

Let the play commence. Kitty positions Mum and Chris across from each other at the table. "Okay. You've just met for the first time so you're both feeling awkward, but excited. Chris, start with a compliment. She's useless at taking compliments."

True.

He hands over a single rose – okay, I don't know where that came from and neither does Mum. She half curtsies; she is not taking this seriously, which puts him off his stride. He clears his throat. "You have beautiful eyes."

Embarrassed, Molly shakes her head. Something seems to happen then. As if he realises she has nice eyes, he pinkens a bit. "Are you blushing?" says Mum.

Kitty takes control. "If he is, it would be extremely impolite to say so, Molly and could embarrass him into not speaking for the rest of your meal. Let's try it again but this time, accept the compliment, smile, make eye contact, compliment his choice of restaurant."

"What if I chose the restaurant?"

"Then something else. His dress sense, the rose he brought." This isn't going as I'd expected. "Forgive her for her rudeness, Chris, for she knows not what she does. Now, let's try again."

"Eyes that would lead a man astray," says Chris, with a cheeky grin. I think he's getting this now, but Mum's having none of it.

"Quoth some Victorian swooner. Sorry. I'm not good on corny. It's been—"

"A long time?"

"Yes."

"Which is exactly why we're here. Let's move on," says Kitty. Chris holds out her chair and Mum sits down. "Ask Chris about himself. Men love to be asked about themselves."

"Is that true?"

"Well I'm not your average guy," says Chris, "but it's worth a try."

Mum takes a deep breath and smiles. "What do you do yourself, Chris?"

"I help out in this really interesting hotel run by a very special lady."

Oh pleeeease!

With Kitty there to keep Mum in check and make her take it seriously, things go okay for a while. Kitty decides to move it to the next notch.

"Okay, Chris, now try taking Molly's hand across the table and Molly, try not to leap back in fright. It's only a hand."

At her cue, Chris obliges, theatrically. But instead of taking her hand, he knocks Mum's glass onto her lap. He leaps to his feet, all apologies, to mop it up. Only Mum starts to get up at the same time – because her lap's all sticky. Chris tries to help, by pulling her chair out, except that he does it a little too eagerly, forcing her to stand quickly.

Trouble is, he's standing on the hem of her dress and when she tries to grab hold of something to stop herself falling, Mum lands a right hook in his eye.

As a first date, it's a debacle. As theatre, it's mighty!

"This is fun," says Grace.

"Shhh."

"I should get back," says Mum.

"Me too. Tyrant of a boss."

"Poor you.

"Absolutely. I don't know how I manage."

Kitty is lost for words. Her phone rings. "Ok. No one is going anywhere. Make small talk till I get back – weather, food. Not sex. Never talk about sex. And try not to do any more damage?"

Chapter 28

"Can I show you this now?"

Without actually waiting for an answer, Grace unfolds the computer supplement from one of the national newspapers. "Didn't know you were a reader."

"Ha ha." She opens it up on the second-last page. 'IS ROMANCE IS BACK IN FASHION? Phenomenon that is the RomanticHearts.com website. The only clue to the makers of this success story – 549 members in a month, up to 30% claiming to have been successfully matched – may lie in an ad for a pub called The Pirate Queen and for the small town of Drisogue in which it resides, in County Donegal.'"

"He put up an ad for Drisogue?"

Grace nods, mutely. "He thought, since my mum had one."

"He was meant to ask. What if someone tracks it back to us?" She's not listening. At least not to me. "Grace?"

"Isn't this meant to be a date?"

"A pretend date."

"Yeah but, like, they're talking business! Who does that on a date?"

Curious we listen in.

"So we find a weekend nobody else is using for anything at all," says Chris. "Transform it into something special, create our own LoveFest."

"Never work." Mum, the pragmatist.

"Course it would!"

"Think of the planning, the organisation."

"Guppy convinced twenty-two single people to come stay in our hotel because she offered them tours to Places of Passion that may not even be real. Kitty has a waiting list for her blind date weekend in two weeks' time. Everyone loves romance, even if they say they can do without. Look at us. Wouldn't we love to have someone to hold us when it's cold, to share special moments with? To spill wine over?"

Mum smiles, as if he's a small child playing make-believe. "I have Angelica."

"And she is special. Mighty special. So do this for her. Make the hotel, no, make Drisogue come alive so she has a future here if she wants one. Think outside of the box for a minute. You've said no to every other idea I've had but what do we have to lose? If we give the people of Drisogue an excuse to celebrate all that is good and positive about this town, it will pay off!"

"Lisdoonvarna," interrupts Mum. "They have it sewn up."

"In October; wet, dark, miserable October. I'm talking spring. Late April. Lengthening, warm April evenings. Magical sunsets. Not so close to exams that the kids can't help. We're a small community, for it to work, everyone has to be involved."

"These things take months to organise. They don't just happen."

He pulls out a notebook, sweeping her objections aside. "I've been doing some research and a timeline. Apart from Lisdoonvarna, there's nothing like this. Remember, this isn't about matchmaking – we're selling the possibility of love and magic. We have everything! Myth, folklore and history, the Atlantic Ocean and whales. We pitch it midway between romantic festival and pagan love fest."

Chris parades around the barn like an evangelist. "We incorporate Guppy's walking tours, one of Kitty's blind-dating weekends, create any number of new events, put up an open-air cinema to show classic romantic movies – Casablanca, Some Like it Hot, La Cage Aux Folles. Keep it to three days, but every hour of those days we offer something different. Every business in town will support it. The County Council has already told me there's a fund there for rural development we can access."

He pauses for breath and looks around the barn as if he had transformed it into a time-travel machine. "Think of it, Molly. We probably have the only Stone Man in the whole of Ireland. We have a dolmen, groves of mistletoe; we have Guppy! We choose a weekend with a full moon and then, on the Saturday, we host a Victorian Ball. Nobody will be able to resist who has an ounce of romance in their body."

"Have you been talking to Angelica?"

"Not yet. Mind you, if we were to add matchmaking, we have her unique talent!"

"She's fourteen."

"So she'd communicate via headphones with Guppy and Guppy does the matching. Wearing a velvet dress and rowan berries in her hair. Or not," he adds quickly, because Mum's not leaping at the idea of my input. "Wouldn't you like to restore the Drisogue Arms to its heyday?"

"More than anything," she says quietly. "I've been trying to bring business in for seven years and we're barely ticking over." She folds the table cloth. "There's a recession, Chris. People aren't travelling and they aren't staying in hotels. Everything's expensive."

"the ballroom's magnificent again."

"People don't sleep in a ballroom."

"So the Drisogue Arms is shabby genteel. Informal chic. A taste of old Ireland. People are sick of impersonal chain hotels. We can give them living history. Look at the scenery we have!"

"The time and money it would take to organise a festival."

"Sponsorship and community involvement."

"You really think we can do this?" He nods. She smiles.

"It would have to be spectacular," he says.

"A LoveFest," says Mum.

"No single supplement, but we give a reduction if they share." They're conspirators now, carried away.

Mum stops for a moment to really look at him. "Why are you so keen?"

"This is my home too. If business doesn't turn round, there won't be enough income or life to keep Angelica here and she loves this daft town. As do you."

"Aww," says Grace – but I've just seen the time and I need to go. Guppy and I struck a deal. She'd keep her walkers out of the Far Field this morning so long as I wasn't late back to serve an early lunch in my Granuaile garb.

Chapter 29

"You're never leaving me here!" Grace hisses as I back out onto the ladder.

"Come on so."

"I can't." She doesn't move. "I can't go down ladders. I can only go up."

"Now you tell me."

"I didn't know we'd have to go back out that way. I thought we could jump down onto the bales of hay."

"Okay, I'll climb down step by step right in front of you. It'll be like a vertical conga." As we go – slow as slow, I remind the dodgy contraption that masquerades as a ladder that it will be called a tree some day, if it doesn't let us down now.

We pass Guppy's walkers at her Leaba Dhrúis, where the grass is now two foot taller and greener than the rest of the field. "Only those men deemed sufficiently virile could join her personal guard. Those that failed—" She gestures towards the cliff. "Well, we'll see their watery grave after lunch."

She's in her element and has them eating her words like honey. I'm sure her accent has got more lyrical too.

"However, it is possible this whole field was used for similar rites back at the time of the Druids. Sex to symbolised the rebirth of the universe in the spring. It was a sacred duty, fertility made the world function."

We slip past unnoticed.

"Now, let's go see the Stone Man."

HOW TO KEEP MUMS HAPPY

Words to use: Cool. Neat. Amazing. Absolutely.

Phrases: I love studying. I REALLY love Maths. Irish is my favourite language. School – why do we have to have so many holidays? I'd far prefer to go to school every week of the year. I wish you could home school me.

Attitudes: Weekends are such a waste. Have you got any chores for me to do?

Sweets: Yuck! Give me a carrot stick any time. Or celery. And hummus. Yup. Life doesn't get much better than hummus, except maybe tofu with salad.

The hotel is buzzing. I was only meant to be handing out sandwiches but Guppy has me in a corner doing spreads for them while they munch sandwiches. After lunch, she's taking them to the Sighing Wall and she wants them warmed up with a little fortune telling.

Mum wouldn't be happy but she's still not back.

The Sighing Wall is the old estate wall in which she drilled a hole last week; big enough for a hand to slip through. The tale she's telling is that on the day of the spring solstice, any single man could place a hand through; if a single woman took it – not literally as in amputated; I mean as in '*to have and to hold*' take, they were married for a year and a day. Part Brehan Law, part Guppy's imagination, part power drill.

At the end of that time, they could part amicably, no harm done. It was internet dating without the photos, the only profiles being the weathering on your hand. And you got to move in together immediately.

I've just got up to stretch my legs and grab a lemonade when I hear Chris's voice in the lobby. "Mum's back," I shout to Guppy and wander out to see how it went, given I'm not meant to know anything about this 'play date'.

"I mean, you're funny, you're witty, you've no facial hair."

"What d'you mean I don't have facial hair! Of course I don't have facial hair! What is it with facial hair?"

"It was a joke."

Chris no longer looks even vaguely fluffy-tailed. Lacking in any form of bounce, it's as if it got exhumed out of him. Where's Kitty and what happened after we left?

"Date's over," she says, smart as you like. "You've got your raise!"

"She told me to kiss you. Nobody made you kiss me back."

"I did not. And it wasn't a real kiss. THAT clearly was the kiss you gave Kitty when she decided to demonstrate how it should be done! Hope you learnt something useful. Oh and look, she's waiting for you outside."

It's true. Kitty's still there, her engine turning over as if it's trying to break some Iron Man challenge or turn into a Transformer Killing Machine with rattly pecs. "I – what?" He looks confused. "I said I'd look at her boiler. What is the matter with you?" And out he goes.

"Angelica," says Mum. "Why are you wearing that dress?"

"What's going on between you and Chris?"

"Nothing. What makes you think there is?"

I can't say, 'The last time I saw you together, you were getting on really well' because technically the whole gig was Kitty's idea.

"He's a fine man," says Guppy. Maybe it's an old person trick, this way of sort of transporting yourself into a scene without anyone noticing.

"And he works for me," says Mum, as if she's sick of pointing this out. "Don't you have guests to look after?"

Guppy gives her a withering look – she's as good at them as I am at shrugs and it has as much effect. Mum's in a world of her own, a grumpy world. Guppy heads into the bar to loudly rally her troops.

"Something happened. Do you fancy him? Did you kiss Chris?"

"Don't be daft. It was a rehearsal. For a play Kitty's writing. She wanted us to do a read-through."

"Oh."

Chris stomps back in as if I weren't there. "Let me get this straight. You think I'd kiss you for a promotion? Kitty and I, we were trying to help you get over your fear of dating. We were trying to help."

"We need you in the bar," says Mum, though we don't. Everyone's leaving to follow Guppy out to the Sighing Wall.

"Angelica," says Chris, "will you explain to Kitty that I won't be over to look at her boiler until I'm finished here."

~ ~ ~

Mum's still in the office when I'm heading for bed. It's been a long day and the walkers are still singing in the bar with Jonas. "You busy?"

"Not really." She has the RomanticHearts.com website up and watches to see how I react so I shrug and say, "Looks like a neat site". Yup, old-fashioned slang works for mums, makes them feel included.

"I thought, with your gift, you could maybe help me pick one?"

"You sure?"

"Uh huh. I want to show Kitty and Chris that I can do this."

Okay, not the healthiest reason, but means justify the ends, don't they?

"These are the ones I've looked at." I can almost feel Dylan's arm around my waist. Goosebumps. "See, the site has been recommending men but how am I to know if they are the person they say they are?"

She takes a deep breath and I hold mine. Is this when it finally begins?

"Since you're the expert, I want you to pick one out for me? And yes, I know this is not normal daughter-mother behaviour but when you haven't dated anyone for—"

"He looks okay?" I interrupt quickly before she tells me something I shouldn't hear.

"Carl?" She calls up his profile. Forty-two. Self-employed, entrepreneur. Loves the environment, animals, ballroom dancing.

Chris knocks on the door to say he's going to the basement to fetch some more whiskey and Mum shuts the site down quick as a tsetse fly. She says sorry to him outside the door, leaving it ajar so I can overhear, which shows she feels bad. He nods and they sort of hug and then she's back, ready to start over again.

"Why don't we look at them upstairs on my computer?"

By now I'm imagining Dylan's arm looping around my shoulders, all five fingers touching my neck where I once wished for a vampire's teeth!

"Okay," she says, grinning. I've never seen her like this. Like a kid going candy shopping full of fizzy drink. "You're old enough for this, aren't you? I'm not freaking you out?"

What can I do but nod? Nod really deeply and well.

By the time I turn my computer off tonight, my mother will be officially dating.

Or nearly.

VERY nearly officially dating.

At last.

Chapter 30

Chris nabs me as I come in from school loaded down with homework, including algebra, the only part of Maths that actively hates me.

"I need your help," he says. "This idea I have – and your mum's on board, well, sort of. But here's the thing, I need to compile a festival package that she can't resist."

He's holding a sheaf of pages covered in half human scribbles and small stick figures. Oh and yes, some small whales blowing heart bubbles. "Can you take a look? "You're brilliant with words and you do have a gift for matchmaking." His ears go red. "It's to help the hotel."

I take the pages. Well, I owe him for not telling Mum about me getting detention.

"See, we talked about this festival yesterday and she was all up for it and then she got mad. She does get mad sometimes; I've no idea why."

"Maybe because you kissed Kitty?"

"You overheard."

"The whole hotel overheard."

"Kitty thought your mother needed to see what it looks like when you're enjoying a kiss. Yeah. I know. I thought it was odd too but she's pretty persuasive. And she made it sound sort of clinical. Do you know, your mum said it's nine years since she kissed a man!"

"Too Much Information! Chris, you know better than to talk to me about Mum!!"

"So just have a look and I swear I'll never mention your mum and kissing in the same breath again."

"Promise?"

"On the dying breath of an albatross."

"Weird, but okay."

"Tell me what you think. Honestly. That's all. Unless you want to, y'know, tidy up the grammar or something?"

> 'Single and mad about film? Come and meet your SoulMate at Drisogue's LoveFest. April 22nd-25th, 2010. Stay at the Victorian Drisogue Arms Hotel, elegantly poised on the edge of the Atlantic, 65 euro pp sharing, includes ticket to SoulMates Ball.'

"That's the pitch. Intro thingy."

"Sounds good."

"Not too over the top?"

"Possibly a bit specific?"

"Ah, but that is part of my cunning plan to target various groups, starting with one your mum's interested in to pique her interest."

"I thought you said she agreed to it?"

He nods. "In principle. It's a blip. She will, oh she absolutely will. Provided it's spectacular!" He grins and heads off with a bounce in his step. "Oh and Angelica—"

"What?"

"It IS going to be spectacular!"

～～～

The bay window near the snack machine in the lounge has become the unofficial headquarters of our festival think-tank. He has some good ideas, like online vouchers that people can print off and redeem against events at the festival, accommodation or food. He's getting pricings for a marquee to run additional events in, like a craft fair or a food market, an outdoor cinema in the Far Field and insurance.

I've helped him pull together an information leaflet that he's going to deliver and post up around town. It calls on the Citizens of Drisogue, Young and Old to come to a Public Meeting at 7pm in the Community Centre on Thursday next.

The date he's pitching for the LoveFest is only two months away.

"You'll need a website ready to go when you get the green light."

"Okay. Can you check prices with Simon?"

~ ~ ~

"Do it yourself. You're well able."

He's trying to make a little rabbit on a crema. Rabbits are Onni's favourite animal. Apparently he had a pet rabbit in Finland, one that answered to his name and shared his sofa.

"I'll give you access to the software you need." Okay, so Simon has decided that he's mentoring me, which is another way of saying I'm his unpaid slave. The last one probably died of coffee poisoning. (His coffee is seriously good now. Everyone's going around town on a caffeine high and the cafe is busy busy busy.)

He wants us to nominate him for Entrepreneur of the Year but since, technically, RomanticHearts.com was my idea and it's anonymous, it's a long shot. I show him how to do the rabbit, not once but three times and when his version is looking like a small ogre with long ears, I start work on the website for Chris's festival.

~ ~ ~

It's nice to be working on something that isn't a secret, or isn't totally. As well as a chat room and Chris's section for vouchers, I add romance, heartstrings and wispy angel wings; everything I had to leave out from my own site because Grace and Simon were looking over my shoulder.

I've added optional panels for music, myth and ritual, history, walking tours, blind-date events, films, a 'mind & spirit' fair, workshops on everything from aphrodisiacs to pottery to candles. I've managed to find some way to incorporate every business in the town; can't have anyone having an excuse not to be involved.

~ ~ ~

"This is amazing," says Chris when I show him the site.

"It's only a rough," says I, feeling chuffed, "and I might have gone a bit overboard. We can't use it until the festival's a 'go' so I set up a blog people can contribute to when you're getting suggestions and want to get the word out locally."

"Where did you learn to do this?"

"School. So when are you showing Mum?" I add to distract him from asking more awkward questions.

"When it's ready."

He has this idea that it has to look all professional and with lots of people already behind it so she can't say no. It's not a great time anyway. She's like a bag full of puppies over her upcoming date with Carl. They exchanged one email before she said they should meet. I think she was afraid she'd lose her nerve.

The highlight of the festival is spread across the top banner: the LoveFest Ball in the Drisogue Arms Ballroom. I'm tweaking it, again, when I hear, "Am I invited?"

Dylan. He looks gorgeous. He looks tall.

What can I say?

"Course."

Dylan and I celebrate with a hot chocolate in Simon's cafe. Any day now, he can ask me out and I'll say yes. I have a good feeling about Carl. I mean, I can matchmake everyone else, why would it be difficult to do for Mum?

Chapter 31

On the morning of the date – luncheon in a garden centre, good sign he's not a rapacious bug-man, I take over her hair because she's all fingers and toes. Even if she refuses to pout, I want her to feel like a film star.

"Not that I will, but if I bring him back for coffee, I mean, literally coffee, no walking in on us and scaring him away."

"I'd never do that!" Especially not with Dylan in the invisible wings.

"Actually, you once told this cute French guy who was about to take me out for a meal in one of the best restaurants in Dublin that your dad had just been released from prison. Apparently, he'd been sent there for murdering of one of my *boyfriends*."

What can I say? "Sorry."

She hugs me and laughs, giddy. "I thought it was quite inventive myself. You were only five or six. You told another man I was desperate to give you a brother or sister."

"Sorry. Again."

"It was pretty inspired: he'd just discovered his ex- was pregnant."

I pile her hair into a lazy bun. Okay, that's probably not the right term but it's the sort of bun that has tendrils of hair escaping all down around her face and neck, so the loose-and-flowing look, yet elegant.

"Ah, none of them tempted me enough to be leaving you all the time." She looks like a movie star again, but it could be the flush of nervousness in her cheek. "Mind you, I'd share you with the world now if it'd get me laid!"

"Mum!"

"Oops, did I say that out loud?"

She lets me do her make-up since I convinced her that she needed the expert touch. Grace clued me in on her mascara techniques and who would have known but Mum has long lashes. I keep it understated, with sexy red lips for contrast.

"This time, I won't say a word. Even if he's gorgeous. I won't flirt with him or anything." Before she can react, I turn her around so she can see her transformation. She puts her hand to her mouth and for a minute I think she's going to cry but she laughs instead; a light, sort of amazed laugh.

"See? He won't even notice me," I say, grinning.

She grins and twirls for a vetting. "No food on my teeth?"

"None."

"Lipstick on my teeth, tremors in my knees?"

I shake my head.

"Wish me luck?"

I slip my thumb around hers. It's a thing we do sometimes.

"You're beautiful and he's an exceptionally lucky man to get a date with you. Remember that!" I know, I sound like her mum but sometimes it's necessary. It's an 'only child' thing.

Then we notice Chris, standing in the doorway. "Did you want something, Chris? If you can't do lunch and you need me to stay on, that would be perfectly fine."

He shakes his head and finds his voice. "Taxi. Your taxi's here."

We are go. Time for the last few nuggets. "Now don't drink too much. If you like him, he'll think you're an alco; if you don't, you might end up thinking you do and that's worse."

"We're meeting for lunch, Angelica. One glass of wine, max."

"Yeah, well, you might just click and hang out all afternoon. In which case we can cope here." I scooch her shoulder strap a millimetre further west. "No harm being sexy, is there Chris?"

"Taxi," says Chris. His voice deeper than usual. "Outside. Waiting."

"Remember, don't tell him where we live or anything stalker-ish. And keep your phone on. Text if you want us to come and get you."

And then she's gone.

~ ~ ~

"He'd promised her boyfriend that, as he would be in Ireland on leave, he'd call and take my sister out. Poor Teddy. He had no idea how far Donegal was from Dublin. Used up half his weekend getting here!"

Guppy is dictating the text of her spiels so I can type them up on the computer. She has an idea of printing a booklet to accompany the tour or even sell in the local shops. It's making her nostalgic. Apparently, Teddy said she had a magical way of telling stories and should write them down. Only their story, it hasn't a good ending – not anywhere at all.

She wants to dedicate it to '*Teddy, wherever he may be*'.

It doesn't seem right.

Why should Guppy still be waiting to know what happened to this man? Surely, she deserves the truth at least? When she goes to stick the kettle on, I slip the photo of the two of them into my pocket. She returns with homemade rye scones. Onni has decided Guppy is his new family. His English isn't great yet and the Donegal accent baffles him entirely, so they communicate with baking.

"Where were we, dear?"

"The Tears of Brigid, Pagan Princess."

"Ah yes. Read that last bit back."

"There, amid the gorse and the tufty grass, she wept for her lover and her tears carved an imprint of his face into the rock."

Guppy picks the narrative up. "And from her tears, on that fateful day, a waterfall sprang from the earth so that perpetual tears would forever run down his face. The spring only runs dry at times of national sorrow. We have no idea what his name was but—What's wrong, Angelica? You need the loo? You're wriggling like an elf."

"Elves don't wriggle."

"They do if they want to be somewhere else. Are you worried about your mum?"

I shake my head. "Wasn't till you mentioned it." Why are adults so good at making us worry about stuff we weren't worrying about until they asked? "I just remembered I said I'd meet Grace in town. We have a school project."

Homework. It's a failsafe excuse for almost anything when it comes to adults.

IN DEFENCE OF FLOWERING WEEDS

Flower centres filled with overgrown, over-needy 'real' plants. What is so wrong with weeds? Daisies, dandelions and buttercups have beautiful flowers. What have they done to us that we feel entitled to behead them, pull them from the ground or drown them with weedkiller?

Example: You can't make flower chains from roses but you can, oh you infinitely can, from daisies. The dandelion can give you tea and cure your warts.

Can geraniuMrs Do that?

Dandelions sit behind your ear neatly because the stem is sort of hollow, easy to bend without breaking and has no thorns.

What other plant in the world can unite us all in the love of butter like the buttercup, regardless of whether we like butter or not? Also, weeds grow abundantly without tending. They're colourful, unpretentious. If we lived in Africa and found a dandelion growing, it would be a priceless bloom.

So, Mr Inventor of Weedkiller, did you sleep well or did weeds swallow your grave when you died?

Simon's cafe is empty for the first time in days, so when he nips out goes to the wholesalers, I turn the sign to 'closed' and scan Teddy's picture into the computer. Starting the search in Canada because that where they were going to live, so I'm guessing that's where he went if he could, I input everything I know. Edward Joshua Bannagher, born circa 1940, American army. Brown eyes.

"Bit old for your mum."

Where does Grace creep from! "It's not for Mum. How did you get in?"

"You should put the lock on when you do the 'closed' sign."

"Oh."

"Tell me it's not your dad?"

I shake my head. "It's Guppy's man." I show her the photo, taken by the oak tree on the front lawn.

"She said she could hardly keep her hands off him."

"Never? Guppy?"

Why are people so easily horrified that elderly people talk about sex? I hope she had lots because she sure as hell hasn't had much for the last forty-six years.

"How did you get her to agree that you could trace him?"

"I didn't."

"You never—"

Before she can tick me off about interfering: "I don't want to get her hopes up in case he's died or something."

"What if she made it all up? My Granddad did. Mum talked to this woman after he died that he swore was the love of his life, separated by religion and politics, but they'd never even spoken."

I take the photo back and study his face. Is she right? Could Guppy have made a romance out of memory and there's nothing really there at all? He gazes at Guppy in a way that seems so open and honest and deeply in love.

"Nope. I have a good feeling about this. If he's still alive, he will want to see her again."

"You're forgetting something. He's 46 years too late."

~~~

I arrive back minutes before Mum. Chris is manning the desk and looks up as I come in so I know he's watching out for Mum. Minutes later, she arrives, mutters something to Chris about freshening up before she takes over and heads upstairs.

This can't be good,

I follow her up.

"Carl's real name is Pronsious." She passes me a photo of an idyllic paddock with a bath in the middle. "This is his business idea. Mud baths. The alternative way to make a living off the farm."

"Isn't it too wet/ cold/ miserable most of the year?" On the site, Carl said he was an entrepreneur, not a farmer. I feel misled. I don't want to live on a farm. "Doesn't Ireland have enough indoor spas?"

Smiling in a way I instantly distrust, Mum hands me a small Styrofoam tub. "But he has a secret ingredient none of the others use." I get a sixth sense I should ask before I remove the lid. Curiosity is such a bad genetic trait; a really foul one.

So is the smell from the tub.

"Manure. From dairy cows. Apparently milk cows make more 'fragrant' poo and it's a magnificent exfoliant, makes your skin glow."

"Sorry. He didn't seem weird."

"I'm tempted to leave it in the bathroom of a grumpy guest next time, with a label saying 'Luxury Face Pack, do not use'. Oh don't look so serious Angel. At least I didn't waste the best fella on my first attempt, right? Plenty more fish. And they say sailors make great lovers."

"Mum!" She only does it to shock me.

"Sorry. I meant whales. Heaps of whales."

Kitty lands in with a flurry of fresh air in her wake "Well?" Like Grace, she has a habit of popping up silently. Must be genetic. "How did it go?"

"Put it this way, next one, I'm going to try and get to know the guy better before agreeing to meet."

"Waste of time," says Kitty. "You'll either like him or you won't. It's 90% visual. And vocal; eye-contact and kindness and gifts. Gifts are good. But if none of that's there when you meet, at least you won't have wasted months writing little love notes and exchanging poetry."

"I'm with Kitty," says I. "Dive in. What the hell."

"Language!" says Guppy, arriving up for no good reason at all except the sniff of drama and to ask me to help her look for a picture she's lost. I grab my bag before Kitty launches into a description of her own recent dates with Marcus.

When we reach Guppy's apartment, I slip the photo out of my bag when she's in the loo. "It was behind the dresser," I shout through the closed door and head back into town.

At least Mum's not upset that her first date was a complete disaster.

And she did say 'next time'.

~~~

The minute I land into Simon's to find Mum's next date, Grace clicks onto the homepage. If I didn't know better, I'd say she was– What? Hiding something? But I haven't time to think about it now. I fill her in as I search.

"What about this one?"

Grace leans over my shoulder. "Lyndon. Sounds like a machine for polishing floors or hoovering cat hairs out of long-haired rugs."

"At least it's original. And it's only a pseudonym, remember. His real name's probably Bartholomew."

"Why would anyone pick Lyndon for a name? Why not Colman or Leo or Jonny or something?"

"Listen to this: 'Most romantic thing? A bathtub filled with essential oils and rose petals, one petal for each year of my mother's life'."

Okay, so I'd prefer a man in his late thirties not to be talking about his mother in the same sentence as his washing arrangements but he's the best newbie on the site since Carl crashed and burnt. "They say you can predict how a man will treat the women in his life by how he treats his mother." I read it somewhere so it must be true.

"Psycho comes to mind."

I give him five 'swans' and slip him into Mum's inbox with a couple of obvious duds so she goes in the right direction. Grace tuts disapprovingly and lands a little thump on my arm to remind me she means it.

Chapter 32

Two pigeons land on the windowsill. When you're faced with a mountain of homework, there's not much else to do in Drisogue but watch pigeons. At least they don't make me feel dimmer than a light switch. Naturally, my pigeons don't just sit and coo in a calming way. Oh no.

They start dancing.

The bigger one puffs out his feathers and tries to be huge, ducking and diving like a toreador in a pigeon suit. They get real close, close and personal.

If I didn't know better, I'd say they are seriously making out on my window sill. Pigeon number one turns to eyeball me. "Your Mum, when she gets a fella, cute ass, nice pecs, randy as a hornet of wasps, you'll have to listen to this all night long."

I leave them to it.

Mum's in the office downstairs. "Mum?"

She looks up from the accounts. "Hey. You okay?"

"Sure." I fiddle with the whales on her desk, putting them into pairs for good luck. Chris must have been leaving them here bit by bit; all told, she has a school of them. "If you bring someone back, can I go to Kitty's?"

"I won't."

"But if you do?"

"We're a long way from that, Angel."

"But down the line or something. Just the first few times or something until you know he's a keeper."

"Of course. I won't let any man make you feel uncomfortable in your own home or anywhere else. Besides, I'll be relying on your judgement too, y'know."

Oh dear.

"Besides, we'd have to sneak past Chris first." She's right. He has been a bit over-protective lately.

~~~

Kitty's blind-daters have arrived. The town is buzzing and where am I? Stuck helping Mum in the hotel. A new group of walkers have arrived, but this time Guppy is there, full of spiel. It's quite a sight, to see her working a crowd. But when the last few arrive into the lobby, she disappears, leaving me to take over.

Figuring something isn't right, I start Jonas off on into one of his stories while Chris makes hot ports and track Guppy back to her apartment. The contents of her carpet bag are emptied across over the big table but she's just sat there, staring at them.

"What does it say?"

Instead of responding, she gathers all the pieces back into the bag and pours them out again.

"Does it say we'll all be millionaires?"

"Everything in here, the bottle tops, the twigs, the bits of water-washed glass, I collected for Teddy or he found for me. It was a game, you see. To give each other meaningless objects and invest them with meaning personal to us."

"Was it that man? The one who arrived last?"

By way of answer, she lifts a cork. "This was the wine he said we'd have for the christening of our first child, Emmanuel."

"He looked like Teddy, didn't he?"

She puts the cork back in its place before answering. "Not really. It was only the way he walked—" Suddenly, Guppy sweeps everything onto the floor violently. As I bend to scoop them all up – however she feels now, these are important to her – she strides over to the window.

"He said he'd come back." She pulls her hair back into a knot and wraps her arms around herself, as if she's cold all over. "'*Dead or alive, I'll come back*', he said. But he hasn't haunted me once. I've said terrible things to make him come and haunt me. And if that means he isn't dead, why didn't he come back?"

I've never heard her talk this way. It scares me to see how hurt she is.

"Maybe it wasn't possible. He must have wanted to."

Oh please let him get in touch and be alive and missing her even half as much as she has missed him. If he has to be dead, please let someone get in touch and tell me that he died with her name on his lips, trying to get back?

"You're very sweet, Angelica but you don't know anything of the sort." She turns and walks slowly towards her bedroom. Guppy never walks slowly. "Ask Chris to explain to the group, that I'm a little unwell and will see them in the morning."

"I'd rather stay with you."

"I'm not in need of babysitting yet."

Now she's grumpy. As soon as I fix one of the grown-ups in my life, the grumpy bug transfers to the next. Compared with Mum and Guppy and Chris, teenagers get an undeserved bad press.

"I will escort them to the Leaba Dhrúis at ten. Don't worry, dear." She gives me a sad smile that doesn't touch her eyes. "Guppy never sinks for long."

~~~

For her date with Lyndon, Mum gets her hair done. She also gets her feet pedicured and her eyebrows sculpted to within a shiver of their lives. I don't get this. It's not a good look. Do it enough and you look permanently surprised, like a shaved wolfhound.

Grace says she's doing all this grooming to keep her nerves at bay, so I lend her my lucky whale amulet before she bankrupts us and see her into the taxi, before heading down to Simon's cafe.

I leave my maths spread out on my desk so it looks as if I've just stepped out if Mum gets home before me and I head for Simon's cafe. In case Lyndon doesn't work out, I want her to be inundated with wannabe dates when she gets home, but Simon takes me aside almost as soon as I arrive in. "You got a message."

"Who said you could check my mail?"

"As long as we're doing this website." He moves me towards the back room, away from customers who might overhear. The place is far too busy and noisy. It's one of the venues Kitty's blind-daters meet in. "Given the number of people you've told already when you promised to tell no one."

Cue Grace arriving in. I'd swear she has a hidden camera on the door of this place so she knows when to arrive. "Simon, Mum says to warn you there will be two blind-dating couples at two thirty, four at three and two at three thirty."

"I haven't." I click open my inbox. Edward J. Bannagher.

"Hope you're not using the site yourselves. Either of you. That'd be dangerous and illegal."

If I didn't know better, I'd say Grace looked sheepish but I barely register it. Teddy has replied. He's alive. "Simon, I'm not. This is Guppy's guy."

He's alive and living in Wisconsin! He wants to know who's looking for him.

Okay, so I could write back and say, '*Why didn't you come back for Guppy?*' but that might scare him off. I settle for telling him who I am and where I live and asking if he knew her. Then, with careful consideration, I pick Mum's next date. A widower with no children, his childhood memory is of dancing on a pouffe to Candles in the Rain.

I've just posted him as a suggestion to Mum, along with a few duds so she knows which way to go. For a beat, I wonder what could happen if she chose one of the duds and decide to pick slightly more interesting ones next time, just in case.

I'm sitting back, job done, when Dylan calls in – perfect timing – with crisps. "Hiya."

"Hi."

Okay, it doesn't sound like much of a conversation, but there are worlds of words and feelings and ideas underneath and we are perfectly happy simply being there, on our own beside each other eating crisps.

Until Simon barges in, ruffling Dylan's hair the way he hates.

"Your mum just flew past in a Garda car," he says.

"Can't be. She's on a date in Gorman's Garden Centre. Why would she be in a cop car?" In other words, go away; not interested in Mum right now.

"Sorry but it was definitely her."

When I roll up twenty minutes later Mum's bent over the computer in the office, dangerously determined. She's muttering too. This is never good. Sounds like, "Normal normal normal."

"Hey, how'd it go?" She doesn't answer. "Where are the flowers? Surely he bought you flowers?"

"D'you know why we met in a garden centre? He wanted show me the only tea-maker that can make 8 cups of perfectly lukewarm tea from one tea bag. Course you could stretch it to 9, but then the grains would get in and damage the motor."

"What has this got to do with a garden centre or the date?"

"Well, isn't that an interesting question! See, if it wasn't for that tea-maker, Mummy's little Lyndon would never have been conceived."

"It was never his real name?"

"Oh yes. It surely was. Lyndon Mary Moore."

"So they sell tea-makers in the garden centre?" I am really confused now.

"Oh no. That was why he'd brought binoculars along. Of course, little naive me thinks, '*He wants to look at the plants in more detail, what's the harm?*' Except that what we were really doing was playing peeping tom at the window of his ex-. The tea maker in question was on her bedside locker. A wedding gift, apparently. She called the police and had us removed."

She looks at me, deadpan. "I think there should be a law against tea-makers." Then she laughs, but it's sharp enough to cut glass. "Angelica, am I a freak?"

"Course not!"

"Then, surely I should be able to meet one man who is relatively normal? Come on. Help me choose another."

"You could take a break?"

"No. I'm not giving up now. Third time lucky is as good a logic as any."

"What about this one?"

I pretend to study Joseph's profile. "Says he likes long walks – as do you. Good food – we wouldn't eat anything else. Swimming – that's similar to surfing. Music. Why don't you ask him to Drisogue? The police wouldn't have as far to come to bring you home."

She smiles, the sort of smile I imagine sharks get when they smell bait. This time I am NOT letting her out of my sight.

"Joseph's a pretty normal name, isn't it?"

"Ach, his real name's probably Hubert."

"So long as he's normal."

"Define normal."

Chapter 33

Normal. Please let Joseph be nice and normal and kind.

Let this be a NORMAL date.

"One kiss," says Dylan.

We're out back of Compton's, supposedly fetching something from the freezer. "Can't. Sorry. Might jinx everything."

I am supervising this date, ostensibly while assisting in the kitchen with the washing up as a pre-trial for work experience during the summer; not that Mum would let me work and get paid for it when I can help in the hotel.

Simon wants Dylan to work in his cafe but old Mr Compton pays better.

"Pays, full stop," says Dylan.

Simon said he'd pay Dylan "in brotherly love". It wasn't a persuasive argument, even to me and I have all sorts of odd notions about how wonderful it would be to have siblings.

"Nobody would know but us."

Compton's is the best restaurant in Drisogue. Mum thought eating here might suggest our own restaurant wasn't fantastic. Kitty and I convinced her that this is a once-off, so she gave in. Though it was hard to get a table, what will all the weekend visitors. Like persuading a sardine to slip into a lime green envelope and posting it to Santa.

All we need from tonight is one good conversation that she wants to continue.

Maybe a slight urgency to meet again, but nothing weird or abnormal or even odd enough to get her worrying. Then Dylan and I can have the longest kiss ever. And hold hands. And cuddle. And go for long walks.

And and and…

When things work out, I can tell her I was here when it all began. Besides Dylan looks super cool in a tux. And sulky. I follow him in with the frozen yoghurt.

"We kissed before and she had disastrous dates!"

He shrugs and gathers dishes to take back out.

I have a good feeling about Joseph. And yes, Grace did remind me that I said the same about Mum's dates with Carl and Lyndon, but I haven't seen a magpie or a rook or a stony-faced crow since and I take this to be a mammoth good sign.

He also chose merlot, Mum's favourite and she looks amazing. Even old Mr Compton looked lechery at her when she came in. Better still, they haven't stopped talking since they arrived.

Dylan returns with their empty starter plates. "He's talking about *duende*."

"I know that word. Mum used it to describe meeting me."

"I can understand that," he says.

Oh, he is so adorable. So, so lovely. So distracting. I think, this is it, we're going to kiss now and that's fine because Mum's okay, only old Mr Compton comes in roaring an order. Dylan grabs starters for another table and I make myself look useful washing cutlery.

Dylan's back in before I empty the sink. "Duende, what does it mean?"

"Passion. No. It's more than that. It's like your life force all in a rush, all at once."

"Figures, since she's talking about you." He squints up his nose. "You being born. Not sure if that's exactly what he was expecting."

"Gory detail?"

"Yup." He holds open the swing doors so I can peek. Mum's in full steam. She looks so full of life. Dylan pecks me on the cheek when the chef goes outside for a fag, before carrying through their mains.

One course to go.

ON HOPE

It's only 'hop' with an 'e' stuck on.

And it's hard to hop for a long time, especially on an uneven road. Or a road with potholes and trip wires and dodgy cardiac conditions.

'E' probably stands for 'eejit' anyway.

"I think you'd better come," says Dylan, his face all grim.

"I don't want Mum to see me."

"Way past that." He holds open the door. I'm thinking Mum and this man are dancing on the table or making love right where they are and old Mr Compton is asking them to leave quietly.

But nope. Joseph is on his back and Mum is kneeling on top of him, trying to bully his heart back into life. Old Mr Compton is calling an ambulance and everyone has gone completely still.

"Mum?"

Chapter 34

She doesn't look at me. Just keeps working his chest and saying, "Come on! Come on! Don't DO this!"

The ambulance arrives really fast. Mum goes outside with the paramedics without seeing me. I collect the red rose he brought. They'll laugh about this later, maybe frame it. I take my time going out, thinking she'll have gone in the ambulance to the hospital, but old Mr Compton says he went alone.

I'm surprised, but then what could she have said to the paramedics? We only met? He chose Merlot? It was a blind date? What would his family say when they met her for the first time by his bedside? There's no sign of her in Kitty's, so I check the church – okay, it's a long shot, but illness– (Death? Oh please not!) It does strange things to your inner superstitions.

Then I hare home.

She's not in the office, the apartment or the kitchen. Guppy is in the office but says she didn't come in. Chris is running the bar and says he's been too busy to see anyone. I've checked the apartment and am heading back down the back stairs to check she's not in the kitchen when I glimpse a thin figure out on the waves from my bedroom window.

I tell myself, at least I've found her. But that's not enough. My mother is playing hide-and-go-seek with the waves under a misshapen moon.

I grab a towel, fetch some big torches from the storeroom and tear down the hidden stairway to the beach, ignoring spiders and cobwebs. I'm half-convinced she'll have vanished into the waves by the time I emerge, just like

Dad. How could she be this stupid? Selfish.

Everyone knows it's not safe surfing in the dark.

Especially not here.

Okay maybe I have a more healthy fear of the sea than any of my friends or, clearly, my mother but still.

I shine both torches in her direction once I'm out on the beach. She finally sees me and heads for shore. I wrap a towel around her as if I'm not waiting for an explanation. We leave the board at the base of the stairs and return to the apartment in silence where she has the longest shower in history.

No singing, though.

When she emerges, I wrap her hands around a hot chocolate and sit beside her.

"When I was pregnant, there were times I thought I was losing you and I was so scared. You've no idea. This visceral fear, this ache, right here." She pats her diaphragm. "I used to sleep with my thumbs linked."

Mum puts down her drink and hooks her thumbs into each other, staring at them and then looking up at me. "That was me holding onto you and you to me."

What can I say? I've known this forever.

"How could I have thought it was that simple? They were *my* thumbs. Both of them were mine but I believed you'd know; that you'd understand and hang onto me. I thought believing and wanting you to be safe were enough."

I try to get her to drink the hot chocolate; sweet things are meant to be good in an emotional crisis, aren't they?

"Know what was the worst thing was about tonight? Joseph – and that was his real name; he said he didn't see the point of lying, he was sweet." She starts to cry, really softly. "They asked me to go in the ambulance and I should have, but I was so scared and I froze. They needed to hurry. I said I didn't really know him." She looks lost. "I should have gone with him, shouldn't I?"

This isn't how it was meant to be. Dating was meant to make her feel beautiful and young and devastatingly attractive. It was MEANT to make her happy and less lonely. I wrap my arms around her but she pulls away and goes to the window.

She takes the deepest, shakiest breath.

"He just crumpled up. I've never seen someone die. One minute he was there and then, suddenly. Oh, you would have liked him. He was a really lovely man."

She lets me hug her then, tight as I dare but she feels light. They say the human soul weighs twenty-two grams but that doesn't seem right.

Doesn't seem enough to hold a whole life.

~~~

Chris has been on to the hospital. "Massive heart attack but he's okay."

She's grabbing around for her coat and a scarf. "I'd better go see him—"

"His… His wife is on her way."

"Oh. Brilliant." She deflates into the nearest armchair.

"Probably his ex-. Lots of people forget to change the name on their emergency contacts list." He's trying to make her feel better. She manages the flicker of a nod. "They said you did everything right. If you hadn't kept working on him…"

"Thanks, Chris," she says and he leaves, quietly.

Before the door closes behind him, Mum takes my hand. "From now on, it's you and me. No one else."

Chapter 35

As far as I can see, the sea shimmers. Winter sunshine or pixie dust, I'm open to either. Or was, until Mum's latest debacle. Now I reckon if there are pixies, they're just taunting us. I fire some lumpy rocks into the Atlantic, as hard and as far as I can. I imagine concussed fish. Dad's whale finally getting what he deserves.

But it doesn't make me feel better.

Odd to think the next landfall is North America.

"Stop hovering."

Nobody hovers like Grace. It's as if she has this special hovering bottom.

"We got our first engagement. Like, for real. Falling in love, wanting to get married, the lot! And you will NEVER guess who it is!"

She's like a bouncy little firework; one that spins and whirls in the wrong direction and blows the noses off chimney pots. I'm focusing hard on throwing rocks to smash into little waves, while she rabbits on, flinging sparks in every direction, hoping to start a blaze.

Mum must have told her where I was.

"Jonas and Ms Willow!!! Can you imagine? They must have been one of the first couples you put together. Remember, behind the shed? When you lectured me—"

"I didn't *lecture* you—"

"Yes, you did. Anyway, you said if she liked the stars (and I thought she meant celebrities) while he was fascinated with alien life and galaxies and time travel and stuff, they were perfect. And they were!"

"Terrific." Thonk! Another fish bites the dust of my unerringly violent rocks.

"D'you think Jonas is really into time travel?"

She skims a few stones. They tiptoe across the water, little rock jehovahs. "It'd explain why he drives the school bus, I guess. I mean, if anything were to time travel in Drisogue, it'd be the decrepit old school bus. It must be centuries pass old. Oh yeah and remember when I told you he'd decorated the bus? I BET that was their first date! Or maybe that was when he proposed!"

Further down the shore towards town, Dylan helps heave Mr Ganly's boat off the water. Grace takes my silence for something it's not and sighs theatrically.

"Okay, so I admit I was against the website and now I'm jumping up and down, but this is like the biggest thing. WE made this happen! We've changed their lives. I mean, here they are, living in the same town, miserably lonely obviously and then POW! Because of us, they find each other's happy-ever-after is their own!"

"Why don't you just go down there and say, 'I was wrong. We don't need to wait'? No matter what has happened to her, do you really think your mum would want you pining like this?"

I hand her my last rock and turn towards the path up to the headland. Dylan waves and the boom swings back and knocks him down. Grace misses it but I don't because I looked back, just once.

She catches up and blocks my path. "What's up Licky Loo, Miracle Matchmaker for the Grumpy & Alone?"

"Did you want something, Grace? Apart from spreading the good news about my super-dooper ultra-successful site that works for everyone except, oh yeah! MY MUM!"

"Oh yeah. We should talk about that."

"What's to say?"

We stand like that, seagulls screeching overhead. Storm's coming back. She's not sure how to deal with my big angry mess, but then neither am I and it's my mess so we start walking up again.

"Dunno why you're so upset," she says, when we finally get up onto the headland. "Not as if she actually killed him."

I have no answer for this. I kick tufts of grass instead.

"I mean it's not like she killed him. That'd be a whole different kettle of fish and great publicity for the hotel. You could host murder mystery weekends!" She sees my expression. "That was a joke!"

"Ha ha. So now it's a joke."

"I was trying to cheer you up."

I push past.

"Stop. Licky! I didn't mean it."

"All I wanted to do was make my mum happy. Was that too much to ask?"

Grace has the kudos to look demure, but not for long. "It's not all bad. Simon says you're a genius."

She kicks the heads off a few dandelions and then gushes on, as if I'd interrupted her mid-sentence and she won't get the Oscar unless she finishes her acceptance speech.

"Your mum will find someone. You know it takes longer when you're unique and successful and stuff. That's what Simon says. Him and Onni are, like, your biggest fans. Especially now Simon's dad is grinning like a pitchfork."

"A pitchfork?"

"Oh, you know the teeth he has. Maybe when he meets whoever he's fallen for on the site she'll persuade him to get some dentistry. Simon says we could use the site to bring tourists in and everything. There's no limit to how big this could get or how much good we could do. He says we'll end up creating jobs in Drisogue and bringing people back from all over the world. The town could come alive again and that will be all down to you!"

"Simon says, Simon says." I turn, catching my heel on a small spiky stone. This does nothing to improve my mood. "Don't you get it? I don't care about Simon. I don't care about all these other people or Jonas or even Drisogue. I care about my mum."

The icy wind bites into my tear ducts.

"I made her feel THIS small." I pinch the air with my fingers and squish a midge, which makes me feel loads better as a human being. NOT. I can't even gesture with my fingers but something dies.

"That's all I've done. She says she's never going to even think of meeting a man again. It's just her and me FOREVER."

I turn towards the hotel before she catches me crying because I'm sick of feeling so rotten and wrong.

"I haven't made her happier, Grace. I've made everything worse."

Chapter 36

Everyone goes silent as I walk down the bus on Monday. Some look away quickly. Others throw me pitying glances. I only make it half way down when I crack. "It wasn't her fault. He had a heart condition."

I should have said nothing. Suddenly everyone wants details.

"I think it's cool," says Denise out of the blue, as if she's defending me or something. "Like Greta Garbo came back as the Grim Reaper."

"Heard she told him how she was going to slice him up and eat him alive."

"I heard she told him what she did to your dad."

"Only one that's likely to happen to is you, Theo."

"Cool!"

The other boys exchange looks of discomfort.

"And he isn't dead. He had a heart attack." I plonk down beside Grace. "Sorry," I say, holding out a slice of chocolate biscuit cake.

"So you should be." She snatches it off me to weigh it in her hand. Thankfully, Grace is useless at staying mad. I've only to ask her about the engagement and she's all better. "You never told me matchmaking was so much fun!"

"Shhh," I say before the whole bus hears her. That's the last thing we need.

"I'm sorry about your mum. Really. It's just bad luck. Really bad luck. I didn't think she'd take it so hard. I mean, my mum—"

"Yeah, well. Kind of different fish, your mum and mine."

"Yeah well," she echoes sharply. "Maybe you're better off, okay? I mean, look at mine. Different man every weekend, me having to tiptoe around them in the morning. Trying not to be too bolshie in case Mum gets the hump. Trying to get to sleep really fast so I don't hear them giggling in the night. And worse."

"She seems pretty keen on Marcus, despite your reverse psychology ruse."

"She was." Grace stares out the window and sighs. "But now she says she's too busy for a serious relationship."

The sigh is odd, since I thought she didn't like Marcus. Maybe she was just afraid to admit she liked him in case he left.

As he has.

"I'm sorry," I say. In case she was.

~ ~ ~

"Come on Mum, you know you're perfect for it! Chris, tell her she's the only one who can do this."

"Angelica's right. No one else has the management skills you have to organise a festival and bully Drisogue into shape. The LoveFest needs you."

"What about you?" Mum turns to Kitty. "You could do it blindfold!"

"Guppy's already got another batch of walkers coming, only someone's trampled her Leaba Dhrúis."

She actually thinks couples have been using the patch for the role she claims it was intended in her fictional history. Which is gross. It's not even that hidden. If you stood on tippy toe, you could see it from the road.

"Chris isn't bossy enough. And no offence, Mum, but would you really trust Kitty to run a festival and not steal all the single men?"

Kitty grimaces but takes her cue. "This one's yours Molly. The Drisogue Arms has to lead the charge. It's our iconic building; the historical heart of the town and I've too much on my hands with the Blind Date weekends. Besides, Chris says it was your idea."

Chris coached her well. Everyone – including Mum – assumed she would manage the festival until she got to feeling so down on the idea of love. The date Chris was pitching is just over six weeks away. We need her and she needs this.

"I'm hardly a glowing role model for a LoveFest."

She's right. In this mood, I can think of rabid bears being better at it and nicer, but at least it would keep her too busy to mope.

"You should choose a couple to front it, all gooey and loved-up."

"Think of the business it could bring in for the hotel," says Kitty.

The hotel argument is good.

"Though if you want to jeopardise the livelihood and potential future of the town?"

"That's not fair."

"Neither am I." Kitty tosses her blonde locks a little too theatrically. "But so long as I keep my dark roots under control, nobody knows."

"Six weeks." Mum shrugs. "I can't do it alone."

"You won't be."

"We'd need an organising committee to manage the various teams. To make sure deadlines are met or it all falls apart. That everyone has a say but it doesn't get chaotic. I need people I can trust to make decisions."

"Absolutely." Kitty winks at me. Mum is on the line and pulling herself to shore.

"And it has to be unique. There's no point copying Lisdoonvarna or trying to be the Rose of Drisogue." Vehement head-shakes all round, all of us trying to keep our faces dead serious, like kids who have persuaded Mum to make the biggest chocolate cake and are now letting her convince us it's the healthy veggie option, source of our five-a-day.

"There has to be something for everyone who might come, whatever their age or interests."

"Agreed." Kitty hands Mum a sheaf of pages. "Some ideas we've got in already. Most romantic couple, best-dressed bachelor, love songs pageant, workshop on making love potions, blind dates using the hole in the wall Guppy drilled. You've seen the flier with the ideas Chris and Angelica put together. The County Council are on board, provisionally, but you're right, it should be a couple at the helm. Which is just as well. Since we have one."

"What?"

"You and Chris of course, Mr and Mrs Drisogue LoveFest. Thanks, Moll."

She's gone before Mum can object. Chris, I notice, has vanished too.

"This is your fault," says Mum. To me.

"Just add it to my growing list of flaws."

~ ~ ~

I call into Guppy for some sanity. She wants to leap right into dictation, now that there's a potential festival audience for her booklet. I'd love to tell her Teddy is alive, but I haven't heard from him since that one email confirming he was alive and he remembered Guppy.

If he's gone all turtle into his shell, what good would it do to tell her that he's been in touch? From where I'm standing, he's a cad who left his girl behind.

I'm going off men, the more I learn.

"So, you ready for the Leaba Druis?"

"Sure."

"The Leaba Druis. Legend has it…"

And she's off. My head is somewhere else entirely and I have to keep asking her to repeat herself.

"Is everything okay?"

I plead a headache and go to bed early.

Chapter 37

Mum drags me along to the public meeting for moral support. The hall is packed and there isn't even free food. Chris is trying to turn the heating off because it's hot as the inside of a spit-roasting pig. Everyone's talking at once but Kitty's up front trying to keep track of everyone's ideas on a flip chart as they shout them out.

The Ark must have sounded similarly noisy when it ran aground.

Big Brenda takes to the stage to correct Kitty's spelling, which can't end well.

"Okay," Mum whispers to me. "Let's do this."

Us? Who said anything about us doing anything! "If we want the world to visit us," says Mum, striding toward the stage. "We have to give them reasons to come that they can't resist."

The crowd parts like waves.

Give over with this biblical imagery! I'm fourteen, I should be using way more interesting metaphors. I find a seat near the back beside Grace. Yeah, she was dragged along too. Most of the teens in town are here. Something about civic duty and getting an education from life.

Mum steps up onto stage. "So let's give them something to really talk about."

She has Kitty pass several pages around so everyone can write down any special skills or possible contacts they have that we might be able to use. "If someone is being too modest, feel free to amend their entry," she says. "We have six weeks to pull together the biggest, best wee festival the island of Ireland has ever seen. This is no time to be hiding our lights behind bushels."

Latching onto the religious imagery in this, Big Brenda wants to know if there's a saint we can attach. "Festivals always have saints," she says. "We can hardly use St Valentine since everyone else does, so who will ours be?"

Fr Lefarge tackles her, bravely "Brenda, Brenda. This is about our community helping itself to grow, not imposing any particular faith. It's a festival of life, Brenda." If he had been able to marry, she'd have been perfect for him. (She's very fond of high horses; he has had lots of practice.)

"But I'm sure," says Rev. Clancy, "we could find room for an ecumenical service on the Sunday?"

"Let's see if there is some class of a saint that matches the date," says Chris and nods to me.

Wi-Fi is lousy in the hall so I slip outside to do the necessary. Every day in April has oodles of saints listed – martyrs and monks, hermits and nuns, but only one is Irish. St Laserian.

"Too close to caesarean," says Grace. "And with your mum's recent experience of talking about childbirth…"

She's right. I go back inside and pass a note up to Chris. He grins, then lands me in it. "Angelica has an idea that might work." He gestures for me to join them on stage.

"Couldn't you just–?"

"No. This is your turn."

So there I am. In the spotlight. I am not a fan of the spotlight. It activates acne, for a start, not to mention a difficulty in getting words out. But there's nothing for it. "St Brigid. It's the name of one of our churches, right, but she was a pagan priestess first, which would make the festival stand out."

There's a general murmur of approval and hedged approval. Brenda likes the Christian element, Mum, Kitty and the other matriarchs appreciate having a feisty female icon while Guppy is already ticking off how she can make use of the pagan aspect.

"There is a rumour," she says, "that she performed one of her miracles in Donegal. It could easily have been in April."

"What?" I mouth at her but she's avoiding my eyes.

Everyone bickers and sort of agrees. Mum gets really bossy but nobody seems to mind. For the next hour, she sorts people into groups with various interests at heart. By 8.30, a central committee has been formed and responsibilities have been handed out to nearly everyone there to clean up various sections of the town. Then they settle down to work out what events should happen and how and when.

I slip away back to my Maths. It's so much simpler than people. I can only take so much of grown-ups in their strange little world. Dylan follows me out. "I'll walk you home."

I shrug. It's a can-if-you-want-but-I-can't-say-I-want-you-to-yet shrug. Then I walk slow, so he'll know I wish I could.

"That was her third date in Comptons."

"She hasn't had a full one yet."

"She's still dating. Technically."

"Technically, they've all gone horribly wrong and now she's fed up with men, even with the idea of falling for someone." It's so dark. Several streetlights need replacing; they flicker on and off and emit a ghostly orange hue. We're passing the gang outside Simon's cafe when Theo calls out. "Hey Dyl, she put out yet?"

Dylan doesn't stop; doesn't respond. It's meant to be a joke. It's a big joke, I'm at the butt end of it and it isn't even funny.

"What did you tell them?"

"Nothing." He pulls his sleeves down over his hands but it isn't even cold and keeps walking.

"Ask me nicely, I'll visit her mum," shouts some boy whose voice I don't recognise. "Speed things up for you!"

"They asked if we were going out. That's all."

"And you told them I had to get Mum fixed up first."

"No, honestly, I didn't put it like that." His voice trails off. "I just said we weren't, not yet."

I stop then, right in front of him and turn so I can see his face. The tears are there, burning inside my eyes but I hold them back with rage. "Try 'not'. Not ever."

As I stride off, I can hear the whistles and jeers but I don't look back.

I will NEVER look back again.

Chapter 38

"What's with you?"

"Nothing."

Grace is not appeased. "Did something happen between you and Dylan?"

"Course not." No point telling her since she'll only tell me it's all my fault and that I was always going to lose him because I was acting stupid. Besides, it's a blip. I'll forgive him when Mum's sorted. And if it's too late, it's too late. I am NOT upset! We have a festival to organise.

I wouldn't have time for a boyfriend now anyway.

And it's official. Drisogue is a treasure chest. Former journos and PR-heads, people who have worked in graphic design, animation, event management, TV; we have them all.

Whenever anyone comes up with a problem, the word goes on the central noticeboard in Simon's cafe and on the blog I set up for the campaign. Within hours someone has a solution.

Turns out that Onni used to do catering for a film company in Finland. They've agreed to come and film a Celtic fly-on-the-wall documentary on the festival if we arrange flights and accommodation. Chris is on to Aer Lingus for free flights.

In this modern post-Celtic-Tiger world, barter is king.

There are committees under committees within committees and beneath it all, the workers. Us, for example. Thanks to Denise's mum buying into the festival so entirely, the school is diving in with all feet blazing. Every student in every class without a major exam coming up – First Year, Second Year (us), TY (Transition Year) and Fifth Year – has been volunteered for a range of practical and decorative projects. Between us, we will manually transform Drisogue into some sort of Donegal Disney, but without the fireworks and cartoon characters.

In Religion, Ms Willow, soon-to-be (maybe, if she changes her name and the bet on is that she will) Mrs Maguire, is in love. She feels she owes it to the world to pass the good news on so we're researching love stories from the area. The best will be included in an exhibition in the Community Centre. I did Guppy's wartime romance (with her blessing and ignoring Teddy's more recent forty-six year silence).

In English, we've been told to, '*Write a news piece about an aspect of the festival*' or '*research and write up a local story/ myth/ character.*' "Use your imagination," says Ms Burke, as if she had any. The best pieces will be printed in The Advertiser and compiled into a special pamphlet – The History of Drisogue, its Myths, Legends and Characters, thanks to a friend of Dylan's uncle who owns a printing press in Letterkenny. He's printing Guppy's booklet too.

It all sounds naff but, surprisingly, it isn't. We're finding out so much about each other and the area and it's fascinating. Dylan's piece is on the Drisogue and Donegal Druids, about which his father is a surprising expert. Apparently he toyed with druidic beliefs before he got married.

Mr Squidgy Fingers (Geography) has us drawing a series of accurate maps of the area, illustrating important historic, mythic and geographic sites. They'll be used in the official guide to the area that is being compiled by TY students. The various language classes will translate it into Irish, German and French.

In Art, we're designing a Life of Granuaile mural to cover the hoarding around the largest derelict site in town, while Grace and four other gifted artists are also doing the illustrations for virtually everything of interest. She has already drawn the dolmen and the standing stones. Next up is Jonas – yeah, for real, he's our official storyteller – and The Whale's Mount. This is a teensie rock island near the Peninsula you can walk out to when the tide is low and feel completely surrounded by the Atlantic.

Yeah, it'd an odd name but better than 'Wrecker's Rock' because that reminds everyone of a history nobody could be proud of anymore. It has been officially renamed for the festival.

In Business Studies, we're working on the information and marketing strategy, while in Computer Studies, the Fifth Years are spreading the word through websites under guidance from Simon who's coordinating the festival's online presence. First Years have the yummy job of cleaning the banks of the river and the memorials.

~~~

While Chris has taken charge of fundraising, Mum has already persuaded the Council to replace the street lighting on the main street in time for the festival. Also to fill in all the potholes and donate tubs full of flowers throughout town, things that people have moaned about for years. Oh to pay for new signs at the entrances to the town.

She is totally back on track, coming up with ideas nobody else had thought of and motivating people. Theo's dad is co-ordinating the music gigs on the stage and various venues around town while Cathie's mum is lending spare office furniture to the new Tourist Information and Ticket Office. It's to be located in the empty shop that used to belong to the butcher everyone called the Gruffalo.

By the time the weekend comes, I've nearly forgotten the website exists. What Dylan did, gossiping about Mum, was bad. Though I still seriously fancy him, I'd have had to let him alone for ages now anyway, so he'd know how mad I was.

With all this LoveFest stuff in the air, Mum won't be able to resist trying again. With so much going on, there will need to be tons of volunteers coming in from outside Drisogue to help out, she might meet some gorgeous man the way you're meant to, accidentally.

Like, in person.

Then, Dylan and I can kiss and make up.

ON WATCHING OTHER PEOPLE IN LOVE

Two people cooing at each other across a table occasionally brings out aahs and oohs and 'how lovelies'. These are, of course, fake unless you are also a couple that is cooing and oozing or wanting to be.

How do people really feel?: "Put it away. Get a room. Do you have to do that in front of me while I'm eating?"

What they really mean: "I want to be cooed at. I used to be cooed at. Am I no longer coo-able-over? What is wrong with me; don't I deserve to be loved?" But without the schmaltziness.

Though it might not feel schmaltzy if it were me and Brad Pitt.

That is, if it were me and Brad, I would accept the schmaltziness and wear it proudly.

I have to say this for Mum, she picks her time.

She could have waited until she was alone with me in the apartment or when we were making up empty rooms. Even down at the beach or in the office but no, Mum saves her meltdown for breakfast and then loses it quite spectacularly in a roomful of guests, i.e. strangers, over two Texan lovebirds.

Which makes sense. If you want the world to know you are miserable because of you lack a man. This is NOT the way she raised me to think!

Granted, this particular couple has driven us all to the brink of insanity for a full week, walking hip-to-hip down the stairs and finishing each other's sentences with the same wee laugh. We bit our tongues and smiled as if everything was sweet.

They were due to leave on Monday so we nearly made it.

The straw that broke Mum was when they tried to drink their fresh orange juice with their arms looped. According to Onni, whose Donegal English has definitely improved since he hooked up with Simon, Mum dumped their toast on the table, snatched the glasses from them and ripped their arms apart.

All without a word but with slightly too much... passion.

"So sorry." Apparently Chris shunted Mum towards the door while smiling apologetically to the couple so they wouldn't sue or write rotten reviews on the web when we'd all been so patient with them.

I hear Mum's pacing the lobby like an antichrist before I arrive down. "They have no right to parade their love around as if it's some god-given right!" I think everyone in the hotel hears this. She's pretty loud when she wants to be.

"What am I doing organising a bloody festival for people so delusional that they think they'll just pop into Drisogue and find their perfect man because we throw up a wee marquee? For people who feel entitled to find true love because they're so special. Unlike me."

I thought she loved the festival.

"You've just had some bad luck—"

She shakes Chris off. "Look, I know you mean well but I mean, even you have Kitty hanging onto every word!"

My mother. The woman who raised me to be thoughtful and considerate and polite is completely unaware of having insulted Chris.

"Me, I get a man who wants to cover me with manure, another who nearly gets me a criminal record and oh, just to cap it all off, the nicest man I meet in decades I accidentally kill!"

"Nearly kill."

Mum becomes aware of me watching then, but I'm not the only one. Several guests, including the Texans, have left their breakfast to see what's happening and Jonas, yes Jonas, is in the doorway; arm-in-arm with his bride-to-be.

He looks younger than he does on the school bus. Maybe it's the way he holds his back straight or their linked arms that tell you this is the only way they can stop themselves whooping and skipping and shouting at the moon.

"We'd like to book a wedding." Jonas smiles broadly. "A very particular and spectacular themed wedding."

"Of course you would," mutters Mum.

"Fantastic!" I chime in with my widest smile because she's not usually rude and she'll hate herself for it afterwards.

Chris is in there with me. "We love weddings here!"

"Why don't you show them our different packages, Chris?"

"Right on it, Mouse," says Chris. He knows we need to get them away from Mum and steers them into the lounge.

I could get Mum upstairs. I could put her behind the computer screen and distract her with festival stuff but I don't.

I don't even wait for her apology or her, '*I didn't mean it/ just letting off steam/ we're practising parts for a new stage play*' excuse. She uses that stage play way too much. One day Kitty will actually have to write one and we'll gather an audience to see Mum perform.

I head out the front door without looking back because I need to fix this. Fast.

Three swans fly past, low and long.

Chapter 39

"I don't open Sundays. You know that."

"You have done. Stock-taking. Clean up. Oh come on, Simon. It's an emergency." My feet are freezing but my mind is clear. "I'll go in from the lane so nobody even knows I'm there and I won't put lights on or anything."

"Where's your doppelganger?"

"Probably helping her mum. Or sleeping. I'll be half an hour and I'll drop the key straight back. Any longer, sure Mum would come looking for me. Promise I won't let anyone else in or drink coffee, not even decaf."

He looks far too closely at me then but I keep my face clear of emotion.

"You okay?"

I nod and he hands over the keys to the cafe with a sigh. "Half an hour. No more."

~ ~ ~

I have the cafe to myself and there's no time to waste. I am typing intently, lost in my own world where Dylan hasn't told tales, where he loves me forever and beyond, even into vampirehood and second lives and beyond Armageddons with seven headed-dragon fish. Love wins out.

It just does.

I completely forget that Grace can walk through walls until she pops up behind me and says, "Whatcha doin'?"

I forgot to lock the back door. For Grace, that's effectively an invitation. "Cafe's closed," I try.

"Exactly. So who are you writing to that requires you to sneak in here on a Sunday when every rightful teen is vege-ing?"

I try, "No one," but she's already reading from the screen.

'Hi Granuaile. Hope you don't mind me contacting you directly but I love the answers you gave to your questions. Like you, I love life in all its complexity, pondered in front of a log fire with a bottle of Merlot. Would love to share these moments with someone special.'

I need to decide on a name. What's the right name?

Grace twigs and when Grace twigs, she twigs really fast. If there were a twigging contest, she would be world champion. "Please tell me you're not doing what I think you're doing because that would be, like so far wrong as to be well the wrongest thing ever and totally MAJORLY cringy."

"He's a sweet and tender man. First wife was squashed by an apple core flung from the Eiffel Tower. Or she would have been if she hadn't tripped over a sheep – the farmers were protesting – and fallen down a pothole instead. Probably rats, but could have been the fall. She was never found, so it's more likely she ran away with a gendarme and that he made those other stories up to hide his grief. Also, he adores old films, whales and Pavlova."

Dave? Gary? What's the right name?

"You've made him up!"

Is it that obvious?

"Angelica." Oh yes, she's onto me. Twig-fast should be an adjective. "You can't send your mum a fictional man! That's like… immoral on so many levels. It's like saying this is Galaxy when it's really dairy-free cooking chocolate!"

I have the perfect name. Signing off, I press send.

"Too late." Right now, less than half a mile away, at the edge of a lonely peninsula with a broken loveseat, my mother's computer is going PING!

"Have you any idea what you're doing?"

"Chillax, Mistress Monster."

"Ugh, I hate that word."

"I know exactly what I'm doing."

She doesn't say anything for a whole twenty seconds. Then I get, "She'll never go for it. Your mum, she'll see right through a smarmy rose-petally guy like…" She squints at the screen. "Like Rick. What sort of a name is that?"

"Mum loves romantic films with unhappy endings; I think she feels safer that way, but that's weird, so I don't go into it much. Anyway, her favourite film is Casablanca and the fact of it is that ANY man choosing Rick for his cover name is already half way to the jackpot."

And here we go.

"Hi Rick," she replies. "Thanks for your email."

Chapter 40

By the time I get home, Mum is grinning like a lemur. "I might have met someone," she says, "but I'm saying nothing yet." This promise is broken by the following morning.

"Well he's thirty-five, runs his own company; filming wildlife documentaries. Mostly endangered species."

"Sounds like Mr Perfect alright," says Chris.

You could cut the air into multiple layers of super deluxe pizza with cheesy filling and nobody would notice. Mum hasn't stopped talking about him since she got up. I had her while dressing for school. She ear-popped Onni all through breakfast. Then it was Chris's turn and now he's in a grump.

Why is it impossible for everyone to be ungrumpy at the same time? Is there some graveyard of grumpy Vikings under the foundations of the Drisogue Arms alongside the ruins of Queen Maeve's harem?

I try to sneak out to school without being noticed but I'm a bit off centre after being Rick all night, so Mum gets a gander at my pasty face. Miracle of miracles, it momentarily distracts her from her personal *Adoration Of The Magi Called Rick*.

It's always nice to be told you look washed-out when you're facing double Science and PE. I hate PE.

"Maybe I need to get you a tonic. Or have a word with your form teacher about homework."

"I'm fine, Mum."

"We need to talk about the plumbing upstairs," says Chris. "Room 25 is acting up again."

"Sure. You really should get out more Chris. It's not healthy."

Pot, kettle... Who's calling who what now?

I duck out the door while she's distracted. Sorry Chris. "Have a good day," she shouts after my retreating back. "Keep away from boys!"

Sigh.

~ ~ ~

"It's a statistical fact that once you have a partner, you are more interesting to other men." Grace nods, trying to figure out where this is going but she'll just have to keep up. "I think it's because you don't need them. Plus you're not available, so you're sexy as hell and you know it!"

"What happens when she wants to meet him?"

Okay so I hadn't thought that far ahead. That's forgivable. Every genius has to have her eureka moment and enjoy it. "Won't come up," I say at last. "Look around you: the festival starts in four weeks. Drisogue will be full of men. Rick, well, he's just a means to an end."

Mum won't want to meet him.

I won't make him that nice.

And sure if she does, he'll find an excuse and by then she'll have her eyes fixed on someone else.

~ ~ ~

Chris and Mum are at it again when I get home from school. Rick seems to be the reason or at least Mum's compulsion to keep talking about him. I can hear Chris from several rooms away. "And if you weren't so pig-headed about shoving your affair—"

Mum's voice is lower so I can't make out her response, for which I'm grateful.

"So, serious thing is it? Wedding bells at dawn?"

"Beats hiding under a rock like a scorpion." Great. I can hear them both now.

"Oooh clever, she knows my star sign. Fine as I am thank you."

I knock loudly, but neither of them hears me. Quarrelsome AND deaf.

"Course you are. Happy being bitter and twisted. The only reason you won't try the site is because if you described yourself honestly, nobody'd reply!"

"What is with you two? You're like a pair of rugrats fighting over a lollipop covered in dog hair."

"The whole plumbing system in this hotel needs looking at," says Chris. "I told your mum that years ago, but did she listen?"

"We didn't have the money then; speaking of which, we don't have it now."

"We've finished the design for the hoarding."

"That's great, Mouse. And Molly, that is not what I said."

"The Growler says we can start painting it the day after tomorrow."

"Brilliant," says Mum, leaving to check tonight's menus.

"I said we needed to get them checked out. Properly. Hold this," says Chris. Which is how I end up holding onto wet pipes for the next half hour when I could have been doing homework.

Next time I am leaving them to it.

"I don't need a website to meet women. I have the Chris Webber charm. It's in the genes. Besides, I'm handy. I can do things. Doubt her precious eco-warrior Rick can do this."

"Probably not." The U-bend comes away again the minute he turns on the tap.

"Well don't just stand there!"

ON THE NEAR-MARTIAL ART OF PERSUASION

Persuasion is a talent that will get you far while enabling you to avoid the work yourself. Although, unlike karate or judo, you don't get a fancy white suit with a range of belts.

Victims of gifted persuaders don't get flung over shoulders but they may end up in over their heads.

Similarly, while you may not get punched in the gut, when you realise what you've agreed to do, it winds you just as badly and there's usually a long-term consequence.

There are many names for being defeated in the ring, but how is it that if you try to say 'no' to someone who is good at persuading people to do stuff he or she doesn't want to do, you become the bad guy?

Chapter 41

Two weeks later and the festival has well and truly taken over life on this peninsula. I'd swear even the whales know something's up if only because drips of colourful paint are washing out to sea since all the boats on the shore are being repainted. Mr Ganly has a notion to run whale-spotting convoys during the festival, especially if there's a full moon.

I've just stuck my head into the kitchen for breakfast when Mum appears, grins at Onni and pulls me aside. "Rick asked how I will feel about my daughter dating."

"You told him about ME?"

I'm good.

Or dissociative, which would mean I'm potentially sociopathic. So I could become a psychopath, which would be messy and is definitely NOT in the career plan.

I grab some toast and run before she can say anything else.

~ ~ ~

Dylan's uncle got a reporter to interview Guppy for The Advertiser: *Community Revives its Fortunes*, which doubled as a call for volunteers and sponsorship. She got interviewed then on local radio and on a chat show on RTÉ radio 1. Now we can't move for the amount that's happening and volunteers are coming in from all over the county.

If Tidy Towns was on now, we'd win for the speed in which we are transforming the town. The cobbles are being replaced in the town centre, kerbs and potholes are being mended or filled, every plot of land is being landscaped and every bit of hoarding in town is being painted.

Simon is running a crash course in the Community Centre tomorrow night on how to use Facebook and Twitter to spread information far and wide. The idea is that from next week, someone from every committee will post daily, drip-feeding updates to pull in possible guests.

Chris is in his element, looking blonder than ever, though I'm not sure how. Grace reckons there must be Scandinavian blood in him though Onni's hair is raven black. He says organising a festival is like building a shelving unit. "First you get the dimensions right, make sure your spirit level is straight. Course you need to source the right wood and varnish it to bring out the knots."

"So you're not just a whale expert," says Kitty, bringing his metaphor to an end, thankfully.

"Pretty face," says Chris. "You meant, '*You're not just a pretty face*'."

"Oh, did I?" says Kitty.

What's this? Has this festival got to everyone?

"How many blind-daters can you pull in for the festival itself?"

~ ~ ~

Having picked everyone's brains and contact lists for sponsorship ideas, Chris has secured crates of beer, boxes of wine, flights to offer as prizes, event seating, marquee and champagne. For free. A couple of crates of heart-shaped jellies have been donated, not to mention fizzy water and some drink company wanting to sponsor Chris's aphrodisiac cocktail competition.

He's determined to get us on the Guinness festival circuit but has failed to persuade Marcus to lend us Albert the whale for a temporary installation outside the ballroom. Probably because Kitty's blowing hot and cold again.

"If we can get on the festival circuit, we'll get a broadcaster."

"Aren't Onni's friends going to film it?"

"A documentary. Which is fantastic, but more use in drumming up interest for the next one. Be nice to get something on the telly before the event."

I preferred it when he talked about whales, though it's still a buzz to see him fired up.

It's as if he's been waiting for this all his life.

~ ~ ~

Alongside Chris's calmness, Mum is a walking, talking whirlwind. She's co-ordinating everything, making sure everyone reaches their deadlines and has all the help they need. No-one can say no to her now. She has become officially cool.

Even Theo is in thrall. "Way to go, your mum!" he said on the bus yesterday, as if he hadn't been saying totally different stuff two weeks ago.

Every time we cross paths, she drags an opinion out of me on something. Potential posters, events, venues, bands, titles for different events.

The Druids Never Left Drisogue

Dowsing – Learn to Channel Nature

The Healing Power of Stone Circles

Aphrodisiacs and how to make your own

Bachelor's Wet Shirt Competition

and the main banner-head:

LoveFest, Drisogue or The Drisogue LoveFest.

~ ~ ~

Rumour now is that Big Brenda is modelling a statue of St Laserian for her ecumenical service, in retaliation for all the attention being given to Brigid and her pagan god-ness.

"But no one knows what he looks like," says Mum.

"Which is probably why she's using Fr Lefarge as her model," says Kitty and the two of them giggle like lunatics.

~ ~ ~

When not discussing festival business, all Mum can talk about is Rick this and Rick that and, "Oh it's a nickname. We have to use nicknames. That's the rule. I guess it makes it more romantic, bit like a masked ball?"

"Yes, I suppose it is," says this poor elderly couple she has cornered in the lobby as I arrive in from school. They back away, nodding and smiling.

She's as full of goodwill as a dog in heat and just as annoying.

"Worse than a teenager," says Kitty.

"Y'know," says Mum with a grin, "that's exactly how I feel," Then she hugs Kitty, thanks Guppy and tries to sweep me into the air, only I still have my school bag on so it doesn't work more than a tight squeeze and that's not really something I want right now.

"You two made me do this. Oh, I know you didn't have anything directly to do with persuading me, Angelica but you gave me the space and encouragement to try. And you didn't let me give up."

Oops.

~~~

I never realised how annoying it could be when someone answers every email INSTANTLY. How do you keep a conversation like that going? Let alone sparkling. Okay, so my Rick-mails probably shouldn't sparkle so much but, honestly, I don't think they do. I'm only talking to her about the weather, politics, hopes and dreams.

It's the name that's doing all the work.

But it's tiring, being some sort of Wonderman for a woman you know is your mother and who can't seem to hear from you often enough. She nearly caught me on the computer last night, staring at her latest email and trying to find something to say.

If I don't find something to write, she'll be on edge all night.

"Oh dear. Is Rickipoo all worn out?" says Grace, right beside my ear.

"Don't sneak up on me like that!" I close down the site and drag her down to the kitchen to finish some Banoffi Pie that has had my name on it since yesterday when it became the last surviving slice.

I can't reply to Mum with Grace hovering around like an accusing angel.

She finally bores of me pretending not to be at all concerned about what she calls the *Fictitious Twat Situation* and leaves. I block the door with my schoolbag and Rick sends Mum an innocuous message:

"Really busy. Travelling with work. Talk in a few days."

Thing is, no matter how busy Mum is, she checks her emails at every opportunity for a message from him. I may have overdone it on the compatibility stakes.

Before I turn off the computer again, I check my face for a beard, convinced I must have grown one by now. But it's clear, apart from a nice little trail of acne that I'm putting down to stress not hormones.

At least, she has learnt not to talk about Rick in front of Chris.

He's agreed to pretend he doesn't notice.

~ ~ ~

A group of us has been delegated to paint the banner that will hang over Main Street. The only place with a floor surface large enough is the Community Centre so the school bus drops us in for double Art to start on the lettering. *Welcome to Drisogue – Home of the LoveFest.*

Catchy.

I'm working on the *Welcome.*

Mum arrives in town just as we get off the bus. She's trailed by wolf whistles from the Council guys working on the cobbles around the war monuments and I would swear she wiggled deliberately. Then, stranger still, she stops and there's a bit of banter.

My *former* mum would have walked past, not responding. This one is new.

Grace notices too.

"Told you it'd work," I say. "She's confident and sexy and that's all down to the mysterious Rick."

"Haven't noticed her accepting any dates yet," says Grace. "From real men. Who exist. In the *real* world."

"Chillax."

"Grrr." Thump.

"It's Phase One: The Power Princess. Mum's starting to enjoy the effect she has on men while she susses out which of them to encourage and accept."

~ ~ ~

When I get home, Mum's dancing on the waves as if she can control the sea with her moods but it's a dangerous game. We know this from the drownings every year up and down the west coast.

The sea is full of tumble and trouble but you forget to worry when Mum is in top form. Because then, she's mesmerising to watch. Like a seagull gliding on gusts of water.

I change and try not to worry about what would happen if she fell badly or hit her head on the board. When I go in search of food, I find Chris holding a vigil of his own on the return of the stairs where the vaulted window faces the sea.

Funny, I never noticed him worrying about her surfing before. Maybe he's afraid she'll hit one of his whales. Before I say anything, he waves some print-outs at me. "Great news! Really great news."

"You should tell Mum. Good news might bring her back to shore."

He looks at me then and we so totally understand each other. We share the Fear of the Bystander.

~ ~ ~

When he gets her back to the apartment, she's still wet and so unable to hold, let alone read the faxes. "Now will you tell me what this is about?"

Chris beams. "I'm happy to wait, if you'd like to shower first? Change into something warmer?"

He's only teasing her. Mum turns to me with that bemused look she gets when she doesn't understand someone's behaviour. "This strange man we know and love insisted on waiting until we got back here so you could hear the news too."

"I know. He wouldn't tell me what it was because you had to know first."

"Chris?"

"Okay. Here it is. As of half an hour ago, our little festival has corporate sponsorship!"

Mum grabs the paper from his hand and reads it, regardless of drips.

"Not any piddling sponsors either. We've got the big buckaroos." When he's excited, he's not in control of his vocabulary. "Mega sponsors. Guinness AND Aer Lingus."

She looks as excited as him. "Oh, the things we can do now!"

He's nodding. Grinning.

"This makes us an important go-to festival. We'll get coverage. All the tourism sites will want to include it."

Delighted, she hugs him and heads for the shower, leaving her wet imprint on his overalls. "Oh but we've so little time. We have to get absolutely everything right! We need to talk to all the committee heads. Tonight."

"I'm on it," says Chris. But then Mum spoils it all, calling from the bathroom, probably to me. "Wait till I tell Rick!"

"Yeah," says Chris. "She has to tell Rick."

If I didn't know better, I'd say he was jealous.

But that'd be daft.

Chapter 42

10am Monday. The sky drizzles; that light sort of rain that masquerades as mist. Some of us had a lie in, since we live in town. After weeks of drawing designs and getting them approved, we're finally painting the mural.

Mum's already in town talking to the team of volunteers painting the derelict buildings. None of them seemed to mind her bossing them about. Brenda, via her hardware shop, has sponsored the paint.

This may account for the vivid colours.

Dylan arrives as the school bus pulls in with the out-of-towners. He's wearing his latest T-shirt, but it isn't until Grace and I walk across to the sweet shop and the gang start grinning at me that I lift my eyebrows into a provocative question mark. He shrugs and unveils his creation.

Get this: Chris's photo of me with the whale is printed onto his T-shirt.

How did he even get hold of it? Serious words to be had with Chris later.

"Creepy," says Grace. I have to agree, but it's also pretty sweet.

He holds out the squeezy button on his whale-decorated jacket.

I shrug and squeeze. This time bubbles come out. One especially ginormous bubble squeezes itself out from the whale's mouth to encase Grace's entire face, making it luminous and large, as if she were in a fish tank. I giggle.

This would be one way to stop her giving out to me... I blink and it's gone. Ach, I know it was never there and no one saw it happen except me, but it was fun all the same.

"What?" She's instantly suspicious. "Is it my mascara again?"

"Nope."

"He's made it run again, the little twat?"

"A little." Well, it's fun messing with her mind sometimes. Makes up for some of the thumps and she is far too precious about her mascara.

"Are you out to get me, Dylan Clancy?" she growls. How could she get squirted in the eye without noticing? He looks confused. "What is it? You hate all girls or just girls who wear mascara? Don't tell me – it's a new cult? That's it, isn't it?"

"Grace, lay off. Nothing happened. Your mascara's fine. I was only messing." As I lead her back to our painting group, I look back at Dylan. Even though I said I never would.

And he looks right back.

Bliss.

When the drizzle stops, it turns into one of those sharp, sunny days. I'm glad we didn't have to wear school uniform, even if it means there's more paint being flicked between us when The Growler looks away than went onto the Sistine Chapel ceiling.

Cathie suggests we paint really slowly so we get the rest of the week off lessons. The Growler says there's heavy rain coming later this week and to work faster.

～～～

All morning, Mum's in and out of town. Everyone wants a piece of her. She's glowing and confident but almost deliberately oblivious to the impact she's having. Even when men keep coming to ask her opinion before doing some mundane task like deciding on which side of a window frame to hang a basket of blooms.

Mid-morning, Louis, the health and safety guy from the Council with the puppy eyes, goes one step further and emerges from Simon's with two coffees, one for Mum. From where I'm standing, under Granuaile's green serpent eyes, it looks as if he's proposing a date.

I hold my breath.

But what does Mum do?

She points to her Claddagh ring, as if to show she's 'spoken for'.

This isn't how it was meant to be.

"When are you going to tell her he's a fake?" Grace is at my shoulder, watching. "I mean, she's not exactly giving in to temptation."

"Granuaile's hair won't paint itself, girls," says The Growler, sniffing discontent in the ranks.

"You said we could have hot chocolate," says Denise.

"When Granuaile is recognisable as something other than a wraith."

So we work hard all day and Granuaile ends up resembling a long-haired glamour model with mascara-effect eyelashes. That's because The Growler left the details of her face to Grace.

~ ~ ~

We're all probably high on paint fumes and looking like miniature artworks ourselves, so The Growler decides not to cart us all back to school for one last class. As I'm walking home, Dylan pops up like a handsome leprechaun on a truth drug (and growth hormones). He falls into step beside me.

Since I'm meant to still be mad, neither of us says anything. If I bring him to the beach, I might forget to be angry and kiss him instead so I keep on walking.

"Angelica—"

"If Mum gets wind of what you told them, she'll kill me."

"Sorry."

"No, seriously! She'll dice me up and feed me to gerbils with lashing of ketchup and Tabasco and—" I've lost track. "Something else really horrible."

"I'm really sorry. It was a stupid thing to do."

"Yeah."

"I'll tell them I made it up if you like?"

"It's okay."

"So I'm forgiven?"

"Is that what the t-shirt was for?"

He nods. "Yeah. I asked Chris what you'd like best and he gave me a copy of this photo."

I grin. But I will have words with Chris. "Yeah."

"Hey, you two!" Mum's car pulls up alongside and I leap guiltily. "Want to give me a hand or just gaze into each other's eyes?"

Why does she say things like this? She opens the back door and hands one box of leaflets to me and another to Dylan.

"Dylan, can you give half of these to your dad to distribute and share with Rev. Clancy? Angelica, drop the rest into Kitty; save me going down into town again. Tell her to make sure every customer she has distributes a batch somewhere in the country!"

Then she pulls out posters and more fliers. "When you've done that—"

"Yup. The rest of town, right?"

"That's my girl," says Mum.

Really, I mean really?

"So much to do. I need to get back to the hotel. I don't know how Chris thinks he can run a LoveFest without being at least interested in the idea of being in love, do you?"

This is EXACTLY the opposite of what she was saying three weeks ago.

I decide not to point this out. I'm finally learning the art of self-preservation. Rule 999: Don't tell adults you know they have changed their opinions radically and irrationally.

They don't like it.

We take a pile of posters too and when I've dropped off the fliers, we paper the town's establishments. I hold the posters, he pins or tapes. Totally co-ordinated, we don't talk about Theogate or my embarrassing mother calling me a girl.

And we never will. Okay?

Chapter 43

Drisogue has come to life like a blushing bridegroom. Every building fronting the main street is the colour of gelato. The flowerbeds throughout town and around the new *Welcome To Drisogue – Population 5,602* signs at both entrances are fluorescent with colour.

The fountain at the entrance to Main Street is even working again. Denise's mum, as school principal, made us all pinkie promise at a general assembly NOT to add washing up liquid to it until after the festival.

Already, for the launch of the 'seven days to go' countdown, there's bunting up over the square and along Main Street while Guppy is in all her finery, ready to cut the ribbon to officially open our new Tourist Information and Ticket Office. Apart from the painting of pigs on the tiles above the main desk, you'd never know it had been a butcher's.

Everyone has gathered to witness the event, from far and near. There are photographers, local newspapers, even a city councillor from Letterkenny whose picture I've seen in the papers claiming he will rejuvenate the whole region. Onni's film crew friends are due on Monday so they can interview us all before and after the event and Onni is planning a special Finnish feast, which means lots of fish dishes and sweet pastries that he's testing on Simon and Guppy.

"It's as I always imagined Drisogue could be," says Guppy. "Slightly brighter in colour…" There's a ripple of laughter through the crowd. "But warm and welcoming. Like a picture postcard."

Mum gives the signal, the banner is unfurled above the street and Guppy cuts the ribbon.

"Speech!" This is Chris, but it spreads until Mum has no choice.

"In seven days' time," she says, with the happiest voice imaginable as the sun comes out, "Drisogue will be at the centre of the world!"

The Councillor tries to hog the reporter from The Advertiser, but Dylan's uncle clued him in so the reporter knows Mum, Guppy and Chris are the people he needs to talk to, not the politician. Chris holds back and lets Mum and Guppy do the talking. He has this layer of niceness about him. Even though the festival was his idea, he lets them take the honour and glory. It doesn't bother him. He just acts happy that it's happening.

Strange to think that this festival germinated in a barn less than two months ago.

I head through the crowd to Dylan.

"Hey you," he says.

"Hey yourself."

He wraps an arm around my waist, which is just the coolest feeling. Like coming home when everything has gone wrong in school for the longest day and your mum hands you a hot chocolate with marshmallows and a plate of spicy wedges as an appetiser to your favourite meal. I'm exhausted.

What with trying to create a love life for Mum, manage school, the festival stuff, homework and trying to make sure nothing goes wrong.

Even when it will.

So, for one delicious double chocolate chip cookie moment, I don't give a damn about anything or anyone. All that matters is the here and now of having Dylan's arm around me, even as we both pretend to pay the utmost attention to what my mum is saying.

But then I see the wording on the banner start to dance and sway. A new inscription appears: *RICK, aka Fictitious Boyfriend. Born February 2010. Died ?*

I pull away from Dylan. Stung. It's not my fault I want Mum to be happy. Why can't anyone understand? Dylan's miffed when I won't let him replace his arm. "What's wrong?"

I can't answer him. Too busy blinking. The image won't fade. Instead, the words re-form into: *MOLLY'S HEART, awoken February 2010 – died April 2010.*

"She's practically engaged!"

I close my eyes for the longest moment, willing the words be banished harshly back into a deep oblivion fog where such Dickensian things belong. "You wouldn't understand ," I say, moving away. "Sorry. I've got to go."

"I've hardly had a chance to talk to you for weeks."

"What, since you told everyone about Mum?"

"You forgave me!"

"Yeah, well, I have to help Mum. And he's only a cyber boyfriend so he hardly counts."

"Seems pretty real to her."

"That's not my fault!" Okay, okay, calm down, he never said it was. This is about me and my mum, not me and Dylan.

"Are you breaking up with me?"

"Course not. Anyway, we'd have to be going out together to break up."

"I thought we were, sort of," he says in a very quiet voice.

"We will. I just… Not right now." I squeeze his hand so he knows I want this more than anything. It doesn't work as a let's-slow-this-down technique because neither of us wants to let go.

A whoop goes up through the crowd as Mum's speech ends and I pull away. "You'll jinx it."

"That mean I'm your genie?"

Oh corny! He looks embarrassed too. I have to save him with a crooked grin. "Yeah, you are." Oh now I'm corny. But it's okay. Everyone's too buzzy to hear us.

"We'll be okay for the Ball?"

I cross my fingers behind my back. "Absolutely."

A single magpie glares at me from a nearby lamp post. I match her look, telling her to go fetch worms for her man and let me worry about my own, before I weave through the crowd. Mum is the centre of attention from more men than this town has ever held and seems only amused by it.

I try to ignore the knot in my tummy that tells me this is all going wrong, by pretending it's pizza-pangs.

"A week to the festival," says Grace, landing up beside me with a softer thump than usual. "Nine sleeps to the Ball. What happens then?"

ON EMBARRASSMENT AND WHY PARENTS ENJOY INFLICTING IT

There is nothing you can do to protect yourself from a parent embarrassing you. The more you react, the more hilarious it becomes. For them. Mum says it is the only free pleasure parents have that will last their entire lives.

Oh you can pretend to ignore them, but they'll find something to say that is perfectly aimed at the underbelly of your apparent indifference. Like they'll tuck your shirt in, try to brush your hair with their fingers or use your baby name in public.

Besides, ignoring them is no deterrent. They know how hard you're trying. Instead of feeling pity, it simply spurs them on to continue until you crack.

The only effective defence is not to care, to laugh back with them and pretend it hasn't worked. This is next to almost impossible.

I follow Mum into the new information office. "The councillor looks nice." Looks nice? The man is dancing around the journo like a gerbil on a treadmill.

"What was that, Angel?"

Okay, bad first choice. He's far too self-interested. I have moments to fix her up before someone comes in looking for her about something. It doesn't matter with whom, not right now, so long as she stops focusing on Rick. "Louis? The guy from the County Council. Or Marcus? Grace says Kitty's finished with him now."

Okay, poor choice of words, but I'm thinking on my feet and I still have the imprint of Dylan's arm around my waist. "You could persuade him to get a haircut and he's a film producer so that has to count?"

"Are you trying to fix me up?" Yup, she's not the fastest in the slot today. "What? Me?"

She shakes her head as if I amuse her. "Sweetheart, I love what you're trying to do."

"You do?" She hasn't a clue.

"Not wanting me not to be the odd one out; the only one without a partner for the Ball."

Oh that. She doesn't know the half.

"But I'm seeing someone, remember?"

"No. You can't say that. That's, like, crazy."

Mum is so obtuse sometimes. Good word that. Chris was using it to describe Big Brenda's insistence that the LoveFest should have a religious aspect.

"Seriously Mum. Listen to me. You can't say you're 'seeing' someone if you haven't met. Has he even sent a photo?"

She shrugs and grins. "We agreed to wait."

Okay, so I knew that. That was my idea. My idea *as Rick* not to swop photos, mainly because I hadn't one, not being real. This is going so very wrong. "People say that when they're engaged, Mum." She just keeps grinning. It's infuriating. "Seriously, you can't tie yourself down to someone you haven't met when there are so many other men out there. And here!"

I wave over to Louis through the window. He gets such a shock at me waving that he manages to fall over his own briefcase and land in the arms of Cathie's mum. My guess? He has a lost daughter somewhere and is now terrified it might be me.

"What if you don't like him when you meet? If he's really smelly or leaves the loo seat up or speaks disparagingly about whales? Or me? Or children in general and especially me? Or turns out to be a woman or a girl. Or I mean a woman who acts like a girl and has this silly high-pitched laugh?"

"What are you on about?"

"What if doesn't live up to– If he's not as–?"

"Substantial?"

"Yeah."

"Well, we'll soon find out." Oh oh. This is going to be BAD. "I've asked him to the Ball!" She sees my face and instantly reverts to being Mum again. "Are you worried?"

"No. Course not."

"Oh Angel, I should have told you but you're not to worry. When this man comes into my life—"

"If."

"Okay. If this man comes into my life, I'm going to take it really slow. We'll still have our special nights together."

"Big deal." Fortunately, this is a mutter rather than the roar it feels like in my head.

"What was that?"

"Big. Real. Rad. Radical. Great. But seriously, Mum, what if he's even worse than the men you already met? How do you know he won't be a huge disappointment and then you've wasted all this time?"

"Instinct."

Grace bounces in then, in time to hear Mum say, "I have a connection with Rick." She gives me one of her best and most cutting told-you-so looks.

"I know it must sound mad to you both, but I feel I've known this man for years. Grace, can you explain to my daughter that she needs to trust me on this one?"

Grace says nothing. Nothing at all. Mum takes this as a yes. Several people come in looking for her to come outside for photographs. There's a hug and a kiss on my forehead (patronising) and she's gone. Grace grabs my arm and pulls me outs back. "Like for fourteen years."

"Shhh."

We race to the cafe to see what Mum has said in her invitation to Rick. Grace covers my back while I log on. "What are you going to say back?"

"I'll say he's thinking about it."

Grace explodes. "Thinking about it? He doesn't exist!!"

"Not for you."

"Not for anyone. You made him UP!"

"He wouldn't say no just like that. He's special. He's kind. He's thoughtful."

"He's her DAUGHTER!"

Yeah. There is that. It's kind of a big that, too. Without a cherry on top or chocolate sprinkles or anything else.

It might even be without ice cream.

Chapter 44

For two days after, I watch Mum to see if Rick's lack of response to her invite dents her confidence that he is The One. To deflect her, I fire the hunkiest, least appropriate men into her inbox with five stars. I even find a Donegal member who likes Casablanca AND surfing.

She doesn't bite.

She gets twitchy but the festival prep keeps her busy so the twitchiness is deflected into bossing people about and not sleeping much. Onni's friends arrive and Mum closes the restaurant that evening to allow Onni to do his Finnish feast.

I'm hoping Mum's giving up on Rick, since he hasn't replied. It's hard not to, when she's twitchy, knowing one little email could make her happy again but I force myself to resist. Exactly how much trouble I'm in is clear when I call into Grace's after school and we hear Mum confiding in Kitty.

"Course he'll come!" says Kitty.

It's a pity I was never able to grow furry ear flaps that would instinctively block out sensitive or damaging material; maybe with pockets for change so I'd never run out of money for chocolate or crisps.

"And when he does, hands off." Mum wags a finger and grins at her friend. "I mean it!"

This sends Kitty into explosions of mock indignation. The '*as if I would!*' and '*I'd never!*' kind that convince nobody. They don't have to. Mum knows Kitty would never get between her and the man of her dreams.

Who, unfortunately and very clearly, still happens to be 'Rick'.

"Oh and I was wondering, just in case, being a love festival and all, y'know I could get carried away… Could Angelica stay with you on the night of the Ball?"

"If he comes."

"Oh he will. He's just playing hard to get!"

Grace pulls me back out of earshot. "You need to sort this, fast!"

I walk home slowly, trying to work out how to fix this now. Onni's friends are following Guppy around her sites, getting some background. I wonder if they realise it's all made up. Or mostly.

Or, at least, *adapted* for Drisogue.

~ ~ ~

Thinking I might be able to confide in Chris, I head upstairs immediately, avoiding Mum. Lying on his worktop is the most beautiful pendant made from quartz and what looks like marble. I can't resist touching it, only for it to fall apart in two pieces. I'm frozen, terrified I've broken it, when Chris comes in with a flask of coffee and shows me how they're two separate whale pendants that clip together into a heart.

"Secret girlfriend?" He shakes his head. This festival is getting to everyone. "Wait, it's never Kitty?"

He has the grace to ignore the question completely. "The weighting of them was really difficult. Put the hole for the chain in the wrong place and the second whale looks like a misshapen two-legged cocktail."

"Chris, this guy of Mum's?"

"Too good to be true, right?"

I nod. He pours himself a cup of coffee and drops it down his throat like nectar. "No way is he for real. Whoever this guy is and whatever his reasons, he's stringing her along, telling her what she wants to hear."

"But Mum's not stupid."

He doesn't even hear me. "I mean we could all do that, but your mum likes honesty, right? Okay, so she was unbearable when all she could talk about was how wonderful he was, but this is worse. Seeing her holding out for him, when he clearly hasn't the guts to admit he has no intention of coming to see her."

"What can we do?"

He puts his arm around my shoulder. "Be there for her when it all goes wrong."

~ ~ ~

What with the last minute festival panics, I don't see Mum again till she's going down to serve breakfast the next day. "Mum, I need to talk to you." Now or never.

"Can it wait? Tell me it can wait, Angel. I've got two new kitchen staff running round like headless chickens in a pie factory saying they can't understand anything Onni tells them to do, a chambermaid with a migraine and forty rooms to make up before Thursday. On top of which Chris pushed a note under the door last night to say the band for the Ball might not be able to make it because of a double booking."

What can I say?

"Sure."

So it's not a good time. I'll tell her later. I mean, she knows now that I want to tell her something and she listens, right? She's my mum; she always listens. Probably knows what I'm thinking half the time.

Oh, who am I kidding?

"We'll sit down later. I haven't forgotten I said we'd do something together before it all kicks off."

Exactly what I need; to be encased in a room with her for a whole evening right after I've tell her I invented her perfect boyfriend and platter-fed him to her like a prize cow. "But you've got so much to do, with the festival and everything."

"Nothing is as important as spending time with my beautiful daughter. Besides, they know where to find me. Now, in return, come help me with these waitresses."

~ ~ ~

Once brekkie is done, I call in to Grace to tell her I have tried; Kitty nabs us for the delightful task of putting pieces of coloured paper into envelopes. Her blind-daters each get a list of venues, times and dates, with matching nicknames for each date like Yum Yum or Choconoodle.

From these pages, everyone has to locate their rendezvous, find the person who answers the same nickname and chat until it's time to go on to the next. They'll be introduced to their 'official match' at the Ball on Saturday night.

"When you're finished, you can blow up some balloons," she adds, "to tie up outside. Make the place look festive."

Great. I feel festive blowing up balloons. Not.

Bursting balloons would make me feel better. Filling them with water and throwing them at the likes of Theo.

"I'm sure Saturdays used to be fun," says Grace.

No sign of Mum when I get home but the computer's on in the office. I move the mouse and RomanticHearts.com pops up. She's still waiting for his reply. Worse, the notepad by the phone is covered with Molly xx Rick over and over, as if she has been seeing how the names look together.

What age is she!

Even I don't do that anymore. At least, not where anyone will see them. Even then, I have the sense to stick to initials. Besides, she knows Rick isn't his real name.

Couldn't be.

Even if he were real.

I'm sat there in a stupor feeling like a bog body corpse when Mum returns. "Looking for me?" She scootches the notebook into a drawer and closes it. I shake my head and make a quick exit. She sits down, probably to check if Rick has replied yet.

Telling her now will do nothing to make her feel better.

I text Grace to come over asap. We are officially going into lockdown until this is solved. "Bring supplies."

My plan, drastic, cruel and simple – but I can't do it alone because of that 'cruel' part, is that Rick will invite 'Granuaile' into the chat room and simply tell her he can't meet her. Ever.

But nicely. He's a nice guy. He would be the best sort of stepdad imaginable. Probably buy cool pressies like cruises to Cuba. But he's a werewolf or a vampire who lives in Peru. Deepest Peru. His passport was eaten by a cheetah.

Do they have cheetahs in Peru?

Chapter 45

'*Granuaile,*' I type while I wait for Grace. '*I'm not the man you think I am. I've been around.*'

Okay it's yuck but what am I meant to say? I've never broken up with a woman who happens to be my mother before! '*You are clearly a beautiful woman, but I think it's better if we don't…*'

Before I finish the sentence, Mum's reply flashes up on screen: '*I like an experienced man.*'

Oh, gross! This is not what I expected. He's telling her he's no good. Why won't she listen? I try a different tack. '*I'm dull: I like football. I have nasal hair. I tape the Late Late and watch it twice a week.*'

That should do it. Mum hates the Late Late Show. Something about feeling she's a teenager living at home again.

Grace lopes in with multiple bars of chocolate and hands me a Yorkie that's *Not for Girls.*

"Very funny."

"Thought it might help you keep in character. How's she taking it?"

"She isn't." I show her mum's reply: '*Anyone who says they're dull couldn't possibly be. I can cure you of your Late Late fetish. There are better things to do on a Friday night.*'

"Yuck."

"Let me." Grace slides into the seat, displacing my bum and types: '*You have me all wrong. I'm not romantic. I just wanted to get you into bed.*'

"Grace!"

"You do want to put her off him don't you?"

"But Rick would never do that."

"Rick doesn't exist. Mum says it happens all the time."

"Too much information."

She hits send.

We nibble in silence like bingeing Easter bunnies trying to double their bodyweight because they're tired of being hollow. Maybe she's right. For five whole minutes nothing comes back. The nightmare is over.

That's what I'm starting to think when the screen pings. "Is it me or was that a really loud ping?"

'*Who needs romance?*' writes Granuaile; writes my *mum*!

'*If I'm completely honest – and I appreciate you have been, I want hot, rampant sex and lots of it. You are going to–*'

Both of us rush to switch off the screen as if our eyes had been burnt. We sit in silence and eat our chocolate, too grossed out to speak.

"Homework doesn't seem so bad."

"Yeah, wouldn't mind being in school right now."

"Even with Ms Willow."

"In a bad mood."

"Double bad mood."

"Detention."

"And Theo being nice."

But some experiences are hard to forget. "Did she really say that?"

We chew it over until the supply of chocolate runs out and the need for crisps emerges. "You have to tell her the truth," says Grace as we traipse downstairs, traumatised. I place one foot in front of the other, saying nothing until we have efficiently raided the crisp stand in the bar.

"She'll never forgive me."

"You can't go online again as Rick," says Grace. "You can't answer her."

"I know."

"Promise me?"

"I promise."

We eat the crisps in silence. The last thing I want is to see Mum's response. Rick is no longer me; he has become this nasty guy and she STILL likes him. Grace tries to sugar the pill for me one last time. "At least, technically, she can't be stood up by someone who doesn't exist."

I prefer it when she gives me chocolate and thumps. Even the thumps are better.

WORST JOKES EVER

On a speeding ambulance: "Won't sell much ice cream going at that speed."

What time is it when an elephant sits on your fence? "Time to get a new fence."

And for the season that's coming: What do squirrels give for Valentine's Day? Forget-me-nuts.

Days pass. Mum's busy, but seems tired. Everyone is, but there's a sort of stoop to her shoulders as if she were expecting bad news.

Grace, as ever, has the solution. "Kill him off. Send an email from a friend informing her that Rick fell from a tree and drowned in toxic waste."

"She wouldn't believe it."

"Give him a wife and kids. A really young wife and gorgeous kids just like us," says Grace, but I can't.

"It'd break her heart, especially after her experience with Joseph."

"And this isn't?" she says, not unreasonably.

~ ~ ~

It's Tuesday; two full days before the festival begins. Despite the risk that Mum might remember she proposed spending the evening with me, I search her out. She's in the ballroom with the electrician who is wiring the venue for the band; the band that still might not come. Onni's friends are there too; they seem to be everywhere.

Chris's cupids are on plinths around the room, banners and fairy lights hang from the coving. It's not elegant but sort of magical.

And slightly weird.

"Mum."

Three of the cupids whip off their togas to cover their ears, eyes and mouth.

"It's not that bad," I tell them and concentrate on getting her attention. "Mum, I really need to talk to you, now."

"Just say 'no'," she says, without even turning round. "Whatever you do, don't be truthful; unless you want to scare him off."

Oh oh! She's talking about what she said to Rick.

The cupids snigger. I try to visualise pigeons dropping really heavy whales and crushing them on their plinths. But they're made of polystyrene; they'd probably bounce into hundreds, millions of teensie giggling mini-cupids, so I blink instead and they're immobile again.

"Besides—" Mum's warming to her theme. "If he's worth it, he'll wait." The banner over the stage is back to front and she sees it when I do. "No, no, NO. Who put that up? Where's Chris gone to?" I'm slipping out when she remembers there are two hundred balloons to be inflated and nobody seems to know whose job it is.

"So you're designating me."

"Chief inflation officer," she dubs me. "Get Grace up to help."

Great. Guilt, the embarrassment of having a boyfriend (without actually having one) and two hundred heart-shaped pink balloons.

Chapter 46

"This is good practice," says Grace. As if she's forgotten how much she gave out when we were doing this in The Pirate Queen.

"For what? Blowing up more balloons?"

"For snogging. We can strengthen our lungs so they take more air in. Then we can kiss for longer."

"Sick."

It's only when we're a hundred balloons in that we find an air pump, buried at the bottom of the box. The next fifty balloons go up more easily, though the air pump sounds like a reverse fart and not a funny one. Fifty balloons later, maybe because she's got her breath back, Grace decides to talk again.

"Since we're telling truths today," she says as I inflate a giant peacock. (Peacocks have nothing to do with St Brigid or love far I know of, suggesting the balloons are one of Chris's eBay bargains.)

"Are we?"

"Yeah."

"So?"

"That's a really ugly peacock. Has it got horns?"

"Yup."

"Weird."

"Was that it? What you wanted to say?"

"Not exactly. Can we go somewhere private?"

This can't be good. She hasn't even mentioned chocolate.

~ ~ ~

"You did what!!!"

The wind rattles the tent as if it totally 'gets' my mood. A barrage of balloons, including my peacock, escape out the entrance as I pull Grace out. Most of them get snagged by the oak tree. They look like chewing gum. I spot one of Onni's friends getting some shots of the tree and drag Grace away. "You could get the site closed down!"

Mum rounds the corner from the ballroom. I lead Grace towards the path down to the beach before she sees us. "I knew you were up to something."

"Takes one to know one."

"This isn't the same thing at all."

"It was just a bit of fun."

I fling the largest stone I can find into the sea. Any day now, I will have built a new Giant's Causeway reaching to America.

"Not as if you care anymore anyway." Grace flings a weak little stone that sinks without trace. Not only has Grace logged on to the site, (which is illegal; she's fourteen) she has been chatting with someone who says he's coming to meet her at the festival.

"I didn't expect anyone to actually contact me."

"We have to tell the police. You say he's thirty-six, you're fourteen. He has to be a perv!"

"He's not a perv! His name's Frank and we talk about films and stuff. Books. And," she adds, avoiding eye contact, "He thinks I'm twenty-seven."

"You hate books!"

It's true. She hates books. Unless they have pictures; lots and lots of pictures. Preferably of film stars, hair styles or, yeah, older men. But Tariq is eighteen *months* older, not twenty-two years. Oh, this is going so wrong.

"You don't even like films much."

"He's recommended some really cool ones—" she starts, but thinks better of it when she sees my face.

"Wait, what name did you use?" I'm having an idea; one of those brain-freeze eureka moments.

"My own," she says very quietly. "But look, it was a double bluff, see, because you're meant to give a fake name and I thought by calling myself Grace, he'd never work out what my name really was." She deflates onto a large boulder. "I never meant it to get this far. But look, I'll go home now and delete my details and log out of the site."

"No!"

"But—"

"He's coming to Drisogue?"

"Licky?"

"Uh huh?"

"Whatever you're plotting, it's probably wrong."

"Me?"

"Yes. Whatever it is, I'm absolutely certain it's really, REALLY not a good idea."

"But this guy, he's definitely coming to the Ball on Saturday night?"

Grace looks uncomfortable. "He's booked a room in the pub."

"But that's perfect! You're *Grace*, right?" She nods. "And Mum called herself *Granuaile*, which, as we know, being erudite little minxes, is another name for Grace!"

Oh I am GENIUS!

Chapter 47

I drag her back to my room, narrowly avoiding everyone who might put us to work. Closing the door, I rest my school bag against the door as an early warning system. "Okay, here's what you do. Tell him to meet you in the hotel lobby before the Ball. I'll do the same with Mum."

Grace doesn't move. "This isn't a good idea."

"1) Rick doesn't exist, so Rick has to vanish. 2) Mum meets 'Frank' but she SEES 'Rick'. 3) She also sees 'Rick' for a liar because he's nothing like he said he would be – and 4) he's history. Only, she breaks it off. She's not dumped."

Grace nods. She has no choice. "So I tell him to be in the lobby of the Drisogue Arms Hotel, 9pm Saturday?"

"And I say the same to Mum, as Rick." I sit down at the computer and log onto the site. *I'll be the daft beggar wearing a silly smile and a rose,* I type. "She hates roses," I explain. "They make her sneeze."

"Then, why?"

"D'oh! I'm not meant to know that, am I? I mean, Rick doesn't. Wouldn't."

"Oh yeah. Hey, Licky, shouldn't we tone it down? He's about to break her heart."

"The more over the top he is, the more likely she'll see through him and the less disappointed she'll be." I slide over onto the bed so Grace can take her turn at the computer.

"Go ahead. Invite your ancient bookworm to the Ball."

If her glares mean what I think they mean, Grace is reluctant to start with me watching. I pick up a book and pretend to read but it's hard not to peek. 'Dear Munchkin!' she types. "Oh please! What does he call you if he's a Munchkin? His little Oompa Loompa?"

Grace lifts her hands off the keyboard. "Am I doing this?"

"Yeah. Sorry."

"Go sit by the door. And turn away."

So I do. For ages. She's either writing it over and over or making tons of mistakes. "You don't have to write a novel!"

Grace places her hands on her lap, again and looks at me with eyes of steel. Where did her sense of humour go? She must be on a sugar-low. "You could leave the room while I write."

It's my room. I don't want to leave. Besides, Mum's everywhere these days.

"Please. It's the last time I'll speak to him. I want to do it right."

"I'll wait downstairs." Reluctantly, I drag my bones out of the one safe place in Drisogue. "But don't forget the rose."

~ ~ ~

Mum's checking bookings in the office. She might not have seen Rick's email yet.

"Now," says one of the whales on the desk. "Tell her now!"

"Mum?"

A commotion explodes behind me in the lobby as the band that nearly didn't make it burst in with all their equipment. Mum rushes out to stop them with a, "Sorry, just a minute" to me and a, "No, no. Not in here. In the ballroom!" to them.

She's up to 999 volts per syllable but she still has time to shout back as she whooshes the musos out: "He's coming to the Ball!"

And her face is all lit up inside.

~ ~ ~

The next few days are a blur.

Yes, we teens go to school but nobody gives homework because all our other waking hours are spent finishing festival stuff. The hotel is booked out, as is Kitty's pub and every B&B for a five mile radius. (Jonas is running a Party Bus to bring people home from the various events.) There's even a small campsite designated on a fallow field to the left of town, as far from the sea and the cliff as they could put it.

Just in case.

~ ~ ~

On Thursday evening, Guppy welcomes Drisogue's guests from the stage that has been built between the war memorials and declares the festival officially open. She looks regal, as if she's been waiting for this event all her life.

Mum's up next, with Chris, to run through the weekend's highlights. The open-air cinema in the Far Field launches with Brief Encounter at midnight tonight, with Casablanca tomorrow lunchtime. There's music in Gaffney's and Kitty's. A night tour of Guppy's sites starts from the hotel at nine, with a complementary cocktail at the end. For those who want a different kind of wildlife, Mr Ganly has organised a flotilla of small boats to ferry visitors out to find frolicking whales.

Tomorrow begins with a druidic ceremony of light at the dolmen at dawn. (Big Brenda's ecumenical service takes place on Sunday morning on the cliff top.) In the marquee and on the stage, events will run all day from eleven. They include a cocktail competition, trad sessions, a local blues band, a workshop on making aphrodisiacs and casting spells. Crowning the whole affair at 8pm on Saturday night is the big Drisogue LoveFest Ball in the ballroom of the Drisogue Arms.

All of this is filmed by Onni's friends. This is what they do, he said. Film everything and then find the story.

If they only knew!

~ ~ ~

Friday dawns crisp with a clear blue sky. The festival has brought hundreds into town and they are all having the time of their lives. Noisily. So are the town's inhabitants, both those with businesses profiting and those who are single or musical, thriving on the buzz. Kitty's blind-daters roll into town at seven pm.

By the time they start scouting for their first dates, dusk is casting a romantic haze over the street and the marquee in front of the hotel is humming with new-agers concocting aphrodisiacs under Guppy's tuition. At the far end, there's a group learning how to imitate whale song on pan pipes but the less said, the better.

Grace and I are kept too busy by our mums to even text each other.

If I could forget what's going to happen – or not happen tomorrow night, it would be fun.

ON THROWING STONES

Every situation is different. Ideally, you need a piece of flint or at least the apartmenttest stone you can find. It should be lacking roundness, serrations, bumps or personality. Finding the right stones works well for sorrow, as well as fear and dread; it takes just enough thought and concentration to skim the edge off the emotion.

Temporarily.

When the stones dance over the surface, it's so beautiful that you don't feel like a failure for a moment or two.

For anger management, however, you need a medium-to-heavy stone. It has to make a satisfying thump when it hits the water and create ripples that will disturb small fish in China, but still sit snugly in the palm.

But steer clear of the really heavy stones. They will hurt your shoulder, your elbow and your wrist and will always fall humiliatingly short. No matter how mad you feel. adding humiliation to anger or sorrow isn't a great idea.

Chapter 48

By the time I catch my breath and look up, it's Saturday evening. The marquee is emptying with the tail end of a speed-dating event while the band tunes up in the Ball that begins at 8pm. Chris created a whole new batch of cocktails for the festival: The *Gilded Granuaile, Awaken The Stone Man* etc so he's in the bar, spinning them as fast as they can, with a couple of lads he trained in for the weekend. There's a buzz in the air that you can almost taste, while everyone gathers, waiting for the ballroom doors to open.

Mum's more on edge than I remember seeing her before. She's watching every man who so much as glances in her general direction. Any of them might be *him*. It's like the hours leading up to an execution. As soon as she has officially opened the Ball, she disappears upstairs to the apartment to pin on her silk rosebud.

Fortunately Onni's friends are busy interviewing people going into the Ball to notice her slip away. This is one story that can *not* be filmed.

I follow her. Slowly.

Now I know what is meant by '*leaden feet*'. If they were actually pinned to the ground with massive galaxy-destroying magnets they wouldn't feel as heavy as the footsteps I take upstairs to our apartment.

"*Please don't expect too much*, Mum." No. Too wishy-washy. I need to make it stronger. More worldly. "*Lots of people don't live up to their emails. It's not a reflection on you.*" The mirror in the bathroom despises every feeble attempt I make to figure out a way to minimise this mess.

I've steeled myself to be honest and brutal when Mum pirouettes out of her room, swirling her new sexy red dress to the four corners of the wind. "What do you think?"

"You look amazing!" Because she does. She absolutely does. This is why I wanted her to find someone. This is how I want her to feel, only not about this man. She twines her thumb around mine.

"God, I'm shaking! What if he really is, y'know…"

"Yeah. Mum?" She ruffles my hair, listening. "If he's a fraud, more fish, right? I mean, look at you! You could have anyone."

Mum hands over a small white whale on a pin. "This came for you. A certain vicar's son?"

It's unbearable and I can't even go to fling stones at the sea or the Stone Man; there are too many people about. "Are you coming down?"

"I thought I'd wait here for a bit."

Okay, I don't want her hiding in the apartment but I don't want her waiting to have her heart broken in public either. "I can give you a shout when he gets here. How will I know him?"

"Handsome, debonair. Wearing a rose."

"Sure," I say and I'm out of there.

~ ~ ~

"I've done a terrible thing Guppy."

"I agree but you had the right motive and you were right to do it."

"I was?"

"Absolutely."

She's dressed in the most beautiful floor-length blue velvet dress, with teardrop pearl earrings; the same ones she wore in her photo with Teddy. I've never seen the dress before. At least tonight, she'll be the belle of the Ball.

But I can't be distracted. She's talking about something else and whatever it is, it isn't what she thinks I've done. "You don't understand." I have to tell someone before I burst. "You don't know what I've done."

"I know that you're here with me when you should be down at the Ball enjoying yourself." She's not even listening. I might as well be invisible.

"I thought I could go with you."

"Oh, Teddy will take me."

Okay. This is worrying. I can almost cope with being the cause of one broken heart but two? This Night of Broken Hearts will go down in folklore. "I'd prefer to go with you." I offer her my arm, as I've seen in old films. "Why don't we both go down and wait for him there?"

"Dear darling Angelica." She pats my arm. "You think I'm making him up."

"I didn't say that."

"After you using that computer net to find him?"

Something in her tone of voice makes me turn. There, coming out of the bedroom is an elderly man in a tux. He fiddles with his cuffs as if he's nervous and it makes him sort of boyish.

"Teddy, this is Angelica, Matchmaker to the Gods." I'm speechless. She turns and takes my hands in hers. "I couldn't say anything till I was sure he'd make it. It was the hardest secret to hold from the one person I wanted to tell."

Then she holds out a hand to him and I step back. As he approaches, Guppy seems to get younger and so does he. By the time they embrace, they're the age they were in the photo. It breaks my heart for her.

"Where were you?"

"Angelica, that's enough."

"She's been waiting decades—"

"Angelica!"

"She's right," says Teddy in this slowly accented voice. "But that's between Genevieve and me. Why don't you go on down to the Ball and we'll see you there."

~ ~ ~

Chris is on reception. The hotel feels like a ghost ship, decorated for a party that will never happen. Course I'm exaggerating again. There are a few punters left in the bar but everyone else is in the ballroom.

Except for Mum.

"I can look after the desk if you like?"

"Not really in the mood, Mouse, but thank you." When Grace arrives, he shoos us out the door. If Mum were a princess, he'd be the dragon guarding the gate.

"Don't worry, I have my instructions. If a man shows with a rose in his lapel, I'll tell him to wait in the bar and call her down."

~~~

The Ball is exactly as I imagined it should be: an enormous roomful of people swirling and flirting and laughing. At the heart of the dance floor, as if they have never been apart, are Guppy and her Teddy.

They seem to be floating on a very elegant cloud.

Jonas is Master of Ceremonies; dressed in a glitter suit that Ms Willow, his fiancée – he uses this phrase at every opportunity – adapted from one of the spaceman costumes he wore to sci-fi conventions. There are so many layers to people that you never see until they fall in love and then you wish you didn't.

Anyway, he's making comments about glamorous couples, couples who won't let go of each other and the aura of love that is filling this ballroom between every song.

"Stop fidgeting," says Grace. "You're making me nervous."

She's right. Absolutely right but it's no use. I can't relax. Mum should be here. It's her Ball and Chris's, more than anyone else's. Only she's hiding in the apartment, sick with nerves. Because of me, she's waiting for a man who may or may not show, who isn't the man she has imagined and who might be a lunatic, while Chris is lurking behind the front desk playing gatekeeper.

Dylan arrives fashionably late and I duck under the table. "Grace, I have to go."

"No way. Trust me, she doesn't want you there. Mums, they like to protect us."

"I should be with her."

Grace catches my arm before I can leave. "You want her to know it's you? You want her to know that NOW?"

She's right. Of course she's right. There's nothing I can do. I'll be really kind in the aftermath. I'll do everything she asks without questioning or moaning and I won't answer back, not until she's okay again.

I will be the best daughter she could imagine.

Just like that, Grace forgets I exist. Tariq is striding towards us. She straightens up, puts on her most cool and nonchalant look. (Think *I've swallowed three frozen hamsters that have just begun to thaw*' and you're close.)

"I knew it. I knew it!"

Only he continues past with a nod to us and invites this Dubliner up to dance. The Dublin guy's hair is weirder than Tariq's or even Grace's Stone Circle hairdo. Think prehistoric jug with cracked veneer and you're close.

"Their hairstyles are from the same historical era," says Grace. "I KNEW I should have got my hair cut. Why'd I let you talk me out of it?"

"One of us making a massive mistake seemed enough. Besides, he looks ridiculous, especially next to Tariq."

"Yeah," says Grace, mollified. "Dubliners are weird. I mean, on Tariq, it'd probably be okay." She draws my eye to the entrance as Mum enters, holding on to Chris's arm and seeming to glow. "See? She's fine." Mum has a word for everyone as she moves through the room. "Don't know what you were worrying about," says Grace.

"Course not. So my imagination?"

She combs through her hair with her fingers. "Over-vivid."

"Right."

"Prone to exaggeration." She's enjoying this too much. Mum's flush from all the congratulations but she seeMrs Distracted.

"And panic attacks."

"Enough already." Chris heads to the bar to get her a drink, leaving Mum with Cathie's mum and dad.

"Wait a mo," says Grace, her voice going quieter than a snail's slime in a vortex. "Was Chris my bookworm?"

Grace is freaked. I let her wallow a little before letting her off the hook. "S'alright. He's not wearing a rose."

"Phew."

We both exhale. Because that really wouldn't be right. Dylan wafts over, as if summoned by mischievous genies.

"This time, try to be nice," Grace hisses as he approaches, too near now for me to disappear. "He won't bite. Though there's no guarantee!" Then she's gone, dragging Theo, of all people, onto the dance floor. Strangely, he looks pretty good dressed up.

Dylan, lovely Dylan, takes my hand before I can think of anything clever to say and I'm out in the middle of the dance floor. With a wriggle of his shoulders he peels off his jacket – a la Grease – and reveals a new T-shirt. The whole world and its pet oyster can read: 'Dylan XX Angelica' printed beneath the image of two kissing whales.

"I didn't know whales could."

He grins and a small cheer goes up from his gang as he wraps an arm around my waist and another about my shoulder. I'm in his arms. We're in a ballroom on a dance floor and it's our first dance. This is the sort of moment you're meant to get lost inside, to tell their children that this was when they knew.

Everyone else is busy having fun and falling in love and not noticing us, so it's not even embarrassing. Even Mum doesn't seem to have seen us.

Dylan holds me really gently.

"It's okay. I don't break."

"Is it sore, your back?"

I shake my head. "Maybe sometimes. I have to do stretches n stuff but really, it's just proof that I was born an angel. The wings fell off cos I never got a chance to fly."

"Cool," he says.

That's when I twig it. All that looking around and smiling that Mum was doing. I know the way she can paste on a smile. I've seen it time and again when she's had to deal with boring guests. She was looking for Rick.

And now she's gone again.

Chris passes us with glasses of wine, looking for Mum among the dancers.

I spin Dylan round, trying to see where she is now and spot Chris taking up position near the Ladies. He's wasting his time. I'd bet you a dozen slow songs that Mum is wandering somewhere, away from all these happy couples, feeling stupid. Or sitting in the dark in our apartment feeling like a wet cloud.

"Sorry. I have to go."

"Again?" Dylan doesn't understand. "Why?"

"Just—"

"Who are you, Cinderella?"

"Sorry." He looks embarrassed. "The loo. In the apartment. Loo here is yuck."

"You'll be back, right?"

Chapter 49

Mum's in the office, which is better than out windsurfing, but she's mumbling, "Seven, eight, nine and ten, then I let him go again."

I'm about to go in when Chris appears. Rather than be caught spying, I duck under the counter.

"Private party or are you drinking with invisible leprechauns?"

"Nah," says Mum. "Sure even they've partnered up. Leprechauns, psychos, predatory pixies. The whole entire world and misfits of every generation have paired up, regardless of—" She gives a bitter laugh, "Facial hair. Look, even your whales have paired up. See."

She's right, but that was me, weeks ago. Seemed like a good idea at the time. The office is in the Feng Shui space of the lobby that means romance and relationships.

"I'm deleting every email the coward sent me."

I was trying help.

"What am I like, Chris? All dressed up and nowhere to go."

"You have a Ball to go to. *Your* Ball. Everyone's wondering where you went."

"I can't. I'm sorry. I'd completely forgotten how it feels, waiting to be stood up!"

Out front, I can hear couples peel across the lawn, disappearing into the darkness for privacy or to witness the witchiness of the sea. I wish I'd stayed at the dance.

Grace was right, there's nothing I can do and now I'm trapped. Chris left the office door open so to get anywhere, I have to crawl past or try nudging it closed and hope they don't notice while I make a dash for the exit.

Chances are that would be the moment Mum's date would arrive, having stopped to help a family in need at the side of the road. He'd actually be nice and they'd fall in love. Then, if they got together, I'd be like this weird girl-child forever that he first saw crawling out from under the front desk of this hotel.

Meanwhile, Mum's sat in the office, trying to understand what went wrong. "It shouldn't be this hard!"

"I know."

"What if he did show up, Chris? What if he came here, took one look at me and fled? Silly old cow, she's not sexy or beautiful or desirable."

"I wouldn't say that."

"You know what I said in my stupid emails? I want someone to love me, to love being in love with me." She shoots each email dead with a precise finger. "Mind you, what I said in my last few emails might have been enough to scare anyone off."

I agree, reluctantly.

"Not going to find love on the other side of a computer screen. Am I? Angelica was right. She tried to warn me not to expect too much."

I want to leave. I want to be deaf. I want those furry ear flaps to block out her voice or fly me through the air like fluffy cormorants. I'd even settle for a deep meaningful conversation with the front desk, one of Guppy's fliers or the woodworms that have to be residing somewhere nearby.

I'm about to risk making a *door nudge-crawl-dash* for the stairs when the reception bell goes on the desk above my head. I peep through a gap in the wood – there are lots, it's an old counter, here from when the hotel was built, but all I see is darkness until the man moves away.

A really tall angular man, sort of lopsided, with grey hair.

"I'll get rid of them," says Chris, leaving the office. I make myself small and invisible under the darkest corner of the desk.

The man drifts, picking things up and putting them down. Chris doesn't like him. You can tell by the way he rests his hands on the desk above my head and waits for the stranger to turn before offering assistance.

The man points at the restaurant menu. "Halibut," he says, approaching the desk. "It has one 't'."

"Can I help you?" says Chris.

"Oh, yes. Hope so. I was meant to meet someone in the lobby an hour ago. Maybe she left a message for me?"

His accent is English; not London but somewhere northerly and a rosebud sticks out of his lapel pocket. The tiniest thing, more like a ketchup stain, but definitely a rose.

"Try the ballroom, around the corner."

"Thanks." The man picks up his bag.

"But I'd say you're wasting your time."

"I beg your pardon?"

What's Chris up to? Just let the man go!

"Drisogue women don't wait an hour for no-shows."

"Around the corner?"

"Can't miss it. Big ballroom. Lots of lights. Music." Chris opens the door to release the man back into the wild before adding, "The Donegal-Spanish variety of halibut has two 't's. Very distinctive taste."

Mum chooses this moment, Chris's last word, to emerge from the office with an empty whiskey bottle. "We need a refill," she says, heading to the lounge. Then something odd happens. She stops and stares at the stranger.

Even odder, he stares back. "Still knocking back the booze?"

Okay, this is weird.

"Still passing comment?"

What is going on? Mum hands the empty bottle to Chris and walks across to stand face-to-face with this man. After a moment they hug, awkwardly.

"God, Molly, you look fantastic!" Mum has spotted the rosebud. He shrugs. "I had a date—"

She fetches hers from behind the counter. "So did I."

The man moves in closer. "No wonder I felt I knew you."

"You don't," says Mum, taking a step back.

"No. I don't."

What is going on? I crawl out from my hiding place holding a festival brochure, as if I'd just bent down to pick it up off the floor. "Mum?"

"Angelica," she says, taking a deep breath.

"You know him?"

She nods, slowly and beckons me over. "This is Jeremy Cummins."

What? What's she saying? She wraps her arm around my shoulders, finally taking her eyes off the stranger.

"Your dad."

Chapter 50

"Why did you say he say he was dead?"

Mum looks out through the window, the way she does when she's lost in thought. Maybe it's regret. Maybe she gets lost in regret.

"It seemed easier," she says at last; in a small voice, monotone and grey. Her body feels heavy sitting on the edge of my bed. I never noticed this before.

But this isn't good enough. You do not tell your child her father is dead for fourteen years and then casually introduce them in a hotel lobby!

"Did he even make films?"

She shrugs, a tiny one. "Commercials. Infomercials. Industrial. Shipping companies. *Health and Safety On Oil Rigs.*"

Brilliant. She romanticised him too. I guess, him being 'dead' and all, she could make him into whatever she wanted.

"I didn't want you to feel rejected. I didn't want his rejection of you to be the first thing you knew."

Great, rejected twice in one sentence.

Way to rub it in, Mum.

"You were always making up romantic stories about him. One day I said, why not? Why not let her think he was something amazing and he didn't merely abandon us both."

Abandonment too. Why not add, as an aside, that he was a serial killer and have done?

"So it's my fault."

"No! Look, Angelica. I always meant to tell you the truth—"

"When, Mum?" I'm sitting up now, my back scooched into the corner. "What if I'd wanted to find him? Would you have even told me he was alive if he hadn't turned up? What if he'd looked for me? Would you have told me then?" I turn off the bedside lamp and slide down in the bed. "You had no right!"

Interview terminé.

I pull my duvet up to my chin and stare at this long tear in the wallpaper. I made it when I was eight and looking for secret maps everywhere. So many things are ricocheting around my head. You're meant to meet boyfriends and princes at balls.

You are NOT meant to meet your DAD for the first time.

Mum doesn't move. Not for ages. When she does finally, it's to stroke the hair from my face. I slide under the duvet before she can kiss my head. As I said, it's a busy and very full head right now and it does not need a kiss as well.

"I told you before – that I never meant for you not to have a dad," she says before getting up to leave.

I remain under the duvet. It's surprisingly comforting, like a warm nest. "He won't just disappear?"

"I suspect it depends on you."

Great. No pressure so.

"Anything else you want to know?"

How can she ask that!

HOW can she ask that?

ON KNOWING WHEN TO BE SILENT

A pause before answering makes people feel that you are actually thinking about your answer.

Result: you come across as intelligent, even if you are:

a) Only trying to figure out how to respond to such a stupid question;

b) So tired you've forgotten how your lips work or

c) You weren't listening and now have to figure out an answer that hides this from them.

A pause within an argument allows you to calm down. Losing your temper doesn't win arguments. This is the moment to count to ten. (I haven't made it past six yet but I'm a Work in Progress, says Chris.)

When being asked if you overheard or did something you were not supposed to do, always pause before answering. This allows you time to gauge from their 'waiting expression' if they are hoping you heard (or did whatever you did) so that they can launch into an interesting discussion about whether it's better to lie in the interests of national security and world peace.

Exception: if the subject is embarrassing and you do NOT want to talk about it at any cost.

Another good time to be silent is when you don't know what to say.

Like now.

Chapter 51

I can't sleep.

The music drifts up from the open ballroom doors and the hotel fills with chatter as tipsy couples start searching for their rooms. Feeling every bit as clever as an underdone stew, I last a full ten minutes before I throw on my dressing gown and creep downstairs to the kitchen.

Might as well eat something as lie in bed awake and hungry.

Low voices in the dining room. Guests shouldn't be in here at night but I ignore them. Bigger things, as they say, going on in my head. I'm scooping hot chocolate into a big mug of milk when Mum's voice makes me hit the spoon off the rim and spill it all over the counter.

"Seriously! *That's* your excuse? You didn't know what you were doing? And you think I did?" She's talking to him in the empty restaurant. "You're saying you didn't receive the photos I sent you. I've just had my daughter in tears because a dad she never knew, who abandoned her, decides to show up. Right now, she's probably crying herself to sleep."

"I didn't know it was you, I swear. I mean, how did you even end up here? It's the tail end of nowhere."

"Oh I guess I wanted to have time to myself or maybe I had to make a living to support my daughter; the child we had together before you ran away?"

"Point taken."

"Drisogue is an incredibly magical, beautiful and safe place for a child to grow up in."

"Okay. I got it."

The lawn outside is full of couples snogging and dancing and even one guy throwing up what sounds like 17 hairless aliens. Magical, maybe. Beautiful?

Her voice starts again, with a shake in it. "Let me get this straight." I can hear her heels pacing the parquet. "You had absolutely no intention of ever looking us up?"

"It didn't seem fair."

"Abandoning your daughter was?"

"Look, I joined a dating site. Don't ask why but I did. Impulse. I'm tired of being alone, Molly."

"You weren't fourteen years ago."

"So I've changed."

"Grown up?"

"Maybe." It sits there, her sarcasm, in the room between them. "I met an interesting woman so I came to see her. If you want me to leave, I will."

"You really are a coward."

She's talking quietly. I have to push the door open ever so slightly more to hear what she says next. Then I wish I hadn't.

"I rang your office," she says at last. "All your obnoxious friends. I rang your home. Let your mother hang up on me time after time. Oh and your ex-girlfriend. I did EVERYTHING in my power to try and find you." Long pause. "For her sake. Not mine."

I can hear her pushing chairs under tables, readying the room for breakfast; keeping physically busy, which is what she does when she's upset and can't get near the sea.

"For the daughter that, even as it galled me to say it then, was 'ours'. I was fully prepared to say, okay, maybe not now, but when you're ready, if you want to be part of her life. You MUST have known!"

Through the door, I can make Jeremy out. He's sitting side on to me, head in his hands. He looks up slowly. "What did you tell Angie?" he says, his voice so low I nearly miss it.

"Her name's Angelica."

I can hear him smile. Yeah, it's ridiculous but there's something about the pause he leaves before he looks up at Mum. "Tell her I was a hotshot director?"

"I said you were dead. Why did you call yourself Rick?"

"Rick? I—"

He hesitates and I hold my breath.

"What does that matter now?"

"I'd like to know."

So would I, because he wasn't. Rick was me. The man who corresponded with Grace called himself Frank.

"That film you loved. Casablanca."

So he can think fast too. And lie. Why am I not surprised?

"Even though you hated sad endings, that was the exception.. Didn't you say, if you had a boy, that Rick was the name you wanted? Guess I was hoping it might be you."

He still loves her. Or has remembered that he loved her, which is something of the same. Mum hasn't booted him out. She hasn't shouted or said she hates him for abandoning us. She still has feelings for this man? But, of course; it all makes sense. I was right – even if I had the wrong reason.

My dad IS the reason she couldn't move on.

Because he wasn't dead.

"Why don't you go in?"

Chris. Has he been listening too? I don't trust myself to speak so I shake my head and move away from the door, but the tears come anyway.

"Come on." He wraps an arm around my shoulders, leading me to the staffroom at the back of the kitchen. "Let's leave them to it. What you need now is?"

"Hot chocolate."

"Exactly." He sits me down on the old sofa. "With cream, marshmallow, cinnamon, chocolate stars, a swirl of caramel dripped into the heart of the steamed milk." Chris makes the world's best hot chocolates, with real cooking chocolate and cream, all frothed up with marshmallows and in a tall glass, dressed up like a cocktail.

"Do you like him?" he says, placing his creation in front of me alongside a slice of chocolate cake cut into the shape of a small brown whale and pulling up a chair.

"Course." I stir the hot chocolate to combine all the flavours. Normally I taste each part separately, but tonight I'm too mixed up. "He's my dad."

"This is me, Mouse."

And he really means it. So exactly when I thought I couldn't talk, not about this or anything, suddenly there I am blurting it all out.

"It's like every school trip, they say, '*Get the permission of both your parents*'. Father's Day we have to make cards. It's not like I can miss something I never had, but it'd be handy. Y'know, for lifts and stuff."

I can't seem to stop.

"There's this part of me that wants to shut people out sometimes, push Mum away, only I can't because I'm all Mum has. Now I'm not, am I? There's this man called Jeremy who says he's my dad, which means he dumped us both and I'm meant to care that he's shown up now?"

And then I'm back in his best-of-the-world bear hug.

"There might have been lots of reasons why he vanished, Mouse."

Chapter 52

The sun glimmers on the sea. Gulls duck and dive for fish the festivals' whale-watching flotilla might have concussed. Fast food. The wind has a chill factor of enough to make me pull my scarf around the back of my head to protect my ears.

April, in Drisogue. A normal Sunday. And yet, so not.

"I tried really hard to reach him, Angel. To tell him all about you, offer him choices to make sure he knew you and you knew him."

I can't say, '*I know. I overheard*', so I say nothing.

Mum asked Chris to look after the hotel so we could spend time together and work it all out. Work everything out. Life, the meaning of the universe and what happens next.

It's not going great so far.

Jeremy is farther down the beach. Farther – Father – get it? It's such a loaded word. He was the farthest father I could have had, being dead, but now? Mum has told him to keep his distance until I indicate I'm ready.

"Looking at you every day. Seeing him in you and knowing he wanted nothing to do with you. Or me. Loving you so much, it broke my heart."

Most people try to skim stones on the surface. Chris can make them go farther than anyone I know but Jeremy, he's bombarding the sea with missiles as if punishing the waves.

"After a year, I stopped trying to contact him," says Mum. She's watching him too and watching me watching him. "He clearly wasn't good enough for you. If I was on my own, then that had to be enough for both of us."

Jeremy throws just like I do.

Every so often he looks across as if he's nervous, wondering what my verdict will be.

"Did he even see me when I was born?"

Mum shakes her head, slowly. We walk on.

"D'you think he's changed?"

"We all have, I guess. I mean, you're not a poopy baby anymore."

I can't take my eyes off him. I'm half this man and that is really weird. I probably didn't get enough sleep last night. It seems forever since I did.

"I know this is so much for you to take in and I'm really sorry, Angel. For all of it."

What can I say? The gulls are steering clear of Jeremy, in case he throws his missiles upwards instead of down. Mum, she watches me watching.

"He has offered to take next week off work, if you want him to stay. Kitty says he can stay on in his room at the pub, so we would have some space. Would you like him to stay for a while, now that he's here? Give you a chance to talk. Or you can take some time to think about it all first and we can contact him when you're ready."

I shrug but I'm excited too, even though I know I shouldn't be. He isn't someone I should make a fuss about meeting – but he's there. For real. My REAL dad.

Not dead.

Not whale bait.

Not a famous film director.

"Okay," I say, casual as I can and gaze out to sea. "It's okay if he wants to stay a bit."

~ ~ ~

Mum decides it would be a good idea for me to pull out a few pictures from my childhood to show Jeremy. It might help us both "to bridge the gap" but I think she's still trying to work it all out. I mean, she last saw this guy that she loved when she was pregnant with me.

How can she still have feelings for him after what he did?

I daren't ask. Not yet anyway. She'll only say wait till you've experienced it and then you can judge. But I can judge. He was my dad and she was my mum. He should have been there for her.

"Not that one. I look like a pickle."

"Nonsense," she says. "You were a beautiful baby." She takes it from me while I root around for a better one.

How many teens get the opportunity to reinvent their childhood as idyllic and golden, with only the attractive pics left in. Suddenly, I'm not sure I want to give him any of our past.

"He only gets to look, right? He's not taking the photos with him."

"Course not," she says.

"I don't want him just getting my past when he wasn't here."

"I know."

"A sad and fat pickle." I put it back in the album, right at the back. "And not that one either."

"Ah no, we have to show him your tooth fairy dress!"

"We don't HAVE to show him anything."

I know he's right there behind me and I want him to hear every word.

"It's not as if he has earned the right to play catch-up. It's not as if something kept him away that was urgent or life-threatening. Did he have to protect us from drug overlords or stop a flood or save the world? I know, maybe he lost his memory or got imprisoned by terrorists or gorillas?" My rage is spent. "It's not as if he ever meant to find us."

"It's okay, Angel." Mum tries to hug me but I don't even want to be touched.

"No. It's not. He gets you pregnant and leaves without a word. Doesn't even send money or keep in touch to see if you're alright. Wait – when did he leave? Was it right at the end or in the middle?"

"He brought me to the hospital. Said he'd go park up—"

"So he didn't even want to know if I lived! If I was a boy or a girl?"

That's when his shadow falls across the pictures and his voice says quietly, "I was a coward." He kneels beside me and offers me a silver necklace with a rather sorrowful pendant of a teddy-bear.

This is awkward.

"I don't want a stupid necklace."

"Angelica."

"No. She's right. You want answers, not gifts, right?"

I shrug. He has a bald patch. It looks as if someone stuck a star-shaped chewing gum on his head and pulled it off quickly.

"I convinced myself you couldn't be mine." He picks up a photo, staring at it; then another. "That I was too young to be saddled with a child." He can't look me in the eye. "I knew that if I never saw you, I couldn't fall in love with you. You'd always be 'just' a child."

He takes my hands and studies them. "It was the biggest mistake I ever made."

They're hands is all; just ordinary hands.

"Look. I can't buy you your first teddy or see you throw your first tantrum."

He looks so completely lost that for a moment, a single moment, I feel sorry for him. He has missed out on the entire life of his child, me. I pick up the necklace. I'd have loved it, maybe, when I was six.

"I threw good tantrums."

"I didn't plan this but I know how incredibly lucky I've been to find you. Would I have had the courage to seek you out? No. I wouldn't. So I realise I don't deserve to get to know you now. "But I'm here. If that's what you—" He looks past me then, at Mum. "What you and your mother want. I have no right to be here. I know that." Then he looks me right in the eyes for the longest minute.

Which is when I find myself in his arms. The arms of my dead dad. They feel surprisingly warm.

Strange.

I wasn't planning that.

"Why don't you both take a walk along the beach?" says Mum.

Chapter 53

I get the feeling Jeremy doesn't 'do' beaches very often, despite his fictional demise taking place on one. He keeps taking his shoes off to empty out sand while asking lots of questions about me growing up, favourite books and music and what I want to be. The weather is starting to change, so when he suggests a hot chocolate in town, I agree.

"Where were you when I was born?"

"Shooting an informational video for Greenpeace. I think it was for their anti-whaling campaign."

Which is good. He was on the right side. Explains where Mum got the whale from.

"Did you two-time Mum, were you married or are you married now?"

"No to all three."

I'm getting the questions in before I have to decide if I like him or not.

"Do you have other kids? Did you have a dog? Why didn't you want to be with Mum?"

"No, not really and I don't know. It was complicated. We didn't really know each other for very long."

Before I can point out he knew her well enough to get her pregnant, he corrects himself.

"No, really, I have no reason except I wasn't mature enough to accept the responsibility. I guess I was scared, so I blocked it all out. You, Molly, the pregnancy; to my eternal shame. I had a dog called Sneeze when I was little.

251

He was photophobic. Sunshine made him sneeze."

I feel awkward walking beside him; my steps are all considered and misplaced so I watch what's going on instead. The town is living on last night's buzz; was the Ball only last night? Full Irish breakfasts are still being served outside pubs for the 3pm risers as we stroll through. Blushing couples emerge from doorways like vampires to lick the scent off the day and see if it is all real.

The strange thing is finding out what Jeremy and I have in common. We both like inventing stuff and we both see things that aren't there, even if he says he only sees them in his head so he can put them on screen in a pitch while I see them for real. He says he loves Christmas, likes making up recipes and puts chocolate in his porridge, with cream and cornflakes.

Which, you have to admit, is a pretty weird coincidence.

I introduce him to Simon, Brenda and Fr Lefarge – basically everyone I meet. Despite the whole thing about him not being Rick and everything I said before this, I want them all to see I have a dad. It's a bit difficult to explain why I thought he'd been swallowed by a whale, but he's very patient, shakes everyone's hand and says he's a lucky man.

Of course I tell them all he's been abroad; very far away.

Deepest Asia.

Under sea.

Africa.

"That's why we thought he was dead."

Then it's back to the hotel and busy with the remains of the festival until everyone finally goes home. Or hibernates and pretends they're home.

The clean-up proper will begin tomorrow.

~~~

You'd think the school would be glad to let us all have Monday off to recover, given how much we contributed to the festival, but no. The teachers seem to have communally panicked at so much time being lost, so Monday is a crazy day of catching up and complaining about the immense tip of homework they feel obliged to drop on our heads. It's not until the bell goes at ten to four that it all hits home.

I have a dad.

Dylan hovers by the bus so we can board together. I realise I can go out with him now. Mum's going steady, if her history with Dad counts. I'm turning left out of the gate towards him, looking all shy because it seems this is where everything gets serious so I might as well make the moment momentous, when Jeremy's car cuts me off. The passenger door opens.

Without even thinking about it, I hop in and he drives off.

Well, it's a lift and lifts are better than school buses on these roads, aren't they? I ask him to stop then so we can go back and offer Dylan a lift. "He was waiting for me."

"There isn't time. I've booked this lovely restaurant but it's an hour away and if that boy really is your friend, he'll understand that you want to spend time with your father."

"His name is Dylan." I say.

Father, I think. It sounds heavy and sort of presumptuous. I try not to think about how Grace felt when Marcus acted like this. Marcus wasn't genetically related. As for her own Dad… Jeremy drops me outside the hotel so I can go change while he parks up. Mum's at the desk, handing over the reins to Chris.

When I come back down ready to go out, Chris is hanging up the new menu but he's watching Mum and Jeremy out front by the car. Mum's laughing. How can he make her laugh so quickly?

"I think I spotted a humpback this morning," he says. "Must have followed the mackerel over. Want to come up with your binoculars and See if we can spot him?"

"We're going out for dinner," I say. "Maybe tomorrow?"

"Sure."

It's odd. Maybe it's that Jeremy is so tall and straight but Chris seems to have shrunk, ever so slightly. He's also taken the second 't' off *'halibut'* in the menu.

"Is this the Big Love of her Life?" he says.

I nod. He must be, because she never got over him. She only imagined him dead in the belly of a whale because she missed him so.

"Nice necklace," he says.

PRESENT-GIVING, THE RULES

People often lie when they accept gifts. These are generally little fibs to make the giver feel better. Let these fibs stand, believe you chose your gift incredibly well until they present you with something very similar the following year.

This is because people generally give gifts that they would like to receive. Follow this and you'll cause intense joy. One exception to this rule: if you get smelly soaps shaped like cherubs, it is possible they were unwanted pressies from an elderly aunt last year.

It doesn't matter what you spend on a pressie if it's something to show that you know what we are interested in but, failing that, chocolate and money go down well for teens. Lots of chocolate and lots of money are even better. Do not buy us socks or underpants. That's just wrong.

"Isn't that your maintenance man?" says Jeremy, as we drive home past Kitty's pub. I am in the back seat carrying food triplets, sated and sleepy. (Me, not the food babies; they're gurgling.) The food was exceptionally good but the toffee ice-cream sundae might have been too much.

"Hard to tell," says Mum, looking away.

But it isn't. Even if they weren't kind of boxed in a corner talking so close by the back door of the pub.

Chris and Kitty.

Okay. Makes sense. I'm happy for them. It's good that everyone is finally finding someone.

So why doesn't it feel right?

Chapter 54

The cupids are back in their boxes ready for storage by the time I return from school next day. They look sort of plaintive when they're all stuffed in together without a pedestal in sight.

"Throw them out," says Mum.

"Come on," says Chris. "You can't deny they brought us luck. Especially you, since they brought the wonderful Jeremy back into your life."

"I said I want rid. Unless, of course, Kitty could find some use for them."

"At least she doesn't pretend to be someone she isn't."

"And what exactly does that mean?"

"Stop it! Stop fighting." They both freeze, like dummies. "They're just crummy decorations!" I'm heading upstairs so they won't see I'm upset when Jeremy arrives on the scene. He takes one look at me, puts an arm around Mum and gives the box a kick.

"Dump them, I say. What do you think, Angel?"

And yes, I should say, "*Let's leave them in the attic*" or, "*Can't we decide later,*" but I shrug and stomp upstairs instead.

~~~

Onni's friends leave with all their footage, promising to send Chris and Mum a rough cut as soon as possible but everyone's too tired here to think about the festival anymore. Jeremy settles right in, like a small tidy clam, asking Mum all about the hotel and catching up on our lives.

They talk for hours after I go to bed, but sometimes there are long pauses and I don't know if they've run out of stuff to say or there's some serious snogging going on. I don't really want to know either. He's my dad. She's my mum.

This is how it was meant to be.

Most evenings, he and I talk and walk. These walks felt really awkward at first. Formal. No great meeting of minds. It's not as if we have a huge amount of conversations to pick up on. As for their relationship, he tells me about how he met Mum and how they about danced all night.

Stories I already know, so they probably don't count.

But that's okay.

He asks fewer questions as the week rolls on and it's not as if I have to answer.

Sometimes I shrug and he doesn't follow through; I'm not even sure he wants to know the answers. Chris says he's probably just happy spending time with me. But I really haven't an answer when he says he wishes he'd had the courage to have been there for us, even if he would have been a lousy dad.

Because his dad was.

"A very lousy dad."

~~~

"It's a reason," says Chris, in his balanced voice. "Definitely a reason. But it wouldn't have kept me away."

I wish I hadn't told Dylan that Mum was serious about me not going out midweek. Just when we're at the point when I can actually go out with him, he's never around. I wanted to introduce him to Jeremy but he's always working in the cafe or Compton's. Except in school and then always in a gaggle of people and everybody too busy catching up with stuff to have any time to linger, even at lunchtime. Why can't I bump into him alone now, like I did months ago? Jeremy says he understands and "I'm sure he's a very nice boy".

Because he's not used to parenting, I'm letting him away with his choice of words.

~ ~ ~

Homework has been oddly focused all week.

In Business Studies, we've to analyse the festival and construct a strategy for next year; in English, we've to write about the festival from the viewpoint of a person living a hundred years from now. "What would seem quaint, outdated? What would you misunderstand or misinterpret a century from now," says Mr Quinn.

"Theo," says Cathie.

Grace has said straight out that she doesn't want to meet Jeremy. "You're making it too easy for him and he doesn't deserve it. I don't see why you haven't just had it out with him or, better still, buried him up to his neck on the beach and wait for the tide to come in?"

And yes, part of me knows she's right, though not about the sand thing. But the other part of me wants to dance and sing and cling to his arm and have piggybacks and get thrown in the air and eat ice cream till I'm sick.

I like having a dad and I don't see why I should have to apologise to anyone.

Mum gets it. I catch her looking at us together with this sideways tilt of her head. All she'll say is that she always knew he could have been a good dad. "It made me sad to see you growing up without him, despite everything."

Guppy's reserving judgement.

She says it's nice to see us so happy but really her focus is on making up for lost time with Teddy. You can't blame her. She's waited so long. It puts everything in perspective. Jeremy's missed fourteen years with me but at least he hasn't missed forty-six.

I heard her giving out to him the other day. He'd made the mistake of wishing aloud that he had been here for something and she laid into him.

"Are you and Teddy fighting?"

"Just clearing the air," said Guppy. "Secrets and lies can poison a relationship."

~ ~ ~

On Friday, in Religion, we have to assess the implications – moral, ecumenical and social – of the festival. "Now pair up." Ms Willow has been entirely able to continue being the most irritating teacher despite being love-soaked the rest of the time. "Theo with Jack. Angelica with Grace—"

Grace's hand shoots up. "Rather be with Denise, if that's okay."

She doesn't even LIKE Denise so I know she is seriously mad at me.

~~~

Saturday morning. I'm waiting on the wall outside Dolan's for Jeremy. I can call him Dad in my head but not out loud. Whatever he's buying at the florists, it's taking forever. Dunno why I had to come down with him. He could have picked me up after he was done. Saturdays are for lie-ins; he really doesn't know parenting at all.

And now it's starting to drizzle.

"Nobody buys that many flowers unless it's for a funeral." Grace lands in beside me. "Who's he planning to kill? His wife?"

"Funny ha ha."

The florists is attached to the undertakers because both businesses are run by Big Brenda's sister Megan, who has already buried three husbands though I dunno how she got one because she is SCARY.

"He is such a creep."

"That's my dad you're talking about."

"In name. I mean, what did he ever do for your mum except, well, the obvious? And then he pissed off for, like, ever."

"There were reasons."

She makes a huffing sound like she's trying to hold something in but then decides to let it out: "Always are. Men are SO good at reasons." She flicks moss off the wall, aiming for a puddle to our left. "You could get rid of him easily. Just tell your mum he was writing to me."

"And explain that I knew you were on a dating website talking to a man in his forties?"

"Easy, Licky Moone! It was just an idea to get you out of your self-destructive loop."

"I don't want to get rid of him."

"Look, I know he's your dad and some of his genes must be alright—"

"No, Grace. Enough!" I'm standing now, every bone at attention. "Why can't you be happy for me?"

"I am, but—"

"You don't even know him."

She doesn't say anything, which winds me up more.

"He's warm and funny and he really cares for Mum. He's trying to make up for not being there for us."

"Whatever."

"Just because I have a dad! Get used to it because he's staying and not because Mum puts out."

She's about to say something but then she picks herself up off the wall, looks at me and leaves. Jeremy arrives alongside before I can go after her and I'm not sure I want to anyway. She has no idea what it's like to have never ever had a dad and then to find you do and he's okay.

"Hi Angel. So, want to show me some more whales?"

"Sure."

He follows my eyes to where Grace joins up with Dylan and some others outside Simon's cafe. "Unless you want to hang out with your friends?"

"Whales are good."

"Penny for them," he says as we move off.

I shake my head.

Chapter 55

Chris is on the shore line, foraging. Most of his amulets were sold over the weekend. He must be replenishing his stock of raw materials.

"What's he doing?" says Jeremy. "Collecting lumps of rock?"

"Yeah."

Well he is. It's what he does.

Jeremy doesn't ask me what Chris does with the rocks. I don't get to explain that he carves them into whales. He asks instead about what I want to do after school, if I've thought of a career.

Again.

"I have homework."

"Can't it wait, munchkin."

That does it. I have to get home. "Not really."

I should have stayed in bed.

~ ~ ~

The following day, Mum calls me for breakfast. It's not often we get to breakfast together on a Sunday, but we had no guests in the hotel last night so she's making coffee and cinnamon toast in the apartment and her phone is turned off on the table. "Oh so that's what you look like. It's been so long."

I growl. It's a primitive response but she's used to it.

"Jeremy had to go back to Dublin suddenly, but he'll be back down on Friday," she says. "Then he's taking a few days off next week because he says this is more important to him now than anything."

But if it is, why did he leave without saying goodbye?

"So, I'm thinking, girls' night in tonight? Long overdue, what with all the chaos of the last few months. What d'you fancy?"

"Dunno. Embroidering vests with broken skulls?"

"I was thinking tattoos."

"With my name or Jeremy's?"

"Oh yours, of course. Seriously, Angel, you want to go out on Mr Ganly's boat? see if we can spot some whales?"

"Can Chris come too?"

"The point is for us to spend time together, love. We've been having quite a hectic time, you and I."

"But Chris knows everything about whales. He could tell us where to go."

We settle for pizza and watch Casablanca.

~~~

On Monday, I walk down the bus determined to sort things out with Grace. I hate not being friends. But what does she do as I approach? She hefts her schoolbag up onto the seat beside her and stares out the window.

I have no choice but to walk past her to the back of the bus and sit beside Theo.

At least he's never liked me, so nothing has changed there. He smells of aftershave but lets me sit down. For the rest of the week, I sit in the first free seat up front. Easier to get on and off without being ignored by Grace. Even Dylan seems to have someone beside him all the time and when we sit nearby, he seems to get distracted by some conversation and we never get to actually talk.

Weirder yet is still to come.

Friday evening, I'm looking forward to Jeremy being back down or, if he takes Mum out, to hiding in my room. I arrive home, full of weariness and swamped by how unnecessarily difficult things are and how unfair and step into an extravagance of roses. The lobby and front desk overflow with bunches of them and the scent is pretty oppressive.

Jeremy, my biological father, is down on one knee right in the middle of them.

He's kneeling in front of Mum.

Mum, who doesn't like roses and never has. She may even be a teensie bit allergic to them, though Chris and I think that's all in her mind.

"I'm not proud of what I did. I look at Angie – sorry! Angelica and you. I've wasted so much time." He seems short of words.

Oh, God! I make myself invisible. It's easy this time because nobody is looking at me or for me or has even remembered I always come home around this time.

I can see her thinking. The roses can see her thinking, she's taking so long. His knee must be beginning to ache.

"Jeremy–," she says at last. Which is his name but doesn't really give much away.

"If you'll have me, I will try to make it up to you and to her for the rest of my life."

Cue Chris, all dishevelled and holding a cracked tile. "Molly, I need a word!"

"Give us a minute?" says Mum, to Jeremy.

He doesn't look happy at being left on one knee in a field of roses. I'm guessing he doesn't like them much either but is trying to be romantic. Roses are what older men do when they're trying to be romantic.

As she moves over to Chris, he gets to his feet. "Hope you're not going to hassle my fiancée for a raise," he says. "I mean, some of the work here is pretty shabby."

"Jeremy, it's my hotel," says Mum.

"Sure, Pumpkin." He kisses her cheek and moves away; only not too far away.

"Pumpkin??" says Chris. Mum does not look like someone you call 'Pumpkin'. She avoids his eyes.

"Chris, you wanted something?"

"That date. I – we… Fiancée?"

"I—" Mum looks at Jeremy, then spots me pretending not to listen. My invisibility cloak no longer operates at full strength; I must have had a growth spurt. She nods without looking at anyone but me and beckons me over.

"Well, yes." She looks at Jeremy and smiles back at me. "Your father and I, we thought we'd give it a go. Be a real family. What do you think?"

What can I say? My mum wants to marry my dad. It's a bit late but if it makes her happy. It's what I wished for when I started the website, so—: "That's great Mum. Jeremy."

Jeremy opens up his arms. "Call me Dad."

I won't.

You can't suddenly call a complete stranger 'Dad', but we can deal with that later. We have a family hug. I can feel Chris's eyes boring into my back but when the hug ends and I look around, the lobby is empty, apart from too many roses.

"Better late than never," I say, as Mum sneezes.

I seem to remember sneezes cancel out good wishes? Still, I had the wish out there before she sneezed, so it's probably alright.

I did not see this coming.

Chapter 56

Normally, I'd have texted Grace immediately or run down to tell her. But after what she said about Jeremy, it's unlikely she'd greet my good news with whole-hearted glee. He wants us all to go out for a celebratory meal in Donegal Town.

I plead a backlog of homework and get to stay put.

I think he was glad to get her to himself anyway because he supported my argument way too persuasively. But I can't stay in the hotel. It's too weird. The scent of roses is everywhere since Mum told Chris to distribute them around the common areas.

Soon as they leave, I head downtown, hoping to bump into someone.

Anyone.

And maybe work out what's going on in my fuzzy little head.

~ ~ ~

Dylan's messing about on the stage with his mates. For some reason it hasn't been demolished yet. Okay, so I'd prefer if he was alone, but at least he's here, so I head across. If I say I need to talk, he'll leave his friends and it'll be okay. He has to be pleased to hear about Mum's engagement. We can go out now for real now and I won't need to see Jeremy so much since he's staying.

I can stop worrying about Mum being alone forever.

I'm still several dead sharks away when I see him put his arm around Denise. Denise!! I stop dead. Frozen, until I'm instantly not. I spin on my clunky little heels as if I never meant to go in his direction at all. But someone in the group must have pointed me out to him because he catches up with me under the festival banner that hasn't come down yet; before I've even tuned in to how I feel enough to cry.

Where Love Begins.

Right.

Dylan stands there scuffing his heels as if I'm meant to say something. HE was the one with his arm around someone else. "Look, Angelica, I can't compete with your mum and your dad. It's your choice."

I don't answer, not trusting my vocal chords to actually work right now. If I did speak, I'd sound like a crow. He hasn't anything else to say and heads back to his gang.

Soul mates. Right.

The pothole cover with the swirly Celtic design by my feet slides open, revealing broad stairs leading down into the abyss I feel. A rat props the pothole open with mega-mouse muscles. *"Come on down,"* she says, in a silky voice. Why do rats have silky voices? All that time underground and in the dark should make them husky. *"It's lovely and warm."*

I walk away without blinking, half hoping the pothole will stay open. Maybe Dylan and his mates will walk this way later and be lost below ground forever.

~ ~ ~

Still, Grace is the one I want to talk to. She's my friend, even if she is judgemental so when I see her outside Dolans on my way back up, it seems like fate wants us to make up. I'd hardly recognise her. She's all done up like Denise. I feel so bad for what I said and how I've treated her. I'm crossing the road when she sees me.

I'm about to wave and see if she waves back, when Denise and half the girls from our class spill from the shop and commingle her down the street towards the Dylanites.

~ ~ ~

What was that about threes?

Good things or miserably, gut-wrenchingly bad? Hmm, let me see. My boyfriend has dumped me – BEFORE he really became my boyfriend. My best friend has turned her back on me and she's the only one I've got and oh, look! There's Chris packing all his worldly goods in to his car.

"Chris?"

He doesn't turn.

"You're going to some sculptors' conference?"

Just carries on packing.

"I know! You got some job down south for a few days? You're going on a holiday? I mean, it's not like you don't seriously deserve one, with the festival and all. A retreat, for artists? To buy a dog, because we really need a dog but can I name him if you do?"

I'm gabbling. See, I know he's leaving and I don't want him to go.

"An elderly relative is ill and needs you. Like you're doing a Jane Eyre, but only for a while. Few days. Max. That's it, isn't it?"

"It's for the best."

What's for the best? Of course! "You're moving in with Kitty, right?"

He shakes his head then, leaning on the car.

"Does Mum know? Because you'd need to say in case Kitty dumps you and you need to come back—"

"Your mother is starting a new life. She has Jeremy." He chokes on the name. "And she has you."

"No." This isn't happening. "Chris. You can't go. You can't leave."

"Jeremy can fix anything that needs doing, apparently. There's no role for me here."

I've heard enough to back off and walk away.

Why does life have to crap on you from a height when you thought things were working out? Why can't anyone just be normal and nice? Not always fighting and not just leaving for no good reason. Why can't they just be there, where they're meant to be?

"Angelica!!"

I don't stop. What's the point? Not like he'll listen to me. Nobody does. Not even my new 'dad'.

I hear Chris's car backfire before I reach the apartment and I know he's gone.

Chapter 57

There's a note pushed under the door of the apartment from Chris. I don't want to see him explain why he's left, because I don't care that he thought he had to leave. I stick it in a drawer and wander the empty hotel. There are traces of him everywhere but I end up in his studio. He was carving all these new pieces and they are achingly beautiful for being only partially drawn out from the stones.

The only finished pieces he left are his whale-twin pendants. I weigh them in the palm of my hand. Rounded and warm from the sun, they may be the most perfect things he's ever made. Since I know he wouldn't walk away without these unless he never meant to return, I slip the chains around my neck so the two whales click together.

Guppy left instructions that she and Teddy were to be left alone but I knock all the same. When she answers, I can't tell her Chris is gone because she looks so happy and sad both at once.

"Is something wrong?"

"Just," I clear my throat and make my voice cheerful. "Wanted to see if you needed anything?"

~ ~ ~

Next morning, Jeremy finds me killing plates in the kitchen. In this foul mood, I'm the fastest kitchen porter in hotel industry even on a Saturday morning when I'd rather be in bed. The plates I wash dry themselves instantly to avoid coming in to contact with my hands a second time.

"Thought we were going out this morning, Angel."

"Chris collects stones from the beach so he can carve them."

"Oh," he says. "Right."

"He makes the most beautiful whales from them." I take off the pendants. "He made these."

He turns them around in his hand, feeling their weight and perfection. "The man has a gift."

"Yeah."

"Angelica?"

"He gave me binoculars when I was eight so I could see the whales properly. His binoculars weighed a ton. I was small, see; didn't start growth-spurting till I was eleven."

"I was the same."

"Which was only three years ago," I'm not interested right now in whatever reminiscences he has to offer. "Chris has always been really protective of us. He took me fishing and he doesn't even like fishing. We get lots of whales here because they like the warmth of the Gulf Stream and that's the coolest name for water because it makes me think of where it's been and it sounds like *gulp*, like the whales are gulping because they've swum so hard to get here. Here, to Drisogue."

I take a deep breath but not so deep it gives him time to jump in.

"He told me, when he handed me my binoculars, 'I've counted seven so far. Aren't they beautiful?'" What am I trying to say? "I'm just saying, you should have been nicer to him."

No. I'm not.

It's too late for that.

"You could have told him to stay. You could still tell him we need him here."

"It's his decision," says Jeremy. "And he's right. There isn't a role for him now."

Brain freeze. It's as if a thunderbolt of pure ice had hit the back of my neck. For a minute I can't breathe or gulp or anything. Then it thaws. I look at Jeremy and it all makes sense. I know what I was trying to say.

I know what I have to do.

~ ~ ~

"Mum! I was looking for you everywhere."

She's making beds but something in my voice makes her stop. "You've been crying."

I shake my head.

She takes my hands. What is it with parents and hands? They're always taking your hands, as if that makes everything okay. As if this shows us that they know best. That they know anything at all – which they DON'T!

"You were meant to be the first person I told about the engagement. It all happened so fast." She fiddles with my fingers. "I mean, I hadn't actually really decided until Chris came barging in and then you were there and I saw it made sense."

Why isn't she making eye contact? Why does her smile feel false?

Why talk about sense when she should be talking about love?

"I'm sorry," she says. "I know it came as a shock."

I pull my hands away. "Chris has left."

"That's his choice," she says. Quietly. And goes back to plumping pillows.

She just doesn't GET it. "No it's not." Sometimes it's as if she is being deliberately dim. "He left because of you."

"Oh Angelica, I know you're very fond of Chris, but—"

"Oh Mum. He loves you. Chris loves you!"

MUMrs DON'T KNOW HOW TO LISTEN

Oh they pretend to, but then so do dogs and cats and seagulls if you have food in your hand. That sounds worse than I meant it to. I'm not saying mums are like cats or dogs or seabirds.

They're much more difficult because you expect them to listen. You want them to hear you, but half the time they don't. Chris says it's the difference between listening and hearing. We're all great at the second; most of us are lousy at the first.

Then there's the interrupting with their own problems or a question. Or the solution to the problem you hadn't even finished explaining, so they get it wrong anyway. And sometimes, we just want to vent, right?

Or talk things over without getting their 'wisdom' in return.

In a romantic film, me saying this to Mum would be enough. She, as the heroine, would rush out of the hotel, steal a motorbike, find her man on the brink of signing his soul over to the Foreign Legion or the Devil and the two would embrace for life. I must have imagined this a thousand times.

Maybe Chris has already broken down by the side of the road so it wouldn't even take her long to find him.

"No," says Mum. "Your father and I—"

"Do you love him?"

"We have you," she says. "And the hotel. He has great ideas about developing—"

Wrong answer.

"It's a building Mum. You can't make choices about who to live with because they like a building! You can't choose who you will be in with on the basis of their relationship to me or because of what you used to feel. Or because it makes sense! You don't even know him, not anymore!"

"What's got into you?"

"Does he make your eyes shine? Or, or your skin? Yeah! Does he make your skin glow?" Come on, think faster! Think faster! Make her listen to you before it's too late! "Does your heart beat faster every time you hear his name?"

Genius.

Mum doesn't seem to be able to answer so I know I'm right. I take off Chris's pendants. "One whale has MM on the back – Molly Moone; the other has CW for Chris Webber and they fit together." She doesn't want to take it but I make her hold it. I wait for Chris's magic to do its work.

"Which is very sweet, but I've made my decision. We're a family, Angel. You, your dad and me." She hands the pendants back but her fingers are shaking. "We should have been from the start and he– *we* both recognise that now."

"Jeremy is not Rick, Mum," I say, quietly. "He can't be."

I have her attention now; her complete and undivided attention. It's pretty scary when you have your mum's complete and undivided attention. Especially when you're about to confess something you know she's going to hate worse than marzipan.

"What do you mean?"

I'm by the window staring as far out to sea as I can, hoping the waves will gift me courage. There's a bare horizon. Nothing for miles. Not even a basking whale.

It's as if they all left with Chris.

"Angelica?"

I'm not being dramatic. Some things are hard to admit. "He can't be Rick because Rick doesn't exist."

Then I walk out. Jeremy is on his way upstairs and I push past.

"Hey! What's the hurry, Munchkin," he says.

I don't respond.

Chapter 58

"One for the flu, two for a cold, three for meningitis and four for being bold."
I fling stones at the Standing Man. Right now, he represents all mankind and
I am my own force nine gale. I know why Jeremy and I throw stones like this.
It feels good.

"Five for a limp, six for pus, seven for the fact that there will never be an
'us'."

"How do you know?"

Of course Mum found me. She always does. This time I needed her to but
still, oh still, at this moment in time, I'd LOVE to be anywhere else; to *be*
anyone else. Only I know it has to end here and now because it has all gone
wrong.

"You had something to do with the website?"

I shrug. Mum's tentative. Probably doesn't want to know the truth either,
not really. She pauses to look around before continuing her inquisition.

"Okay. So. You found it. Is that it? Someone told you about the site and
you thought—?"

"I set it up."

"Okay." She absorbs this incomprehensible fact. "But I was matchmade.
The matches were…"

"Guilty as charged."

"So Rick was Simon? Grace? Chris?"

I shake my head, not trusting myself to speak. I know my voice would be tiny and insufficient.

"You?"

I nod. Mum takes a deep breath. I'm holding mine and staring at my hands. If I could blame them – they did the typing – but I can't. Then, after moments longer than several hells freezing over and opening ice-cream parlours, Mum ups and walks away.

I can't believe it. Doesn't she even want to know why I did it?

"I wanted you to be happy!"

Mum spins so sharp she could have dislocated her hip. "By making someone up? You know more about me than anyone else, Angelica. I can't believe that you would BETRAY my trust like that!"

"Yeah well maybe you shouldn't have lied to me about Dad." It's true. She's not squeaky clean but I still can't look her in the eye. "Maybe I'm my own self, an individual. Maybe I'm tired of you being sad and lonely and alone because what chance have I if that's how you ended up?"

"Didn't realise I was such a burden," she says and walks away.

~ ~ ~

"Give her time. Your Mum will understand." Guppy wraps a velvet throw across my shoulders while Teddy makes me a sweet tea. "It's a bit of a shock, that's all."

I've been walking for hours. I couldn't go to Grace or to the cafe because, well because. Guppy and Teddy found me up near the Marrying Wall or the Wall of Foolish Hopes or whatever it's called now and brought me home to her apartment.

"Your mother will be worried sick by now."

"NO. She won't." Then I told her why. It didn't even faze her.

"You are the most precious thing in this world to her." She folds my hands around the mug of tea. "More than any man, more than any hotel, more than silly fights and websites and imaginary men."

"Chris is gone."

Now Guppy looks as shocked as I feel.

"It's because of my father and me."

"What do you mean 'gone'?"

"I'm sorry. I've messed everything up." But I shouldn't be sat here feeling sorry for myself. I put my mug down on the table. "Oh Guppy, I have to find Mum. Then I'll come back."

~~~

Jeremy is in the lobby. Says he's heading back to Dublin and the wedding is off, all the time watching me to see how I'll react. "What did you say to your mother?"

"Nothing. The truth. Some of it. You should have told her you weren't Rick."

"Yes," he says. "I should."

"I've nothing against you. You're my father and you're a stranger. Like an old friend of Mum's I've never met. I'd like to get to know you better, just not all at once. Maybe we could email and meet for coffee or go to a film and do stuff together but right now, I've got to find Mum. Have you seen her?"

He shakes his head. "Want me to help you look?"

"You could stay here for a bit, in case she comes back. And if she does, keep her here. No matter what."

~~~

Mum's like me. When she's wounded really bad, she needs to be near the sea. I check that her board is still in place, which means she's not playing kamikaze with the waves again. Probably too many people on the beach but it's still a huge relief.

I pick my way around the headland and find her on the Whale's Mount that used to be Wrecker's Rock. When the tide is out, you can walk across this sort of isthmus and climb on top but it's the loneliest place I know. If you close your eyes, even before the tide cuts it off like a mini headland, you can feel the vibrations of the waves crashing into the rock beneath your feet.

For ages, I stand there watching. I don't know what to say to her. But I don't want to make things worse so in the end I follow her out and sit nearby, because silence doesn't work either.

"I never meant for you to get hurt. I just thought if I can do it for everyone else, why not my mum?"

I wish I was seven again. I wish things were less complicated. I wish I was small enough to sit on her lap and be cuddled to sleep.

"You want me to shut it down. I mean, you're right. It was a mistake."

"Not so sure it'd be fair to close it down," she says at last. "It might have saved the hotel."

Does she mean it? I sneak a quick look to see if she's playing with me but she hasn't moved.

"Not to mention the town. Which, let's face it, needs all the help it can get." She lifts up an arm and I snuggle in against her, gratefully. "Promise me one thing."

"Anything."

"No more meddling? No matter how great an idea it seems to be."

I nod. Mum holds out a thumb and I wrap my own around it. This time I'm holding on.

"At least not until you're old enough to face the consequences yourself."

"What about Chris?"

"Let's just work with what we have here and now," says Mum. I'm not exactly in a position to argue.

Before the tide turns, we head back to the hotel and I leave her to talk to Jeremy. They're going to keep in touch. Access to me and such.

Chapter 59

"That nice young man who works here? Who makes the little whales?"

"He doesn't work here anymore," says Mum. "Anything I can do for you?"

With a shake of their heads, they decline. "We liked him, that's all." It must be the tenth time someone has asked about Chris this week. There's a chasm in the hotel where he used to be and it feels wrong. Completely, unfairly wrong.

"Maybe we should try and find out where Chris has gone?" She's uploading pictures from the festival onto our new website. "Lure him back."

A photo comes on screen of Guppy and Chris.

"He made his choice," she says.

~ ~ ~

"Yes, a plumber. As soon as possible, yes."

We have a blocked sink in Rooms 25 and 26 and taps that drip in baths all along that corridor. Chris warned Mum about this. Now is not the time to mention it. I'm getting good at not mentioning things now Mum is as touchy as a Venus flytrap and has entirely lost her sense of humour.

When the contractor's van pulls up, Mum looks sort of disappointed. As if she expected it to be someone else. She retreats into the office as soon as she's shown him to Number 25. Normally she watches tradesmen at work, to learn all she can for fixing the problem herself next time and to make sure she's not overcharged. This time, she tells me to keep an eye on him, but it's half-hearted.

I stay there anyway because I'm not sure she wants me around her either.

The plumber needs to see Mum before he leaves. When I track her down, she's standing in the middle of the store room, holding Chris's overalls to her face as if she's trying to make him real by inhaling his smell.

I slip back and approach noisily, calling out that I'm going down to help Grace with some homework and that the contractor wants her.

"Can't you just ring Grace?" she says.

"No," I say. "It's Maths. She needs hand-holding. I'll be home for tea." I have to fix this.

Somehow.

~ ~ ~

Grace, who still isn't talking to me, grunts when I rush into the bar. "Is your mum in?" Her hair is normal again.

"Wholesalers."

"I really, REALLY need to talk to her."

"Everything not perfect in Paradise then?"

"No." I sit down to wait. "It's really, really not."

Chapter 60

"Are you sure she wants him back?"

I nod. Emphatically. "She pretends everything's fine but it's not and it won't be and it's all my fault."

We unload toilet rolls and industrial strength bread as if I hadn't said anything. Then enormous sacks of pasta and toilet fresheners. Why won't anyone listen to me? Mum needs Chris and Chris needs Mum and I need both of them.

"I need to put it right."

Only when everything is out of the car and in the store room, when my heart's about to fall off my sleeve into a pail of potatoes, does she respond.

"If this all goes pear-shaped?"

"Absolutely. It'll be all my fault. End to end." I put on my most earnest face, the eyes that speak volumes. "You have to help me find him."

For the longest moment, she considers me and Grace watches us both. Finally, she nods and grabs her car keys.

"You know where he is!"

"Might do."

I grin. A big grin. A big self-satisfied-just-swallowed-an-elephant-and-it-tasted-good grin. Grace is out the door after us but Kitty's having none of it. "You stay here. Catch up on some study."

"No way!"

We clamber into Kitty's dilapidated Ford. I've never been so glad of a rattly car.

~~~

Out of town, southward. Deep countryside; boreens, bog roads and bonky donkeys leaning on walls as if they were having their ears manicured by tiny beetles. The car hurtles along, with both of us in the back feeling just a little bit car sick.

"I never meant," says Grace. "All that stuff. To hurt you."

"Jeremy's not so bad, when you get to know him." She grunts. "Okay, some of it you were right about. Sort of. I'm working on him. He'll be okay – but he's not Chris."

"So your dad, has he gone again?"

"Yeah. Back to Dublin. But we're going to email and stuff, get to know each other better. Slowly."

"Sounds good."

I nod and stare out the window at hedgerows made of gorse. "It was a dream I had, that's all."

"I know," says Grace. "They're bummers, those dreams!"

~~~

We end up in the middle of nowhere.

Worse than nowhere.

This is scenery. The sort parents point out to kids on a sunny day in Connemara when you'd rather be home watching very grey paint very slowly dry. The speed sign still says 80 km/h, but there's grass growing down the middle of the road and the only way two cars could pass would be in one of them levitated.

"Maybe we took a wrong turn?"

"Trust me," says Kitty. "Chris said he wanted somewhere quiet to pull his head together and my friend needed work done. There!"

How could we miss it? See, Kitty neglected to mention which friend had helped her out. Turns out he is the clown Grace disliked intensely. Apparently children's entertainers have breakdowns all the time and they come to here to rest and recover.

The house – is it actually a house? – has whitewashed walls covered with giant colourful spots, with a red circle covering the door like a nose.

Grace goes pale to the gills. "Tell me this isn't the guy who turned my breakfast into a petting zoo?"

"He became a friend," says her mum with a shrug.

Grace is NOT impressed and stays in the car.

~~~

"Chris, she needs you."

He's up on the roof fixing a gutter and is SOOOOO not listening to me. What is it about grown-ups that makes them so bloody stubborn?

"Chris!"

Nothing. Nada. Zilch.

Maybe he's gone deaf in his old age. Too far from the sea to hear normal conversation. Maybe he's morphed into a mute clown. This house could do that. A flock of crows spin upwards from a nearby field, complaining loudly: *Wasting your time! Save your breath! Feck off home!* I pretend to hear nothing.

A tiny bird lands nearby and leaves me a feather. There's a shimmer almost of gold. Is this my consolation prize? No. I'm not giving up. "Chris! Please."

He finally speaks through a mouthful of roofing nails. "She should have thought of that before taking up with that letch."

"Don't talk about my dad like that!"

"See, nothing changes."

The crows land on a derelict cottage in the next field and settle their pecking order quickly. I swallow my pride and Mum's. It doesn't taste good, but it has to be done. "Look, she made a mistake. We both did. He's my father so I can't talk about him like that. Not yet. But he's not my dad."

I can't even look up at him, realising something I never realised before: "If anyone's been my dad, it's been you."

I look up then to see if my words have had any effect but the roof is empty.

Well, that's it! I tried.

I can't believe he could be so stubborn and pig-headed and mule-eared. I'm officially OFF men for life. They don't make sense. They don't KNOW how to listen, let alone actually HEAR what you say!

"I thought you didn't care anymore."

And he's there, right behind me, wiping his hands on his jeans, same as ever. I fling myself into his arms. Into the warmest, bestest hug. Then I pull back, because I'm a teenager and we're cool; we're not meant to be into hugs and stuff.

But the grin, the grin I've suddenly acquired, runs from ear to ear and is going nowhere.

"It was Mum's cobwebs. They kind of blurred things. For both of us. That and Brad Pitt. You do know he's her ideal man?"

Chapter 61

THE WHALE AS ROLE MODEL

Whales don't pretend to not feel something they already know they feel. They care for each other and for their young and besides, there are so many other things to do, like catch mackerel and skim the Gulf Stream and avoid fishermen.

And when they surface, they leap as high as they can. Every time they breathe, they fire spumes of water in the air! When they slam their tails on the surface of the sea, they send up harmless mini tsunamis. Nobody knows why they do this but I think it's just another way of saying, "I'm here. I'm in love with life and I don't care who knows".

They do it to show how big their feelings are.

Mum's working on the accounts when I run in. I have minutes at best and she looks like a browbeaten mouse.

"What's going on?"

I pull out her pigtails and fluff up her hair, while fighting off her hands.

"Angelica! Why aren't you in school?"

"It's Saturday, Mum." Told you she wasn't with it these days! "Lipstick?"

"There. Why?"

No time. "Purse!" She purses her lips and I apply salmon-pink lippy. Not her best, but it will have to do. "We need to go shopping. You need new clothes and new lippy. Pronto."

"Angel, will you stop for one moment."

Before she can continue, because I really don't think I have many more of the right words left in me today, I fling the door open so Chris can come in. "Tell him how you feel."

They look at each other. Being grown-ups, this goes on for a while. "Do you want me?" he says, finally. Mum nods. About bloody time! A girl could waste a lifetime getting these two together! He holds out a hand and she takes it. It's all I can do not to barf right there and then, but it's so gorgeous and right!

"Come on so," he says, folding her hair back behind her ears. "Let's get away from prying eyes and sort this out."

They take their feelings to the beach and stand there, holding each other as if they'd just been washed up on shore. I've hidden myself inside the staircase that runs from the hotel. I need to know everything's alright and if it is, I promise myself I will never spy on either of them again.

"Remember our first kiss?" Mum doesn't answer. He kisses her neck. "I don't know about you, but I thought it was amazing. Better than amazing. It was—"

"Between you and Kitty?"

"Ah but I was thinking of you." Yes, Chris is back. Amazing what knowing someone loves you, finally, can do to your confidence. "See, what you didn't know (and were too pig-headed to ask at the time) was that you fancied me and I fancied you. I had my eyes closed all the time, pretending it was you."

She's looking sceptical.

He grins. "The second kiss was better anyway," he says.

"What second kiss?" says Mum. I mean GET ON WITH IT! Stop toying with each other. Why do adults do this? It makes everything so complicated! As if he heard me, Chris kisses her. Seagulls swoop in off the sea and circle them; you'd swear they were bait. Out at sea, two whales surface and the water they blow into the air conjoins into a heart before falling into the sea.

They pull apart, FINALLY.

"That one."

"Not sure I remember exactly," says Mum in a voice I've never heard her use before.

"I could try, y'know, to recreate it? Might be tough, but I'd be willing to try?"

Chris is savouring every minute of this! I can feel the electricity from here. All my little nape hairs are standing up and dancing a frenzy. (It's a new type of dance, sends shivers down your spine in little gangs of twelve.)

"That might be helpful."

When did she get so coy? And why can't I walk away back up these stairs and into the kitchen and chat with Onni until it's all done? Even Onni going on and on about Simon, it has to be less frustrating than these two!

"If you're sure?"

He's just as bad. They SO deserve each other!

"I mean, I wouldn't want to…"

She kisses him. When the kiss finally ends, they are silent.

"…Disappoint," he says, finally. They both smile, sheepishly. "Howabout next year's festival?"

"Oh." Mum looks disappointed. Why is he talking about the festival now?

"Unless you don't want to be seen walking down the aisle to marry an employee in front of half the world?"

Mum's face opens then into the deepest, happiest, most surprised smile and I find myself out on the beach. Not even pretending to hide. A stray flock of sparrows spin into a ring above Mum's head, as they do in cartoons when you get concussed. I like the picture, even if I'm the only one to see it and I try so hard not to blink it away.

Then the sun comes out of a gap in the clouds right above my head and extinguishes my cloak of invisibility.

But I don't really mind, not now. I don't really mind anything at all.

"Come here, you," says Mum, pulling me to her. "You spying on us?"

"Oh Angelica needed to know what was happening?" says Chris. I nod. "So, what do you think, Mouse? Can't say I match your father for looks and charm."

Enough already!

Such nonsense calls for a bear hug that knocks the air out of him. Mum joins in then and this three-way hug feels right. Warm and strong all at once. But then I step back. I'm not a child after all. I don't do bear hugs.

Do bears even hug? I mean, they have claws and all.

In case Mum and Chris haven't understood that a bear hug when you're a teenager is a definitive YES, I give him a shrug. I am masterful at shrugs. "Be okay. I guess." Don't want them getting cocky either. I, after all, am the one who brought them together. "Unless something better turns up. I mean, let's face it both of you could do soooo much better."

The insult and compliment drips off both their backs like warm oil. I can almost smell the lavender.

"Now will you tell us where you're from?"

"No," says Mum. "He won't. Everyone's entitled to a few secrets."

"My father was a fisherman," says Chris as we stroll along the beach towards the harbour.

"See, that wasn't so bad!"

"Well, when I say *fisherman*, what I really mean is that he talked to fishes. But only really small ones. He reckoned they held the secret of the universe. As for whales…"

He's useless! I can get NO information out of this man whom I love to bits. "You two kind of need get married," I say, really casually. Well I never said I wasn't romantic. It's in the blood after all, no matter how I fight it. "Chris needs a daughter like me to keep him in line."

"Do I really?" he says, mock-scowling.

"Go," says Mum, when we're down near the harbour. "Find that boy of yours and tell him the good news."

Ah now. That's not fair. "You knew?"

"Oh yes. Kitty told me."

How come everyone can keep their secrets hidden in this town except me?

"Saw him skulking around reception earlier. Seemed a bit shy." They're so busy being amused at my love life that they don't see me blush. "Told him you might be in Simon's cafe later. At three o'clock, I think."

"But it's three now!"

"So it is." She turns to Chris, smiling up at him. "Can you believe how fast time goes sometimes?"

Grrr. I think I preferred her miserable!

Chapter 62

Dylan is perched with his mates on the wall opposite the cafe. Like a line of rooks sort of squeezed onto a telephone line, they turn as one to stare at me as I cross the road. Might only be a distance of twenty yards, but it feels as if I'm crossing the Valley of Death on a pogo stick, especially after the last time.

Two of them nudge Dylan. The first he ignores, the second knocks him off the wall so he's standing there waiting for me.

This isn't exactly how I mapped it out, but I have a feeling this is the time. Maybe the only time in my life when I have to bite the bullet, step up to the mark and all those horrible clichés grown-ups use when they want you to do something you'd rather not.

Except that this time I want to do it. .

I stop right in front of Dylan, block out all the onlookers and the idea that he could blow me out of the water and make me a laughing stock again. Because I know deep down I wouldn't be doing this if he wasn't a good person as well as entirely hot.

"Dylan Clancy, would you like to go out with me?"

The look on his face, well, it's hard to read. It's like shock and amazement and double chocolate chip cookie dough ice cream in a blender. As far as I am concerned, right now we are the only two people on earth. The WHOLE of Earth. Earth and the universe and galaxies and infinity and beyond.

"I mean, like properly. No mention of parents, not even once. I'll even snog you in front of Simon, no matter what he says. And I promise not to run off without explaining why and without coming back. Or to keep secrets unless they're to do with mammoth birthday pressies or Christmas or something. And I'm sorry I went a bit obsessed over Jeremy, but it was such a novelty, really, I didn't know how I felt."

Then I sort of run out of words. So I look down at my scuffed shoes – any day now a toe will shoot out and start growing like a tree – because Dylan hasn't said a word. I don't even see the kiss until it lands on my lips, like a feather.

"I'll take that as a 'yes'," I say, grinning. He shrugs and we kiss again.

This day I will never forget.

This day is SPECTACULARLY good!

~~~

"Just because it worked for your mum – and let me remind you, it DIDN'T, this doesn't mean you are EVER to matchmake me," says Grace when I call in to break the news.

ALL the news.

"So you don't want to meet Dylan's cousin?" I fiddle with her mascara set. "He arrived over this morning from Glasgow. He's called Rod."

"Course not," she says, but in the sort of way you say things when you've backed yourself into a corner and there's a dragon slobbering over the thoughts of eating you, but which bit to eat first? Then someone says, '*So you don't want me to, like, kill the dragon then?*'

"You could always come along and say hello? Warn him about my matchmaking skills?"

"S'pose I could," she says. "The Scots accent is pretty awesome."

"Might want to do your usual walk through a spray of perfume thing. This room's pretty ripe."

She flings a cushion at me.

"I can't believe you were actually chatting up my dad online."

"Yeah. Yuck." She engulfs the room in enough perfume to keep a hot air balloon aloft, if it was gas, that is, not perfume. We both walk through the haze into our new lives as fully-fledged women of the world.

"I think I've gone off Brad," she says as we emerge be-fumed, casually dumping years of shared fantasies about Brad arriving in Drisogue and declaring undying love for us both – but really only for me. "What d'you think of Johnny Depp?"

"Apart from the weird little beardy thing?"

"Yeah. I mean if he shaved it off, he'd be really hot. Probably only grows it so people don't recognise him when he shaves it off."

So Grace prefers Depp to Brad. I can't even speak. I let her go on and on. It's as if she has swallowed every movie he's ever made. When did this happen? She quotes lines from them. This is so wrong! Whatever happened to best friends for life and sharing everything and knowing each other inside out?

Okay, that'd be disgusting. I didn't mean it literally.

"I also kind of fancy Angelina Jolie."

"Well, okay then." I slip my arm through her and I think, more of Brad for me and it's not fair to expect best friends to be perfect. "Yeah, they're both okay."

~~~

As arranged, Dylan has brought Rod to the cafe. They're sitting in the window with their backs to us, but I can still tell which one is Dylan.

When they turn, like reindeer on a sharp corner, we both take a deep breath.

Twins might be less alike, though while Dylan is pale and poetic, Rod looks positively Spanish and long-lashed. I have to pinch Grace's arm to get her to move forward. Dylan and I, we feel like proud parents but I'm the one who does the introductions.

"Hi. I'm Angelica and this is Grace. We're not vampires or werewolves and my father wasn't swallowed by a whale."

Did I mention that Drisogue is the best place in the world to be fourteen?

Acknowledgements

On Angelica's behalf, I'd love to thank all my beta readers who took the time to read my early drafts and give me invaluable feedback and additional insight. THANK YOU to Patricia Groves for laughing until she cried, Caroline Farrell, Jean O'Sullivan, Martina O'Reilly, Caroline Finnerty, Ann Newall, Nicola Depuis and Libby Sedgwick.

Without readers, writers would not have an audience and beta readers may be the bravest and most self-less of all!

Thank you also to Maynooth Uni. The first rewrites of this book were done in room 1.17 while I was Screenwriter-in-Residence at Maynooth University and Kildare Co. Council Library & Arts Service 2016-7.

Also to Javaholics cafe in Fairview where I escape to write, inspired by Al's flat whites to write faster and better and to Leo Lundy for still somehow thinking it's cool to live with a writer.

To Barbara Henkes for the photo of me and to Liam Boland for his help with marketing.

To Aoife Henkes, sublime graphic artist and wonderfully talented person, for her beautiful cover.

L. J. SEDGWICK is addicted to words. It's the way things are. Okay, so it wasn't a great thing to use five syllable words in the playground of her junior school, but she stored them away for later. Her love affair with words and dialogue launched her onto the unsuspecting world, first as a freelance journalist (for publications and papers in Ireland, Australia, the UK and the US) and playwright.  When she decided to write fulltime, she became the worst waitress ever. Think *'dropping a tray of flaming sambuccas, another of tiny (full) milk jugs and knocking over a bowl of round mints'* and you're close. Several hours of TV later and a couple of award-winning plays and unpublished books she headed to Leeds to study screenwriting.

Her screenwriting credits span genres and form, from feature films, television drama and children's series, to short films, radio plays and game narrative. Her award-winning animation series, *Punky* has been recognised as the first mainstream cartoon series in the world in which the main character has special needs and is available globally. She also teaches screenwriting, creative writing and visual storytelling in libraries, colleges, universities and festivals around Ireland.

In addition to screenwriting credits, Lindsay's plays have been produced throughout Ireland and her writing has been described as 'gripping,' 'gut-wrenching' and 'seductive'.

For more information on The Angelica Touch and her other books, you can visit her website www.lindsayjsedgwick.com or have a gander at her blog, thiswriterscrazylife.blogspot.ie. She is available for readings and workshops and can be contacted at ljsedgwick@lindsayjsedgwick.com.

Other books by this author

Dad's Red Dress.

Jessie wants her family to be 'normal'. It's never going to happen. Kid sister, Laura (7) thinks she's been abducted by the Virgin Mary. (Twice; once on a motorbike). Step-mum, Eva makes feminist installations while Dad becomes Mandy as soon as the front door closes. Which is fine. She loves them all to bits but they've just moved back to Ireland and this time she wants to try and avoid the bullying that usually kicks off when some school friend finds out about Dad. Trouble is, she really has no control over what's about to happen.

Reviews:

Filled with vivid, genuine characters and complex, conflicting family drama, it is joyous, loving and truly unique among the vast canon of coming-of-age stories…a delight to read. Simply wonderful - Children's Books Ireland

A beautiful story excellently told…one of the best novels I've read in bloody ages - Patrick Chapman, author of Slow Clocks of Decay

What a great story, filled with complexity - original and believable, every character so well developed…Jessie is just a delight, I was with her all the way! A beautiful relationship with her Dad, and her little sister! It's wonderful, just wonderful!! - Caroline Farrell, author of Arkyne and Lady Beth.

Write That Script!

After teaching screenwriting for 21 years and even longer working as a screenwriter, Lindsay has designed this book to enable people to write the script they've been talking about or threatening to write. It covers idea, character, structure, plotting, how to avoid procrastination, kick start your imagination and get your first script done because finishing your first script means you can write the next. Due out early 2018

Made in the USA
Columbia, SC
09 February 2018